Navigating Austerity

Anthropology of Policy

Navigating Austerity

Currents of Debt along a South Asian River

Laura Bear

Stanford University Press
Stanford, California

Stanford University Press
Stanford, California

Printed in the United States of America on acid-free, archival-quality paper

Bear, Laura, author.
  Navigating austerity : currents of debt along a south Asian river / Laura Bear.
    pages cm. — Anthropology of Policy
  Includes bibliographical references and index.
  ISBN 978-0-8047-8947-9 (cloth : alk. paper) — ISBN 978-0-8047-9553-1 (pbk. : alk. paper)
  ISBN 978-0-8047-9554-8 (electronic)
  Typeset in 10.5/15 Brill

Cataloging-in-Publication Data are available from the Library of Congress

To Tara and the River

Contents

Acknowledgments

I HAVE WRITTEN THIS BOOK on my own at times of joy and of sadness. Yet I have never actually been alone. My writing has always been a conversation with friends and informants on the Hooghly. I can't explicitly name many of these people. To do so would affect their livelihoods, but even those not named know who they are. Only they can measure my debt of gratitude to them for opening up their lives to me. I have interpreted their experiences against vistas of history and the scale of global patterns, so they may not always recognize themselves in these pages. This book is not intended as a mirror but instead is a tribute to their endurance, which builds creatively on their perspectives. I would especially like to thank Shankar Das, Viswanath Samantha, Viswanath Sardar; and Vasantho Lal Shaw.

These pages are also the fruit of dialogs with, and support from, colleagues at L.S.E. over several years. Many thanks to Catherine Allerton; Rita Astuti; Mukulika Banerjee; Maurice Bloch; Fenella Cannell; Matthew Engelke; Chris Fuller; Katy Gardner; David Graeber; Stephan Feuchtwang; Deborah James; Nick Long; Martha Mundy; Johnny Parry; Mathijs Pelkmans; Michael Scott; Alpa Shah; Charles Stafford; Hans Steinmuller; Harry Walker; and Gisa Weszkalnys. The Anthropology of Economy writing group has been a lively source of ideas and debate. This included, alongside L.S.E. faculty, Max Bolt; Dena Freeman; Jason Hickel; and Insa Koch and Mitch Sedgwick. My doctoral students have provided much inspiration as well, so many thanks to Lexi Aisbitt; Chiara Arnavas; Indira Arumugam; Rebecca Bowers; Kimberly Chong; Sarah Grosso; Michael Hoffmann; Juli Huang; Thomas Joassin; Ken Kuroda; Jovan Lewis; Georgia Nichols; Itay Noy; Fernande Poole; Andrew Sanchez; and Yasna Singh. I am grateful, also, for the gift of two years of research leave funded by the Economic and Social Research Council (RES-062-23-1000) and a sabbatical from my department that allowed me to complete this project.

Beyond L.S.E. this book has been enriched by friends and collaborators in the "Conflicts in Time: Rethinking Contemporary Globalization" research network that I led with Stephan Feuchtwang from 2008 to 2011 (ESRC grant RES-451-26-0456). These include Simone Abram, Catherine Alexander, Nicolas Argenti, Andrew Barry, Richard Baxstrom, Eeva Beglund, Xiang Biao, Georgina Born, Beverley Butler, Sharad Chari, Tony Crook, Jamie Cross, Harriet Evans, David Featherstone, Sarah Franklin, Neil David Galway, Olivia Harris, Casey High, Mette High, Eric Hirsch, Matt Hodges, Mekhala Krishnamurthy, Michael Lambek, Penny McCall Howard, Sian Lazar, Luo Pan, Nayanika Mathur, Morten Nielsen, Frances Pine, Rebecca Prentice, Dinah Rajak, Josh Reno, Felix Ringel, Mike Rowlands, Nicolai Ssorin-Chaikov, Olivia Swift and Sharika Thiranagama. A workshop on "Waterscapes, Labor and Uncertainty" I held with Nikhil Anand, Sarah Bell, Kate Crawford, Samantha Hurn, Lyla Mehta, Edward Simpson, Linda Waldman and Anna Zimmerman contributed much to my thinking on inequality in waterscapes. My writing has also grown with the help of a stimulating, nurturing School for Advanced Research seminar organized by Fenella Cannell and Susie McKinnon that also included Gillian Feeley-Harnik, Michael Lambek and Elana Shever. I have been very lucky to receive constant encouragement for my work from Veronique Benei; Janet Carsten; Thomas Blom Hansen; Danilyn Rutherford; Shivi Sivaramakrishnan; and Jonathan Spencer. Their invitations to speak at their departments and willingness to review my writing have allowed my ideas to bear fruit.

There are three other cooperative projects that have flowed into the concepts I explore here. Karen Ho, Anna Tsing and Sylvia Yanagisako will recognize our shared attempt to think critically about capitalism from within anthropological and feminist traditions of thought. Arjun Appadurai, Ritu Birla and Stine Puri will feel their presence in the discussions of speculation. Nayanika Mathur will find echoes of our mutual interest in the public good. Akhil Gupta, Matthew Hull and Brenda Chalfin contributed greatly to the refinement of our ideas on this theme. I am so very grateful for all these stimulating fellow travelers in inquiry and for our conversations in Cambridge, Copenhagen and Stanford.

The Anthropology of Policy series editors Cris Shore and Susan Wright, and Michelle Lipinski at Stanford University Press, have supported me with their enthusiasm. It is because of their faith that I have been able to finish this book. They have been exceptionally generous in their attention, making sure that I speak clearly and boldly on vital current issues.

It is my companions on the river of life, Griselda, Jeremy, Subhrasheel and Thalia, who have carried me through all the joys and difficulties of writing. I thank them last because they know how much, and how little, these pages mean.

L.B.

Navigating Austerity

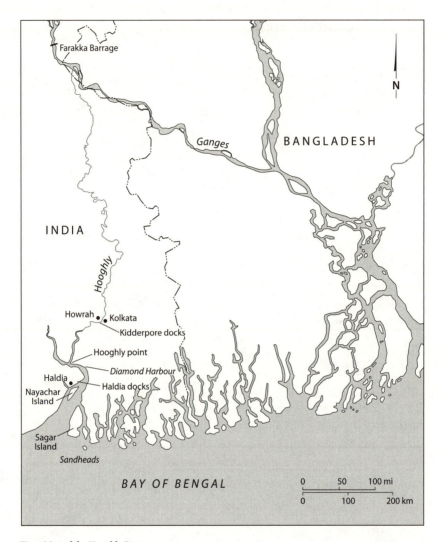

Fig. 1. Map of the Hooghly River

Introduction: Navigating Austerity

ACROSS THE WORLD public debate and political decision-making now center on the problem of sovereign debt repayment. Collectively, we are faced with the question of how to navigate public austerity and fiscal crisis. Our standard answer to this dilemma proposes urgent financial solutions, but this book aims to change the terms of debate. It explores how we have come to focus on financial rather than social or political solutions. It examines the growth of a new form of policy in which state debt has a primary economic value. It traces the new kinds of ethical and political engagement, as well as the social relationships and physical environments that emerge out of such measures. By navigating through the history and contemporary reality of austerity policy on the Hooghly River, this book offers a new lode star for fiscal policy. It proposes a reorientation toward a social reckoning of state debt. This book is a transforming journey along the Hooghly that allows us to glimpse other possibilities for fiscal policy. It is created from my own movement on this river during eighteen months of ethnographic research with port officers, marine crew, river pilots, boatmen, entrepreneurs and shipyard workers.

For more than 150 years the Hooghly has been a vital artery for trade to South Asia, Europe and East Asia. Now it carries the hopes for an economy based on international finance, privatization, contractual labor and flexible technologies. Container ships move along it to the Bay of Bengal, from where they travel on to the Indian Ocean, South China and Mediterranean seas. Shipyards produce huge vessels for national and global companies. Other firms improvise cheap, adaptable technologies such as "virtual" jetties. This waterscape has emerged since the 1980s from changes in state fiscal policy. Linked to a global pattern associated with IMF restructuring and new markets in sovereign debt bonds, state debt has radically altered in India. Fiscal policy since Independence had treated it as a political relationship expressed in financial form—a national debt. Debts were taken to make a long-term investment in the future prosperity of the nation. Since the 1980s these were redefined as primarily financial transactions and were linked to attempts to increase bond market transactions in sovereign debt. They were financialized and economized to a much greater extent than ever before. The central government imposed fiscal discipline on public-sector institutions such as the Kolkata Port Trust in order to repay these debts. This generated permanent crisis and austerity measures. That in turn led to new forms of speculative planning and entrepreneurial citizenship. From our journey along the Hooghly in this book, a hidden history of state debt crises (and alternatives to them) will be revealed.

A Voyage on the Hooghly

To begin this passage we must step away from policy statements about debt or liberalization in India onto the Hooghly itself. It is here that river bureaucrats, workers and entrepreneurs attempt to navigate austerity. The nature of their work and the waterscape it has generated will become clear if you follow me as I join a hydrographic survey team on a small steel launch on a monsoon day in 2008. Daily, teams travel the 125 kilometers of the river that flows from the city of Kolkata to the Indian Ocean at the Bay of Bengal. They track changes that threaten the movement of vessels or augur environmental threats. Without their work the trade that has long sustained the livelihoods and cosmopolitanism of the city of Kolkata (and the eastern region of India) would halt. The consumer goods displayed in the shopping malls of the city or the precious vapors of the petrochemical plants of Haldia would disappear. Steel plants in China would lose an important iron ore source. Cement factories in Bangladesh would be stilled, deprived of fly ash waste from local power plants. Since 1991 the flow of cargo along the Hooghly has steadily increased from 15.240 million tons in 1991 to 47.54 million tons of cargo in 2011 (Ministry of Shipping 2011). The Ministry of Shipping reports in its twelfth five-year plan that this is a result of the freedoms of liberalization that have led to gross domestic product increasing at an average annual rate of 8 percent. But these figures reveal little about either liberalization or the effects of new state debt policies. More can be learned from a voyage with the men of the hydrographic survey.

We cast off from the ruins of Ash Ghat in the Kolkata docks, commanded by Captain Kumar, a port marine officer. Abandoned giant buoys and chains marked where two hundred marine crew used to work, until they were laid off in the 1980s. Since Captain Kumar's memories stretched back to the 1970s, when he had first been apprenticed to the river, he recalled these men as we passed. He pointed out the ruined port warehouses as well, where thousands of men used to work until the

1990s. The helmsman carefully swerved round the side of a towering container ship poised outside the dock gates waiting to race the flood tide down river. On the right bank he drew my attention to a successful private enterprise, the shipyard, Venture Ltd, where the launch we were traveling on had been built for the port. Here two huge hulks of brown steel were being shaped into vessels for a Scandinavian shipping company with almost no equipment. In the open air of the muddy shore men balanced on beams hundreds of feet above the ground.

Kumar looked nervously at the thickening rain. He began to speak of the many dangers beneath the surface caused by reduced state expenditure on dredging. He warned of the wrecks around which silt tirelessly collects, threatening the passage of ships. Midstream at the treacherous Sankrail and Panchpara stretches of the river the crew set about the task of preserving safe passage with austerity technologies. Accuracy was ensured by combining the ancient quintant and chart used for two hundred years on the river and an aging echo-sounder. Captain Kumar recorded the siltation of two meters in some places. His pen moved from tracing the ideal lines of movement in the charts to recording recent barriers to it.

As the rain diminished, we moved farther south downriver. Midstream, small wooden boats harvested sand for the booming construction of a new town northwest of Kolkata in Rajarhat. Men stood up to their necks in the river lifting wooden buckets, and the boats bowed under the weight. Wearily Kumar explained that he has to keep a close eye on all activities on the river. He warned that any changes such as sand extraction were potentially life-threatening because they altered the flow, creating new islands of silt or eroding currents. He described how recently a ferry jetty filled with passengers and a fly ash barge from Bangladesh had sunk because of such changes. He complained that he could not prevent such dangers. He said he was now powerless against the private businesses of sand extraction, shipbuilding and other more illegal activities that had developed over his working life. He whispered that behind them are political leaders who will make a complaint to their party cadres if you try to stop them. He added that they might even send someone to assault or kill you.

As we moved northward back toward the docks the vessel shook as it pushed against the flood tide. Here in the open water Captain Kumar grew optimistic, anticipating a more prosperous future. He explained that he had spent his spare time walking the clogged canals of Kolkata so he could write a paper on them. In this he had argued that the fortunes of the river and the city could be restored by rejoining them to the inland waterways to Bangladesh that had been cut off by partition. The ultimate force behind this waterscape, he suggested, was the goddess Ma Ganga (Mother Ganges).

But then Captain Kumar grew distracted as calls came on his cell phone. A strike had been called. As a port officers' union member he was rallying support. These protests were against the permanent pay freeze for port staff that had been in place for ten years. Finally we pulled into the jetty at Ash Ghat, which was pock-marked and thinned by rust. Captain Kumar's impossible work was to be a guardian against changes that were as unpredictable as the silt that swirled around the wrecks beneath us. This was a disturbing task because each day the river revealed the instability that austerity policies created in the waterscape.

In this precarious, ruined, but productive waterscape, people are challenged to make the return of each tide fruitful. In this book we will navigate in each chapter the connected efforts to generate value from the Hooghly encountered on this monsoon journey: the ruined but productive docks (Sections I and II), private-sector enterprises such as sand extraction and shipyards (Sections III and IV) and container ships on the river (Section IV). In them we will trace attempts to combine fiscal policies and popular ethics of productivity. In recent years there have been important calls for studies of urban environments and waterscapes as forms of technonature (Agrawal 2005; Rademacher 2011; White and Wilbert 2006). While building on these perspectives, this book explores a question that concerns people on the Hooghly, and all of us living under similar policy regimes. That is, How can productivity be created in a time of public austerity? By focusing on the strategies of people negotiating new public-sector policies, this book ultimately reveals how debt, circulation and time work in austerity economies. It moves toward a conclusion that draws on people's restoration of the hidden ethical meaning of fiscal policy to argue for a social calculus of state debt.

Why the Hooghly River?

The Hooghly River is a particularly revealing site for exploring the unplanned effects of state debt policies for several reasons. First, it is one of the many public infrastructures across the world that has been radically transformed by austerity policies. These policies produce a deep contradiction between the redistributive and extractive aspects of state institutions. This conflict has a great impact on public infrastructures. Such complex structures require patient capital to sustain and renew them. However, austerity policies emphasize the short-term repayment of central debts. This leads to an intensified extraction of value from public infrastructures—for example, through the selling off of assets; use of decaying machinery; and employment of cheap outsourced, contractual labor. In addition, public infrastructures become an intensified source of accumulation for the private sector. This is enabled by new financing mechanisms such as infrastructure bonds; government guarantees; and direct private lending to public institutions. Overall inequalities between already prosperous nations, regions and cities with low public debt and attractive investment potential and more indebted, "risky" places increase. Mounting contradiction and inequality produce material dilemmas for bureaucrats and public-sector workers. Therefore a focus on the infrastructure of the Hooghly reveals key alterations in the public sector associated with austerity measures and their spiraling, unintended effects. These effects are material, but also political and ethical. Infrastructures are a variety of *res publica,* or public object. Their physical extent, scale and shared usage provide the topography of a public (Chalfin 2014).[1] Some forms of infrastructure can contribute to the generation of a care for the world and common feeling (Arendt 1958). Others do not provide such a ground. Attention to the changing forms of an infrastructure such as the Hooghly River can fully reveal the material, ethical and political entailments of austerity debt policy.

Secondly, the Hooghly River is not just an infrastructure, it is a *water*scape. Sensory experiences of water such as ingestion, physical contact and immersion are the primary medium for metaphors of regeneration, life, death, time and space (Strang 2005). The movement of water between solid, liquid and vapor also evokes many symbolic associations, along with its responsiveness in unpredictable ways to human intervention. As a result, alterations in the management of water are frequently experienced as changes with significant ethical consequences (Gandy 2004; Swyngedouw 2004; Zandi-Sayek 2000). Bureaucratic policies draw on the imagery of the generative power of water (Alley 2002; Rademacher 2011). In addition, interventions are often strongly opposed as people object to the appropriation of a vital symbolic and material resource (Baviskar 1997, 2007; Doron 2008; Mosse 2003; Haberman 2006; Jalais 2011; Mehta 2005; Subramaniam 2009). Therefore when austerity debt policies are applied to a waterscape they escape their financial framing. This makes waterscapes an especially fertile arena for exploring how capital circulation emerges from multiple, intimate projects of self-fashioning and status (Yanagisako 2002). In them we can follow the interactions between the hidden ethics of formal economic policy and the diverse life-worlds of popular economies.

Thirdly, the Hooghly is not just an infrastructure and a waterscape, it is a river. The fluidity of rivers draws human attention to connections between spaces. Their ebb and flow provokes engagement with rhythms in time. To make them productive requires a careful spatiotemporal orchestration of labor and technology with recalcitrant nonhuman forces. Therefore focusing on a river can reveal key shifts in the management of timespaces (Adam 1998; Thrift and May 2001) linked to austerity policies. In particular new conflicts between various human and nonhuman temporal rhythms come into view. We can trace the short-term and long-term crises generated from austerity policies alongside the social experiences of space and time connected to them.

Therefore, the Hooghly as an infrastructure, waterscape and river provides a highly significant microcosm. Within it we can trace the unpredictable material, ethical and political effects of public debt policies. But what are our current theoretical resources for addressing questions of debt, circulation and time in austerity?

State Debt Crises: An Unexplored Phenomenon

From the fears of default in the EU zone, to attempts by national governments to reduce structural debt, to the news of bankrupt local municipal governments in the United States, there now appears to be a sudden, mounting catastrophe of public deficit. We should be skeptical of such claims of urgent, new problems. Since the 1980s, policy reform has advanced through claims of imminent crisis (Peck, Theodore and Brenner 2009; Roitman 2013). People in most of world, such as South and East Asia, Latin America and Africa, would be mystified by the idea that state debt crises are recent. They have lived through earlier fiscal crises in the 1980s and 1990s. I look beyond current events to examine this longer history of sovereign debt and to reflect on the deeper significance of state debt. Therefore I challenge the usual interpretation of austerity policy as a recent phenomenon (Blyth 2013). Instead I show that current fiscal policies that focus on cutting public spending are a consequence of a longer history of alterations in sovereign debt.

Given the rising visibility of state fiscal crises it is surprising how little they have figured in our accounts of neoliberal policy. Neoliberalism is often presented as a response to economic crisis, rather than as a redefinition of fiscal policy as primarily a financial question. For example, anthropologists frequently chart how new policies are introduced in relation to an external event of financial adversity or collapse (Song 2009). Yet such an approach leaves three key questions unexamined. First, how does state debt and/or financial crisis come to be understood as primarily a question of fiscal responsibility? Secondly, what new practices of the public good does such an emphasis on financial calamity generate? Thirdly, what happens to class relations, politics and environments when financial responsibility dominates policy? We need to examine how state revenue crises have become primarily resolvable through financial responsibilities and financial market mechanisms (Mbembe and Roitman 1995; Wengle 2012). How, in other words, does the ethical, political and fiscal question of state debt become narrowed to a technical issue of monetary debt?

My focus here on state debt aims to create greater precision in debates about historical changes in economic policy that are often labeled "neoliberal." Anthropologists have shown that neoliberalism is not a single coherent project, but an assemblage of techniques and institutional structures (Collier 2009; Ong 2007; Murray-Li 2007; Shore and Wright 1997; Shore, Wright and Pero 2011). They have argued that we should focus on the partial realization of neoliberal policies, tracing their incorporation in social relations (Kipnis 2008; Kingfisher and Maskovsky 2008; Shever 2012). I follow such approaches, but advance them by arguing that many of the recent changes in public-sector policies attributed to "neoliberalism" are linked to specific alterations in the relations and mechanisms of state debt. Economic governance becomes newly constrained by the public good of interest repayment and the use of debt bonds to underpin financial markets. This creates a contradiction between the redistributive and extractive aspects of state institutions. It also leads to austerity policy, which is decentralized, creative, short-term and chaotic. Importantly, to a greater extent than in postwar centralized economic planning, the institutions, technologies and urban environments that emerge are formed by popular expertise and diverse ethics of productivity.

A focus on state debt also offers a new perspective on liberalization in India. Standard accounts center on changes in trade regimes, the private sector and practices of consumption initiated in the wake of the acceptance of an IMF loan by the Congress government led by Narasimhan Rao in 1991. Liberalization, as this book shows, involved a much longer process of change in the public sector. This is an alteration that was explicitly planned by the architects of liberalization, even though the results of their policies have been unpredictable. Importantly, recent widely discussed social welfare initiatives (such as NREGA) do not reverse this more subterranean phenomenon (Chatterjee 2008; Corbridge and Srivastava 2013; Dreze and Sen 2013; Ferguson 2009; Harriss 2011). It is in the management of public infrastructure such as the Hooghly River that the consequences of this longer-term shift are most clearly seen. As explored throughout this book the *res publica* of infrastructure becomes problematic when state debts are narrowed to mechanisms for underpinning markets (Graham and Marvin 2001; Arendt 1958). Such infrastructures are made from and sustain political and ethical life (Bear 2007; Elyachar 2012b). Alterations to their purpose and form, as I show in the chapters that follow, have spiraling social and political effects (Collier 2011).

Toward a New Anthropology of Debt: Sovereign Debt and Collective Obligation

How then should we approach the significance of state debt? Although economists and legal scholars have specifically addressed sovereign debt crises (see Conclusion), general questions about state debt have been remarkable by their absence. Credit as part of capitalist economies has, on the other hand, been widely discussed. For Marx, all credit attempts to fix contradictions in the rhythms of realization of capital. For Weber, it is part of the rational technologies of accounting that generate predictability in capitalism. For Schumpeter, it allows the entrepreneur to act to creatively destroy old forms of productivity and generate new ones. More recently credit has been considered as a mathematical representation of social hierarchies (Finn 2003; Poovey 2008; Roitman 2003). These arguments cannot help us to understand the particular qualities and significance of state debt. This is because it is not like private credit. It is not an exchange with an individual or institution based on a dominant fiscal logic. On the contrary, it is a collective ethical, fiscal and political obligation.

This characteristic of state debt is not addressed either in the classic anthropological or theoretical literature on debt and time (Mauss 1990; Derrida 1992; Bourdieu 1990; Lyotard 1993). These approaches focus on acts of exchange between individuals. Yet state debt is an explicitly collective obligation. The responsibilities it generates apply to every citizen and every public resource, although its origin lies in the specific acts of administrators. Its rhythms of repayment are set in motion by an individual act of giving credit. But these rhythms can come to dominate all the diverse cycles of obligation at work throughout society. State debt, therefore, conjures into being a national economy to which we all have obligations. It orients centralizing annual rhythms of repayment and taxation. It also generates through its accounts, the nation as a simultaneously fiscal, ethical and political entity.

State debt has been tangentially discussed as part of theories of the origins of money. These perspectives have more potential because they stress collective debts. Recent revivals of the Chartalist account of the origins of money focus on the collective obligations of citizenship (Aglietta and Orleans 1998; Theret 1999; Ingham

2004). Aglietta and Orleans, for example, suggest that it is the social debts that citizens owe to the state for the sustenance of their lives that leads to the creation of a collective bill of exchange in the form of money (1998). Importantly, Graeber, with his critical stance on the state, reverses this argument (2012). He suggests that it is capitalist money that creates a social debt to the state and an abstract quantified measure of labor value. It makes a dual claim on the future creativity of human action both fiscal and political. Money therefore does not reflect pre-existing social obligations to the state. On the contrary, it secures the legitimacy of the institutions of the market and the state. It also makes all other forms of value, debt and exchange subject to these institutions. It is through an extension of Graeber's argument that we can begin to understand the particular features of state debt. State debt is a mechanism that mediates between ethical, political and economic relationships. It creates differences between these forms of human value and allows conversions between these. Taxation creates a relationship between the citizen and the state (Abelin 2012; Munoz 2011). Centralized money links state authority to market exchanges (Peebles 2008). State debt brings the citizen, state and the market into a network of interconnected obligations.

We can understand this fully if we examine one of the "original" sovereign debts, the foundation of the Bank of England in 1694. This (along with the Swedish Riksbank, founded in 1668) provided the historical model in relation to which forms of sovereign debt were developed by various states (Goodchild 2009). Sovereign debt, monetary credit and state guaranteed bills of exchange (paper money) emerged as a system from the negotiations between William of Orange and Parliament over how to manage a crisis in public finances resulting from the cost of war with France. To solve this issue a permanent loan of £1.2 million for the king was raised from the public with a guaranteed return to creditors of 8 percent per annum. The administration of this system was placed under the control of the newly formed Bank of England. The return on investments was secured by the diversion of future taxation toward the repayment of the loan to the king. In addition the bank was given a monopoly on bills of exchange (paper money) that had previously been a private matter between merchants. It also became the lender of last resort for both the state and the public. Goodchild emphasizes that this produced a situation in which the state was indebted to its creditors in financial terms, and creditors were politically indebted to the state as taxpayers and as an issuer of reliable bills of exchange (2009). Yet, importantly, for our understanding of state debt, this event also established the collective responsibility of all citizens for the repayment of interest on a loan made by financiers to the sovereign power of the state, the king. State debt created by a specific authority figure became the collective responsibility of all citizens. In this manner the potentially limitless public obligation to repay the debt of the sovereign was founded as a political, ethical and a fiscal responsibility. It is this structure that still underpins our financial systems in the present. Yet as we will see in the next section, since the 1980s its mediations have radically changed.

The Financialization of Sovereign Debt 1980–2012:
The Example of Liberalization in India

Across the world the 1980s marked a significant change in the forms of sovereign debt from those established in the post–World War II period. Commercial bank lending to state governments to finance public deficit or investment has always formed a part of sovereign debt. Many countries also have long histories of issuing state debt bonds into financial markets or to individual investors through the agency of central banks. However, in the postwar period these mechanisms were under the control of political institutions. Most public financing was dealt with through monetization, the issuing of long-term treasury bonds with interest rates fixed by governments or international loans for specific infrastructure investments from the World Bank. Monetization is the mechanism first created with the foundation of the Bank of England. The government issues debt to the central bank and the central bank creates money to increase the monetary base with which to cover the purchase of this debt, causing an overall increase in the money supply in society. Although this was ruled illegal by the Federal Reserve Act of 1913 in the United States, it is a practice that continued well into the 1980s in many other settings across the world (Currie, Dethier and Togo 2003). When governments needed funds they also relied on the issuing of treasury bonds into open markets. Even in the case of the US Fed, which is historically described as "independent" from political and private interests, interest rates for borrowing were kept low through back-door mechanisms, and markets were captive to the needs of states to borrow (Sylla 1988). This system creates fiscal mechanisms of sovereign debt that are controlled primarily by political institutions and have long-term rhythms of investment guaranteed by permanent political relationships.

With the end of the Bretton Woods fixed interest rates agreements in 1971, a new system of sovereign debt began to develop from the intense fiscal instability experienced by states and the innovative international lending practices used to deal with this. Commercial bank lending and new IMF loans to states steadily increased as sources of public finance through the 1970s. These loans were usually taken to deal with the consequences of the new dramatic fluctuations in the value of currencies. These developments intensified through the 1980s–90s, leading to the emergence of a new orthodoxy on central bank independence and sovereign debt relations. Official lending by multilateral and bilateral organizations such as the World Bank, IMF and Asian Development Bank increased exponentially. The conditionalities of these loans to emerging and transition economies led to the increasing management of sovereign debt by technocrats who focused on loan repayment, market mechanisms and sovereign debt markets. These technocrats emphasized the necessity of central bank independence from political influence and fiscal austerity imposed by the market discovery of interest rates on government debt in primary and secondary financial markets. These became recommended principles for transitional and EU economies as well and were enshrined in a series of OECD, World Bank and IMF documents (International Monetary Fund and World Bank 2001; Arvai and Heinin 2008). They were extended to their logical conclusion in some contexts by the formation of separate government debt management offices that now dealt with sovereign debt as a matter of managing risk portfolios and were run by former financial market brokers (for example in Portugal, UK and Ireland) (Currie, Dethier and Togo 2003). This new model of sovereign debt made the fiscal policy of governments increasingly dependent on the volatile, deepening and internationalizing financial markets in state bonds.

The history of the World Bank and IMF policies of austerity loans, structural adjustment and HIPC initiatives is very well known. These organizations created incentives for speed and volume in lending (Roodman 2006). These practices have been widely criticized even from within these institutions (Stiglitz 2006). But the new commercial bond markets in sovereign debt are often represented as relatively efficient and reasonable. The example given is that of the attitude of commercial bank lenders in the 1982 Latin American crisis who accepted the Brady plan to make their bond terms more favorable or write off debts owed to them (Porzecanski 2006). The point missed in these debates is that there has been a radical shift toward the technocratic management of sovereign debt in relation to market concerns. It is no longer primarily a matter of long-term political institutions and relationships, but is a financial matter that underpins bond markets in debt. State debt of course still mediates between ethical, political and fiscal relationships, but now it is treated as if it is solely a technical financial problem. If issues of citizenship or political concerns appear in these calculations, it is in terms of the rights of citizen-bondholders. As a result economic policy becomes focused on appearing as a well-behaved debtor to an atomized market place of multiple bond holders and debt-instrument investors. This is a fundamental shift in the meaning and practice of sovereign debt. Economic governance is increasingly conducted in relation to international ratings agencies, interest repayments and the volatile short-term rhythms of financial markets. It is this convergent historical process: the growth of official sector international lending; the growing dominance of debt technocrats; and the deepening and internationalization of primary markets and development of secondary derivative markets in sovereign debt that has transformed sovereign debt in India. India is not alone in this; similar structural forms have been put in place across the world as a new orthodoxy on central bank independence has combined with various institutional histories of sovereign debt. It has been imposed in some cases for example through IMF/World Bank lending initiatives and the EU 1992 Maastricht Treaty. In others, such as the case of the Federal Reserve in the 1980s, Ireland and the UK in the mid 1980–90s, it has been enthusiastically adopted as new best practice.

What occurred during the 1980s–2000s in India was a gradual shift in the form of sovereign debt. It began as a source of public finances for national social investment but became a fiscal mechanism that underpins markets and the rights of citizen bond-holders. This change has had a profound impact on the possibilities of, and aims for, public-sector policy. It also turns public-sector institutions into a source of accumulation for a broad base of middle-class and institutional investors. This follows a worldwide trend. This has led to the main debtors in recent debt crises being public or quasi-public-sector organizations and their creditors being predominantly holders of securities in local and foreign markets (Marx, Echague and Sandleris 2006). These debt crises are quickly resolved so that market trading and private accumulation, which are now key rationales for sovereign debt, can continue.

How then did this transformation of sovereign debt occur in India? This was a long, gradual process that began with the return of Indira Gandhi to power in 1980. With her economic advisors such as Arjun Sengupta and L. K. Jha she moved toward selective liberalization measures and sought an IMF loan. These policy moves were driven by the short-term economic goal of reducing the fiscal effects of declining exports and the increasing cost of oil in world markets. They were also related to the longer-term political goal of building support for the Congress Party among the business communities in North India that had been lost during the Emergency

from 1975 to 1977 (Dash 1999). Government control on the limits to some manufac-
tured imports were lifted, taxes were decreased on the middle classes and controls
on the expansion of national firms were reduced. The IMF loan request of $5.8 bil-
lion was the largest in the history of the institution. Approval was achieved through
the interventions of Robert McNamara (head of World Bank, 1968–81) and Indian
economists on the negotiation team, who had previously worked at the World Bank
or IMF. These technocrats knew the techniques and perspectives of these institutions well. The longer-term consequence was that at the heart of Indira Gandhi's
government public deficit began to be managed by World Bank and IMF trained
technocrats seeking to conform to the fiscal policies of new multilateral lending
regimes. They pushed hard on public-sector spending. They restricted central government loans and expenditure to make repayments on the IMF loan. This was fully
paid for in 1984, and the third segment of the IMF loan was not taken up.

During the second half of the 1980s Indira, then Rajiv Gandhi's administrations,
increasingly resorted to the growing financial market in international commercial
loans (Ghosh 2006). These bore comparatively high interest rates and shorter term
periods of time for repayment (Gupta 1994). They were used more frequently as
government tax revenues declined. This was due to the policies of the Rajiv Gandhi
administration. These policies cut taxes on the middle classes and corporations and
reduced government business licensing regimes. Debt servicing as a percentage of
gross national product, or interest payments on these loans, rose sharply from 17.5
percent in 1984–85 to 28.8 percent in 1991–92 (ibid.). Further loans at higher than
previous interest rates were taken from official sources such as the Asian Development Bank. The requirement of paying the interest on public-sector debt came to
gradually dominate economic policy, restricting the parameters for decision-making by its annual rhythms and figures. This increase in interest payments on public financing contributed greatly to the balance of payments crisis in 1991 (Mohan
2000, 2008). External political events such as the collapse of the Soviet Union, the
loss of East European markets, a global recession and the rise in the price of oil
because of the Gulf War in 1990 added to the growing problem. In 1991 IMF loans
to the value of $1.8 billion were taken by the Janata Dal government under Chandra
Shekhar. However the economic policy reforms introduced by the Narasimhan Rao
coalition government later that year fully developed the trend toward the financialization of sovereign debt.

These reforms were designed and led by former World Bank and IMF technocrats. Manmohan Singh, the new finance minister, had acted as technocratic advi-

sor to both Indira Gandhi and Rajiv Gandhi on matters of sovereign debt (as head of the Reserve Bank of India 1982–85 and deputy head of the planning commission of India 1985–87). As secretary-general of the South Commission (1987–90) he had discussed his ideas for economic reform in India with IMF managing director Michael Camdessus (Ghosh 2006). Montek Singh Aluwalia was brought in from a distinguished career in the World Bank and was made the key economic advisor to the government. These men placed colleagues from the World Bank and IMF at the head of most government ministries or in key advisory positions. Other proreform ministers such as P. Chidambaram (commerce minister), N. K. P. Salve (minister of power), and M. Arunachalam (minister of state for industry) were appointed to cement the coordination between the IMF and the Indian bureaucracy. In 1992 a new head of the Reserve Bank of India, C. Rangarajan, who had long argued for reforms, was appointed. In 1993 Shankar Acharya was made chief economic advisor to the government after a long career at the World Bank. These technocrats started to "dominate the upper echelons of the bureaucracy" (Ghosh 2006, 417). These policy moves were strongly supported by business lobbies such as the Confederation of Indian Industry, which organized a press campaign in favor of opening the economy to foreign direct investment and privatization. The opposition Communist Party (Maoist) had little ability to resist economic reform given the balance of payments crisis and the assertions that there was only one possible technocratic solution for it. Indian trade unions, as they had in 1986 when Rajiv Gandhi introduced his reforms, threatened national strikes. But their protests were ended by government guarantees that they would retrain laid off public-sector employees and create new jobs through a national renewal fund. The key policy idea of the technocrats was that a "rebalancing" of the economy was necessary. This would be achieved through a turn toward free markets and away from a controlling public sector that was described as starving the private sector of credit, savings and growth (Aluwalia 1994; Mohan 2008). The Congress-led government swiftly introduced changes to achieve this through reducing taxes on and licensing of trade; removal of investment limits; cutting tax on imports; and removal of public-sector monopolies in all but six industries. A second IMF loan that was negotiated in 1991 was intended to stabilize the economy during these reforms. The World Bank also supported these policies through a structural adjustment loan in the same year and further loans to the center in 1993.

How then did these economic policies and external loans further consolidate the financialization of sovereign debt? First, an institution, the External Debt Management Unit, was introduced into the Reserve Bank of India (RBI). The aim of this was to manage as a purely financial problem the question of external sovereign debt. With the close technocratic links that had now developed between the RBI and the bureaucracy, the public sector was pressed hard by this office to find the revenues to prepay high-cost external loans. As a result the borrowings from the IMF were liquidated in 2000. This trend continued as from 2002 to 2003 the Indian government prematurely repaid US$2 billion and a further $3.8 billion from 2003 to 2004 (Ministry of Finance 2004). As a result austerity policy dominated in the public sector with an increasing trend toward using public-sector income and further loans to repay interest and deficit arrears in state and central budgets (Vithal 1996). State debt was increasingly managed at the high levels of government as a financial problem of debt repayment not as form of social or political investment. While at the same time, taxes were reduced on the middle classes and corporations so that the money supply would remain more in the hands of "entrepreneurial" forces in society (Mohan 2008; Piketty 2014).

Direct policy moves toward the financialization of sovereign debt were also taken. These initiatives were to create a dynamic and expanded internal financial market in sovereign debt bonds. This would replace previous strategies for financing state debt through monetarization, government fixed interest rate bonds sold mainly to captive banking institutions or loans from external agencies. It was also argued that these moves would release the creative energies of finance capital in India by underpinning financial market institutions. If institutional regimes were set up for greater dynamic trading in government bonds, then a new financial infrastructure could emerge of laws, products, services and derivatives markets. In addition a market in sovereign debt would form the foundation for efficient measuring devices, yield curves, through which the value of other debt bonds and derivatives could be calculated. Yield curves are the key forecasting devices for bond markets that track the measure of market expectations of future interest rates on securities given the current market conditions (Zaloom 2009). Government securities are the zero base for these calculations, as they are considered risk free unlike other debt bonds. These also act as a basic measure that would integrate different segments of the domestic financial market and could establish a scale through which domestic and external financial markets could be linked. In the reforms that followed, Indian state debt was taking on a new role—it would underpin financial market speculation. As the RBI report on Indian sovereign debt suggested, the yield curve of sovereign debt bonds "acts as a kind of public good that is used constantly by participants in the financial system" (Reserve Bank of India 2007, 166).

The new technocrats at the RBI and finance ministry set about constructing this market following other government initiatives. Citing the model of the Bank of England reforms of 1986, they tried to develop a "deep" and "liquid" market in sovereign debt bonds. Government securities would be issued on a fixed routine that would facilitate sufficient market liquidity, not in terms of the borrowing needs of public-sector institutions. Tax revenue should only be raised on the trade in these securities in a way that would not hinder market liquidity. Issues of the social benefits of accumulation occurring from the public sector and its resources through this mechanism were not addressed in this technocratic model.

So what measures were put in place for this financialization? In the early 1990s these began with three policy moves (Ministry of Finance 2008). Auctions in government securities at fixed annual intervals by the Reserve Bank of India were started. The fixing of government bond interest rates by the RBI in coordination with the finance ministry was ended. The requirement of banks and financial institutions to purchase a certain percentage of fixed rate government securities was also stopped. In 1996 primary dealers were designated who could also trade in government stocks as investment vehicles. These moves were followed by the ending of the automatic monetization of fiscal deficits in 1997–98, which reduced the finance ministry's ability to independently handle government debt. In the ways and means agreement of 1997 the RBI and central government discontinued the practice of issuing ad hoc treasury bills to replenish the cash stocks of the center. These would be met instead through ways and means advances from the RBI that had to be fully repaid on a short-term schedule of three months from the date of advance, accelerating the rate at which public debt repayments had to be made. The aim of these moves was to improve the "fiscal discipline" of the public sector and create a monetary policy independent of political authorities. These policies were strengthened in the FRBM act of 2003 that mandated central government targets to eliminate revenue deficits and to reduce fiscal deficits to 3 percent of GDP by 2008–9. They also set the investment market freer from control by the RBI, which was no longer allowed to act in the primary market in government debt. Recent suggestions in the RBI's Kelkar and Mohan reports, taken up by finance ministers Chidambaran in 2008 and Pranab Mukherjee in 2012, to found a debt management office independent of the RBI represent a further attempt to fully separate the market in bonds from the management of government debt. Rather than reducing the cost of government borrowing, these moves have led to a steady increase in interest rates and the cost of borrowing for the government (Mohan 2008). This situation has become so chronic that it has led key government economists such as Rakesh Mohan (economic advisor ministry of industry 1988–96, RBI deputy governor 2002–4, author of infrastructure financing reports 1996, 2010) to argue that the public sector should be dismantled (2000). He suggests that there should be a radical privatization of all but strategic sector public enterprises and the revenues derived from this should be used to retire public debt interest burdens. The election of a Bharatiya Janata Party government under Narendra Modi in 2014 has not altered these policies, which are seen as technocratic necessity. Here the new form of sovereign debt meets its full realization. The only public good of state debt is that it should be repaid.

In the chapters that follow I trace the unpredictable impact of this new practice of sovereign debt. As we will see from the Hooghly waterscape it contributes to increasing instability and inequality in the circulation of capital. It also leads to contradictions in the extractive and redistributive aspects of the public sector. Public infrastructure is generated that becomes increasingly difficult to manage or make a livelihood from. The *res publica* of urban life are transformed. I will also reveal how people attempt to remake the ethical and political aspects of public life that are undermined by the management of state debt as a financial problem. Ultimately these measures have produced new relations between market and state institutions.

Toward a New Anthropology of Economic Governance: The Conduct of Productivity, Speculation and Timespaces

State debt policy and mechanisms of government financing originate with high-level central government technocrats, but related policies are implemented through widely dispersed practices of economic governance. I propose a new way of analyzing this economic governance as composed of popular ethical projects and forms of speculation that take place in complex timespaces.

In anthropology, we have concentrated on economic governance as an application of expert knowledge and heuristic devices (Callon, Yuval and Muniesa 2007; Riles 2004, 2011). We have focused on how officials classify the economy demonstrating the social costs of this activity (Mitchell 2002; Murray-Li 2007). We have undermined the authority of this expert knowledge by showing that it is based on dramatic performances and generates ambiguity (Best 2012; James 2012; Silver 2010). We have illustrated how knowledge procedures create uncertainty for bureaucrats and their clients (Bear 2007). Knowledge techniques have even been shown to work through routine ignorance (Anders 2008; McGoey 2007). In my approach I build on these critiques but I move away from their emphasis on formal knowledge. Instead I trace how economic governance emerges from the interactions between such formal practices and popular ethics of productivity. In this move I am guided by Herzfeld's emphasis on the qualities of bureaucratic relationships and the forms of intimacy and distancing they involve (1993, 2005). Formal devices from debt agreements, accounts of profits, models of markets, projections of future income to money itself are used by people to convert between diverse forms of value in strategies aimed at ethical goals (Bear, Ho, Tsing, Yanagisako 2015). This is even though these devices themselves are also technical forms of a moral order (Maurer 2002; Miller 2002). Capitalist social action can only be understood if we trace the pursuits of class status, of the public good and selfhood that are both troubled by, and orient the uses of, these translation devices.

All formal models of the economy from utilitarianism and probabilistic risk analysis to macroeconomics are ethical projects. They hide this in their mathematical languages, procedures and models (Maurer 2002; Li Puma and Lee 2004; Blyth 2013; Poovey 2008). Yet they all contain transcendent ordering principles, concepts of the public good and models of ideal conduct. Critiques of economists also take place in ethical registers. For example Marx combined Protestant, agricultural and chemical analogies to understand the fertility of labor (Arendt 1958; Bellamy Foster 2000; Bear 2013). Yet, knowing this, we have rarely examined the ethics of everyday transactions that aim to govern the economy and generate profit (Weber 1978; Patico 2009; Wilson 2012; Zaloom 2004; Yanagisako 2002, 2012, 2013). I draw on the anthropology of ethics to enter into this reality (Herzfeld 2004; Laidlaw 2013; Lambek 2010; Stafford 2013). I examine how bureaucrats, entrepreneurs and workers understand acts of labor and entrepreneurship as part of a larger project of, what I call, the conduct of productivity. In this case, and most likely in many others, people combine concepts derived from science, economics, ritual and kinship to create a sense of large-scale generative processes that persist through time. They seek to harness these productive powers for the public good through forms of action on the world. Importantly, their broader ethics emerge from the specific experiences of particular timespaces of work. At the center of the conduct of productivity are senses of workmanship. These are forms of practical knowledge and descriptions of the world that are generated from encounters in labor with it. Senses of workmanship include skillful human practices, aesthetics of well-made objects and expertise about nonhuman processes (Veblen 1924). To act according to a sense of workmanship and in relation to a wider conduct of productivity is to be an ethical person and to assert a distinct class position. In my case, this personhood is unequivocally male. Masculine potential and status is at stake in the fortunes of trade and business on the river (Chopra, Osella and Osella 2004; Fernandes 1997; McDowell 2003). Although, of course, my theoretical point could be applied to any capitalist situation from professional economists or financial markets traders to feminized labor such as direct selling agents or data entry (Freeman 2000, 2007; Wilson 1999; Upadhya and Vasavi 2008; Zaloom 2004). It is important to map the diverse conducts of productivity that exist within structurally related state and market institutions. This is because it is the combination of such microprojects that produce forms of class inequality and accumulation.

Alongside senses of workmanship the conduct of productivity also involves forms of social action that seek to anticipate the future and creatively bring it into being—speculation. My argument is that such speculation is central to capitalism—especially of contemporary forms of economic governance—rather than an illegitimate exception to it. Derived from the Latin word *speculatus*, meaning to spy out, examine or explore, speculation has acquired negative associations and is now a label given to illegal or risky financial behavior (Birla 2009). But I use speculation in a neutral sense to describe a particular form of social action. This is the sharing of secret conjectures about hidden, opaque realities. These acts of disclosure form the foundation for creative social relationships intended to realize the potential of these obscured realities. Speculation, unlike the sense of workmanship, exceeds existing ethics and knowledge. It is associated with a heightened state of anticipation of the future in which normal ethics and routines of work and calculation are often suspended (Bear, Birla, Puri 2015).

The conduct of productivity takes place in specific time-spaces of circulation. Economic governance has rarely been analyzed in relation to time. Only factories and markets have been explored in this manner (Thompson 1967; Bestor 2001). In recent years we have traced how bureaucracies plan the future through risk analysis and scenario planning (Adam and Groves 2007; Reith 2004; Lakoff 2007). But this is just a first step in an important area of study—how people attempt to govern timespaces of productivity. How do bureaucrats, entrepreneurs and workers on the Hooghly use and experience various disciplines, technologies and representations of time (Thrift and May 2001)? In the complex timespace of the river they try to reconcile the rhythms of international trade; the seasonal tides and patterns of the river; debt repayment schedules; representations of the Hooghly's divine and human history; visions of the future; speculation; and predictive technologies. It is only through such analysis of timespaces that we can understand how circulation in austerity capitalism (or any form of capitalism) works.

Economic Governance on the Hooghly:
Bengali Nationalism and Hinduism

The bureaucracy that governs the Hooghly was first put in place in 1890 and its authority has remained largely unaltered since then. The Kolkata Port Trust has a wide jurisdiction that goes beyond control of the labor and traffic in the two docks in Kolkata (Kidderpore docks and Netaji Subhas Bose docks) and the newer, downriver Haldia dock. It governs the Hooghly and all the land within 10 kilometers of the high water mark at spring tide on either side of the river from Konnagar north of Kolkata to the sea, 125 kilometers away at Sagar Island. From 1969 it also gained control of the Bhagirathi River that runs from the Ganges down to the Hooghly. All the traffic on, and the physical resources of, the river are controlled by its rulings and licenses. Each boat that plies along it has to be licensed by its officers. Ships must be guided through the river by pilots who take over command of the vessels until they reach the sea off Sagar Island. Navigable channels up the river are maintained and mapped by its hydrographic survey department. The port trust deploys dredgers to clear the river of silt. Wrecks and obstructions must be removed by its agents. Any use of the water, sand or bank along the river has to be licensed by its offices. Land along the banks must be leased from it on short-term contracts. The port trust is, in fact, the largest single landowner in Kolkata.

This vast enterprise is divided into key departments of the Port, Estate, Personnel, Marine, Hydrographic Survey and Mechanical Engineering. Most bureaucrats work far away from the river in BBD Bagh at the center of Kolkata. A smaller new office, built in the 1980s, facing the gate of Kidderpore docks houses the staff who have direct knowledge of the river and manage its daily operations, the traffic department and the departments of the harbor master river and harbor master port. At the top of this governing authority stands the chairman and his deputy. They are Indian Administrative Service officers who have been appointed from outside for four or five years, with no specialized knowledge. The schemes and ambitions of departments are presented once a month to the trustees of the port in board meetings. The board sanctions expenditures and programs of work and decides on future plans in relation to precedent and rulings from the Ministry of Surface Transport. Since the 1960s the trustees have included the leaders of the Port Sromik

Union (PSU) and National Union of Waterfront Workers (NUWW); the head of the Shipping Corporation of India in Kolkata; the head of the Central Water Inland Trading Company; representatives of the West Bengal government; powerful local politicians from the Kolkata Municipal Corporation; the head of the navy in Kolkata; a bureaucrat posted from the Ministry of Surface Transport; and the regional chairman of the Indian Oil Corporation. They adjudicate the fate of the waterscape.

Importantly, the river governed by this complex bureaucracy is a resonant presence. Everyone who worked with it reflected and drew from its colonial and nationalist history. Older economic endeavors rise up from its depths and on its banks as wrecks, ruined schemes for prosperity and vital infrastructure. Eighteenth-century merchant trade is visible in the Chinese Buddhist temple at Achipur and the Portuguese church at Bandel. Nineteenth-century colonialism appears as sunken ships such as the James and Mary at Hooghly point and the Kidderpore docks. Partition is marked by a Sufi shrine south of Diamond Harbour that is saluted by men as they pass it, which revives the presence of East Bengali Muslim lascars (skilled boatmen and sailors who declined in numbers after partition in 1947). The decaying infrastructures of the Indian socialist nation-state exist as stilled vast cranes in Kidderpore docks and spurs that still shape the river. Working on the river compels attention to the past because its material remains are central to the practical work of the present. In river charts, ruins on the waterfront and wrecks orient navigation along the river. It is the old equipment built by the public sector in colonial and Nehruvian India that is recycled now into new uses. The past forms both the material infrastructures and resources for reflection on the most recent changes in the waterscape.

These material fragments are overlaid with well-established nationalist representations of the river (Cederloff and Sivaramakrishnan 2006). From 1937 an elite environmental nationalism, first popularized by Radhakamal Mukherjee, has argued that the Ganges in Bengal is declining because of silting caused by the wrong kind of human activity along its banks (1937). The sentiments of this nationalism are thickened by a much more widespread popular sense of the river as a link to a lost, but potentially redeemable, Golden Bengal (*Sonar Bangla*). This is fueled in particular by the genre of *bhatiali gan,* or boatman's songs, collected by the well-known folklorist and poet from prepartition East Bengal, Jasimuddin Mollah (1903–76). These were widely broadcast in Bengali radio programming in post-Independence India. They now circulate on tapes, are used in Bengali films and are sung by enthusiasts. In the songs *majhis* (boatmen) working the river offer an image of endurance and represent a longing for a rejoining of territory with Bangladesh. On the back of buses *majhis* and their boats appear bearing the Indian flag, often in rural scenes of a *Sonar Bangla* (Golden Bengal). Governing or working on the river is an intervention in a longer-term project of generating or hindering the national prosperity of a Golden Bengal.

As well as these resonances, the Hooghly's recalcitrant force is framed through the ritual associations of the goddess Ma Ganga (for different examples of the potent symbolism of Indian rivers, see Alley 2002; Feldhaus 1995, 2003; Haberman 2006). In popular Hinduism, Ma Ganga brings life and energy to a world filled with polluting death (Ostor 1980). She descends to earth to restore the life of the ancestral relatives of Bhagirath burned to death in anger by a sage disturbed in his meditations. She is controlled in her movement by the male principle Siva, because otherwise her force would be destructive. Her descent marks a new life-giving beginning. It is the moment when the landscape itself takes its present permanent form. This is made clear in popular religious pamphlets that contain geographically accurate maps of the Hooghly, Bhagirathi and Padma and descriptions of how these rivers were formed by Ma Ganga's descent. The Padma breaks off because Siva could not let all of Ma Ganga down in one place without destroying creation with her force. Bhagirath leads into the Ganga/Hooghly as it runs down to the sea at Sagar Island because he himself called her to earth to reanimate his dead ancestors. There is no distance between the physical, material river and the mythological Ganga in this Bengali popular Hinduism (for other different examples of these associations, see Alley 2002; Doron 2008). In fact, everyone I met during my fieldwork called the river the Ganga not the Hooghly. The productivity of the river and its agency were framed for bureaucrats, river workers and entrepreneurs through this ritual mythology. Whatever negative force existed in the waterscape was, in contrast to this, as we will see, dealt with through the manipulation of relationships with the goddess Kali.

As I will explore, the economic governance of the Hooghly occurs through the articulations between these forms of popular nationalism and Hinduism and austerity policies. The management of nature here looks very different from that predicted by many existing theories. It does not only rest on a short-term market logic, nor on a single split between the human and nonhuman (Adam 1998; Latour 1996; Escobar 1999). Instead, economic governance is rich with ethical meanings that both sustain and challenge the extraction of value from the river.

Fieldwork in a Liberalization Waterscape: Public Records and Speculative Friendship

How is it possible to approach research on such a complex bureaucracy and waterscape? The answer I found was to start with two key elements of economic governance on the Hooghly—public records and speculative friendship. My initial encounters with high-level bureaucrats at the port trust head office at BBD Bagh were shaped by their attempts to control access. As a result, instead of starting in the docks and on the river, my research began in the small port trust library set up in 2000. This was intended for employees and more recently for the public, who could access it under the Right to Information Act of 2005. Judging from the attendance ledger, no members of the public had ever been here. This was not surprising, since the Central Industrial Security Force (CISF) guarded the entrance. I felt isolated from the bureaucracy in the library, which was on the outermost edge of the offices next to an unattended reception for visitors. This proudly displayed international quality management certifications and an old social realist painting from the 1970s of thousands of men at work in the Kolkata docks. The librarians, two middle-aged female clerks, were kindly protective and strictly supervisory. They meticulously reported my reading to officials. They attributed the tight security to friction with the port unions. One morning evidence of this arrived in the form of twenty men from the PSU stripped to their waists shouting at the bored CISF officers demanding wage and benefits settlements. But my sense of exclusion was misplaced. It was from this library that I began my journey into the interplay between official records and speculative friendship through which economic governance on the Hooghly is being transformed.

In the library, as a matter of public record, were stored the published board meetings of the port trust stretching from 1880 to 2004. Bureaucrats were not worried about my access to these. As I spoke more to officers and clerks in the head office, I realized that this lack of concern existed for many interlinked reasons. Bureaucrats did not expect the records to contain anything controversial. They assumed that they contained indifferent rulings, which they still referred to in order to regularize decisions and make them impersonal (Herzfeld 2005 [1997]; Hull 2012). Because they used the records as bureaucratic tools of indifferent authority in the present, they thought they would tell an uncontroversial history. To think otherwise would undermine the very official basis of their own actions in the present. Bureaucrats also expected them to be filled with mathematical accounts, which were records of irrefutable neutral facts (Poovey 2008). They assumed too, that because these were public records, they would confirm their standard narratives of what had produced the crisis of the present. This was, bureaucrats argued, the inefficiency and activism of the working classes along with the growing natural problem of a silting river. They assumed that by their inherent nature as official records such documents would not breach the security of the kinds of secrets they wanted to preserve. Official records, by definition, could not contain secrets. Yet these did contain a secret hidden in plain view. This is the long-term history of institutional decisions oriented around changing forms of state debt that I tell in this book. Ultimately this is the enchanting power of official records within bureaucracies. Their very form as a public record generates an amnesia in the bureaucracy about their controversial origin in political struggles, autocratic decisions and forms of impotence. These are turned into mathematical facts and neutral rulings. These then become the unexamined foundation for actions in the present. Therefore to work in this archive was to uncover both the agency of official abstractions that enable economic governance in the present and a hidden history.

Importantly, as I spent more time in the library, I met officials who began to convey sensitive information to me. In addition, permission was finally granted for me to interview high-level officials. I began to be passed along networks in the bureaucracy, and officials asked me to accompany them in their work on the river. The relationships generated by these disclosures were unpredictable because bureaucrats would switch abruptly from gestures of intimate friendship back to official statements (Hertzfeld 2005 [1997]). These interactions were not specific to my encounters. They were evidence of a relationship that is central to the creation of links between state and private capitalism in liberalization India. The forging of such connections has a specific name. It is to *jogajog kora*, or "to create useful friendships." This verb has its origins in a play on words. To add and subtract is to *jog bijog kora*, but to *jogajog kora* is to add and then add again, thereby building limitless, expanding connections. These relationships have as an explicit aim the accrual of potentially endless influence. Accountancy and affect combine in a pursuit of ties that have future potential. Although this term and practice are widespread throughout West Bengal, the term has taken on a heightened significance for bureaucrats and entrepreneurs on the Hooghly. It is the medium through which a decentralized economic governance of speculation occurs. I did not understand how *jogajog kora* worked until I had spent several months moving along key brokering relationships. These shaped the arcs of my research, taking me outward from the port trust and the docks into private businesses on the Hooghly. Through these connections state plans and revenue streams were linked to the projects of entrepreneurs and their informalized workers. The official documents I read in the archive and more recent publicized schemes often formed the means for negotiating these connections. Through this activity of *jogajog kora* the creation of contemporary forms of economic governance was laid open to me. The networks I joined, along with the records I consulted, were the substance of bureaucratic action on the economy.

These networks led me outward from the Kolkata Port Trust Office to four key sites and networks for in-depth participant observation. These we have encountered on the monsoon journey I described at the beginning of the introduction. First the docks and launches at Ash Ghat, where men in the port trust marine crew worked. Second the networks of marine officers and river pilots who navigate the container ships on the river. Third the interlinked boatmen and private entrepreneurs associated with a port office at Water Ghat. And fourth, the private shipyard, Venture Ltd, where state vessels, and now international ships, are built. From 2008 to 2009, for a continuous year, I divided the days of each week between these locations and networks, joining men at work and at home in their neighborhoods in Kolkata and Howrah. This was supplemented by several shorter month-long research trips in 2010 and 2011. I have renamed these places and my informants to protect them from any negative outcomes of my research for their livelihoods.

In each successive chapter I trace this journey outward from the Kolkata Port Trust offices and docks into the private businesses on the river. The structure of the book echoes the arc of my research. We begin in the heart of the bureaucracy, the port trust library and its records. In Section I, I reveal from these the hidden past of state debt crises on the Hooghly moving through the history of changing forms of debt from the 1960s to the present. I track the emergence of everyday financial crisis within the Kolkata Port Trust and its unintended consequences. These included unstable forms of austerity: labor, property, technology and nature.

In the ethnographic chapters that follow I explore how contemporary economic governance emerges from the conduct of productivity among river bureaucrats, entrepreneurs and workers. In Section II, I focus on practices of the public good that seek to create regeneration on the Hooghly. Among marine crew, marine officers and private entrepreneurs individual and collective conduct is directed toward a project of renewal that is understood through nationalist and ritual frames. I show how managerial hierarchies and class inequalities between public- and private-sector labor emerge from these popular ethics.

In Section III, I focus on speculation, or, how the Kolkata Port Trust has turned into a speculation machine. I examine the practices of *jogajog kora* that stimulate links between public and private economies on the Hooghly—in particular those associated with a marine office at Water Ghat and its networks. These networks contribute to the emergence of an entrepreneurial society on the river in which the working poor are both brought closer to the state and are exploited by it in new ways.

In Section IV, I highlight the contradictions produced in the timespaces of circulation and production on the Hooghly by the financialization of state debt. In Chapter 5, I move out onto the Hooghly with river pilots. I show how accidents with container ships emerge from uncontrollable and increasing disjunctures in forms of capital accumulation. River pilots attempt to solve these by creating more efficient uses of time aided by technological devices that reflect their heroic ethics. In Chapter 6, I enter the informal workplaces produced in relation to the new state practices on the Hooghly, which have also become part of global production. In particular we encounter the short-term capitalism of private shipyards that are riven with uncertainty and instability. Here men attempt to forge a future through faith in the powers of exemplary men or worker-brothers that are manifest in the products of their labor. These are associated with the eternal returns of natural and ritual rhythms.

My section "Beyond Austerity" explores the significance of the realities of the Hooghly for our own analytical, ethical and political engagements with austerity policy. The first chapter explores how the ethics of shipyard workers and their families might lead to new theoretical and political insights. The second returns to a general discussion of state debt policy and can be read as a stand-alone chapter. In this I trace the global crisis in the practice of government that is created by current sovereign debt policies that emphasize financial and market mechanisms. I suggest that a social calculus be applied by policy makers, politicians and the public to government fiscal measures.

Section I

The Circuit of State Debt

Everyday Crisis

In the Kolkata Port Trust fiscal crisis is a permanent condition that guides daily decisions and acts of work. The signs of this chronic predicament are everywhere in rusting equipment, ruined buildings, malfunctioning machinery and threats of redundancies. Yet trade on the Hooghly and the revenue raised from its resources has steadily increased since the 1980s. Surrounded by this contrast of decay and productivity, marine bureaucrats often contemplated their fate.

I encountered this meditation from my first journey on the Hooghly when a high-level officer, Captain Verma, took me on a port launch. He is a man who enjoys movement and he wanted to show me the Hooghly, so he suggested a dusk voyage from Kidderpore. The port launch churned into action. We sat on the prow with the few lights of the city turning it into a distant shadow. The dark water parted before us. On the river Captain Verma began to describe the past and desolate future of the port. He pointed out the lascar's monument to Muslim sailors long gone and the Calcutta jetties that he said had been given away for a paltry 1 rupee to the state government to use as they willed. As he looked at the river he saw traces of the ill-fated actions of men. Pointing at the bank he explained that the Hooghly was widened here by the British, but that such measures caused dangerous contrary forces and increased silting. He grew sadder remembering how water levels were higher here before the Farakka barrage had been built. We sped past fishermen in the middle of the river anchored to old abandoned port buoys. Reaching the second Howrah Bridge, it suddenly cast light on the waves with its bright illuminations similar to those strung through the streets during puja festivals. Captain Verma said, "They spent so much money on this illumination, but none on my docks." He laughed and added that the current chairman had told the unions that they could do all the "Marxist-Leninist show" they wanted, but they had to work to make the port survive. He continued with deep sadness, "My port is just remaining not progressing."

He then asked what had happened to the London docks so that they were closed in the 1980s. A flash of lighting lit up the west and a freezing wind rushed over the water, making it writhe. The launch labored hard against the flow of the tide turning back to land, but at full speed it hardly moved. Caught between the river and the shore surrounded by signs of decay, we all willed the decrepit vessel forward.

This was one of many such conversations. Men often asked me about the docks in central London—why exactly they had been shut down. They grew quiet as I described the combination of political and economic reasons for their closure almost overnight. Then they spoke sadly of the rumors that the Kolkata docks were going to be turned into a marina for pleasure yachts. At other times they suggested that new jetties opening downriver at Diamond Harbour or the new virtual jetty at Sagar Island would redeem the fortunes of the port. Yet no one could explain to me why there was a persistent financial crisis when trade levels were high. Marine officers sometimes ventured the idea that this was because of the bad reputation the port had gained in the 1980s–90s for labor disputes. They also suggested that silting caused by the construction of the Farakka barrage to regulate water flow into the Padma in Bangladesh was steadily overwhelming their efforts to make the Hooghly productive. Importantly, in these conversations nobody questioned the fact of a fiscal crisis or attempted to trace its origins in long-term bureaucratic decisions.

In the chapter that follows I examine the historical origins of this fact of fiscal crisis. The chronic situation in the Kolkata port is unlike the spectacular events of sovereign default or financial market collapse that have been widely discussed (Bryan et al. 2012; Engelen et al. 2012; Poovey 2012; Roitman 2013; Samman 2012; Sewell 2012). It poses a different analytical challenge. It is necessary to explore how fiscal crisis takes on a quotidian bureaucratic life and how routine extractive mechanisms come into being. It is also important to trace the spiraling, unintended effects of these policies, including the inequalities they produce. Or, in other words, the social forms of austerity capitalism need to be traced.

As we will see, it is changes in the management of state debt that have generated the new forms of austerity capitalism. Significant work has traced how accounting practices hide their ethical and political underpinnings in representations of fact (Maurer 2002; Poovey 2008). Other research has examined the discipline of numbers in the context of structural adjustment policies (Anders 2008, 2010). I do not focus here on the general power of accounts and statistics, but on the precise social effects of figures of state debt. These deserve special attention. The numbers involved in state debt are a compelling simplification of complex bureaucratic histories. No one asks how they have arisen, only what needs to be done in the present in relation to them. The actions taken in their name are oriented to a fetish of increasing or decreasing a number without reference to the social relations that are produced. The figures of state debt are wide in their reach because they represent a collective debt. They make everyone within bureaucracies and ultimately in society responsible in the present for actions in the past that they did not take. As the chapter that follows shows, how state debt is practiced profoundly affects the governance of labor, property, nature and technology.

Fig. 2. Ruins at Kolkata docks

Chapter 1

Unpredictable Circulations

FROM 1965 a particular figure, the accumulated revenue deficit (the gap between net revenue profit and operating income) appeared at the end of the annual accounts of the Calcutta Port Trust. Despite its debut in 1965, this number came to dominate policy on the Hooghly only from the 1980s. Its annual return then created a year-long crisis. It had to be responded to by immediate short-term policies aimed to reduce its size during the following year. It became a *financial* legacy that required no analysis of the reasons for its existence. It was not attributed to specific policy actions or decisions from which different strategies could be learned. Instead, it dispersed a general responsibility throughout the Calcutta Port Trust. Gradually the bureaucracy and its highest body, the Port Trust Board, became a site of struggle over how to reduce this figure.

In this chapter I breach the status of the accumulated revenue deficit as a mathematical fact. I trace its origins in the era of centralized state planning, restoring its complex political history. I then explore the new fetishized agency that it acquired as public deficit was increasingly managed as a technocratic fiscal problem. I show how this shift created an accelerating, volatile rhythm focused on repayment of debt within the Calcutta Port Trust. This replaced an older emphasis on state debt as an endlessly deferred, long-term political obligation. I follow the unplanned alterations to relations with labor, property, nature and technology that developed out of everyday fiscal crisis. Austerity capitalism, as we will see, is characterized by increasingly unpredictable forms of capital circulation and unstable, dangerous livelihoods. It proceeds through the devaluation of labor; decentralized speculative planning; and improvised low-tech investments.

State Debt and Long-Term Political Obligation: Nationalist Capitalism on the Hooghly, 1965–84

The accumulated revenue deficit had its historical origins in ambitious political schemes for the remaking of the Hooghly through technological intervention.

In the 1960s and 70s the future of the Calcutta Port Trust rested on three projects laid out in the first four five-year plans. These were top-down, centralized schemes orchestrated and financed by the Ministry of Surface Transport (MOST) and the World Bank. The first of these, the Farakka barrage, was for the benefit of the port, but was not under its control. This was under construction across the Ganges in order to regulate the flow of the river into the Padma and the Bhagirathi River (the tributary that joins the Hooghly to the Ganges). Water levels had been declining in the Hooghly since the 1930s. The plan was that the Farakka barrage would divert 40,000 cubic feet of water per second into the Bhagirathi. This would guarantee flow into the Hooghly, reviving the fortunes of the Calcutta port.

The second project, which was directly under the control of the port, was the refurbishment of the docks in Calcutta. In 1958 and 1962 two World Bank loans were negotiated by the chairman and the government of India to finance this. The total loans were for $29 million and had a long, slow repayment term of twenty years at a low interest rate. This was to be used for the expansion and modernization of the berths at Calcutta docks. It would also pay for new heavy equipment such as cranes, dredgers and pilot vessels. An infrastructure of repairing workshops and mechanical cargo-handling would also be put in place. But the majority of the loan was to set up a hydraulic survey department.[1] This department was seen as particularly crucial, as it would remake the river into a productive artery.

The third large-scale project was the building of new docks downriver from Kolkata on the west bank of the river at Haldia, only 40 kilometers from the sea. In 1958 the port had considered introducing a deep draft anchorage at Diamond Harbour on the eastern side of the river, but the deputy conservator suggested in 1959 that a place on the opposite bank at Haldia be chosen. From this small seed the project for a satellite port to Kolkata at Haldia took on momentum. This was in spite of the fact that in the same year the channel at Haldia had become impassable. It was only re-opened through twenty-four-hour dredging. Ignoring this inauspicious beginning, MOST and the port trust pressed on with this location. They were confident that the World Bank loan to support the development of the hydrographic survey department would allow them to overcome these limits to their ambitions.[2]

The expectation of MOST and the Calcutta Port Trust was that that any debts taken on to support these three schemes would be paid off by future productivity. Bureaucrats and politicians were confident that a combination of hydraulic science and long-term investment in national prosperity would have a transforming effect. So when the amounts of loans steadily increased from 1967 onward, the central government was not concerned. Instead they kept on renewing their political commitments to the possibility of future national wealth. When the accounts of 1967–68 revealed a deficit of 3.13 million rupees, resulting from the costs of borrowing to finance Haldia, a central government Port Finances Inquiry committee was convened.[3] This concluded that the government should keep lending over the long term to guarantee future success. As debts mounted, MOST even began to suspend the fiscal responsibilities attached to its loans and subsidized the Calcutta Port Trust. It introduced a complete moratorium on the repayment of government loans for Haldia.[4] This continued into the 1990s, even as costs for Haldia rose. When the accumulated revenue deficit rose to Rs10.56 million by March 1972, the central government also agreed to give a retrospective subsidy of 80 percent of dredging costs in the Haldia area. Confidence in these expenditures continued because all concerned were convinced that hydraulic science and the effects of the Farakka barrage would solve current problems. In 1973 it was estimated that each year 4 million tons of cargo would move through 40-foot-deep drafts in the Hooghly near the new port.[5] In 1976 the board confidently predicted that the full amount of the debts would be paid back to the government within eight years of the opening of Haldia.[6]

Yet these ambitious political plans for prosperity were already looking as if they were unlikely to ever be realized. They had been sacrificed to a greater national good—the building of diplomatic relations with the new state of Bangladesh. All the hydrographic and economic modeling had been based on a particular quantity of water reaching the Hooghly on the commissioning of the Farakka barrage. Yet these amounts never flowed into it. The new Bangladeshi government were very concerned about the diversion of large amounts of water from the Padma into the Hooghly. Negotiations in 1972 ended with the board of the Calcutta port being presented with scientific evidence by the Ministry of Irrigation and Power that only 25,000 cubic meters per second would be necessary to make the Hooghly viable. Promises were made that in a few years the amount of water might rise, but they never reached the full discharge of 40,000 cubic meters per second. Debts between the central ministry and the port trust had been accrued on the expectations of Farakka's miraculous results. Now these would never be achieved because a greater national political good had intervened.

By the financial year 1978–79, when Haldia first came into operation, the debt that the port was now liable for was enormous. As would be typical of each year going forward, the accounts showed that the cargo, port and dock were making an operating net profit in both Haldia and Calcutta, but that total outstanding loans created a deficit of Rs1558.41 thousand.[7] This debt had been built on the expectation of the productivity that would be generated by Haldia and the Farakka barrage. Faith that these would be achieved was sustained by long-term political promises of financing from MOST. It was also built on a representation of time in which the years stretched forward organized along the trajectory of five-year plans that required only political and technical will to be realized. These long-term plans were a commitment to the ever-growing future national economy. State debts created a gift of time—a pause in current processes of accumulation in which prosperity could be generated for the future. Political relationships dominated over the fiscal aspects of state debt. As long as this situation continued, the debt burden of the Calcutta Port Trust would have limited social consequences. However debt policy was about to transform radically.

State Debt and Short-Term Fiscal Obligation: Austerity Capitalism on the Hooghly, 1980–2010

The Origins of Austerity Capitalism

From the 1980s there was a dramatic shift in the practices of state debt at MOST. These followed the changing fiscal policies at the highest level of the Indian government. Public-sector austerity drives were imposed to repay the IMF loan taken in 1980 and to cover the cost of high-interest payments on the commercial loans taken from 1984 to 1990. In this environment MOST consistently reduced its subsidies and delayed payments to the Calcutta Port Trust. They also increasingly treated the port as a source from which to extract repayment revenues. For example, in 1982 MOST added a condition to their 80 percent dredging subsidy and moratorium on Haldia loans. The condition was that the dredging subsidy would be adjusted against the defaulted government debts of the port that were not under moratorium until they were liquidated. In effect this reduced the dredging subsidy to almost zero. In 1984 the ministry raised the dredging subsidy to 90 percent, but only on the condition that the amount owed to the government for dredging for 1980–81 and 1981–82 was recovered from the port. They also threatened that if the port failed to make repayments on loans from the government not covered by the Haldia moratorium, the defaulted amount would be taken out of the subsidy. As a result of these new conditions the dredging subsidy became a mechanism for moving funds centrifugally toward the center. State debt had abruptly become a punitive fiscal relationship.

Through the 1990s the financialization of state debt intensified. The new external debt management unit in the Reserve Bank of India pushed hard to limit public-sector spending and speed up repayments to the center. This was to enable the prepayment of high-interest international loans. State debt thus became a matter of austerity and repayment. In addition it became more short term and subject to the rhythms of domestic financial markets. The automatic monetizing of sovereign debt ended, along with the issuing of long-term treasury bills. This was replaced with short-term loans to the government from the Reserve Bank of India (RBI) under ways and means agreements. These had more aggressive, faster repayment cycles. In addition the newly developed bond market in sovereign debt was inaugurated. This raised the cost of central government borrowing and made it subject to the rhythms of the bond market. The effects of these measures are visible in the increasingly extractive and short-term fiscal policies of MOST. In 1994, MOST converted its old political gifts made for investment in Haldia into monetary debts. The ministry ended the moratorium on government loans made until 1977 for the construction of Haldia. The amount of Rs1.6 billion of the original loan and the interest up to 31 March 1992 of Rs2 billion would have to be repaid in twenty equal annual installments from the financial year 1993–94.[8] To secure the return of these amounts to the center, the ministry agreed to give a 100 percent reimbursement on future expenditures on river dredging. But this move was not made to suspend the fiscal aspects of the central government relationship with the port trust as with previous subsidies. It was designed to contribute to maintaining revenues on the Hooghly, so that these could be used to repay the vast debts it owed to the central government. These moves profoundly altered the national political project on the Hooghly. It was no longer a public resource in which investment would be made to generate future prosperity for citizens. It was a fiscal resource that could be used to repay central government and, ultimately, sovereign debts swiftly. Most strangely of all, in these new measures the debts created by the decisions (and mistakes) of high-level bureaucrats were becoming a source of revenue for another generation of central government officials.

MOST did not stop here in its transformation of national political debts into fiscal ones. It began to transfer its funding responsibilities to other state and commercial agencies. From the mid-1980s it steadily devolved debt relationships at commercial rates through the lower levels of the bureaucracy. The ministry encouraged the Calcutta Port Trust to take loans directly from domestic and international banks. Beginning with the plans for the financing of the sixth five-year plan in 1985, MOST instructed the port trust to take an Rs431 thousand loan from the Bombay Port Trust in order to fund the plan of works in the Calcutta docks. The repayment of this would have no moratorium and would be at commercial rates of interest.[9] By the seventh five-year plan, in 1989, the Calcutta Port Trust was informed by the ministry that the amount of Rs19.05 million needed would be provided in loans of 6.05 million from the government, and the balance would be funded by intercorporate loans from other port trusts and commercial banks.[10] By 1991 the port trust had already borrowed Rs214 million of intercorporate loans to finance these schemes.[11] Public debts were becoming decentralized and transforming into diverse commercial relationships with various institutions acting as financial creditors.

Year after year these policies brought the port finances into crisis. In 2000 the Calcutta Port Trust experienced the most severe financial crisis in its history. A similar pattern was visible right across the public sector as a result of the change in state debt funding policies (Vithal 1996). Calcutta docks would start the financial year with a cash balance of Rs40 million but would require an extra Rs164.81 million to meet establishment costs. Haldia began the year with Rs127.28 million, but all of this would be fully spent by the end of the year, leaving it without any cash balance. Part of the problem was that MOST had reimbursed only just over half of the total expenditure made for dredging maintenance, leaving the port with a shortfall of Rs229.87 million.[12] This annual nonpayment of the full amount of the dredging subsidy continued until 2004, after which access to public records ends. The consequences of the technocratic management of state debt as a fiscal problem are starkly visible in these figures.

This repetitive, cyclical internal fiscal crisis in the Calcutta Port Trust was entirely distinct from the external face of liberalization reported to the press and public. For example, in the influential report of the interministerial group set up by MOST to examine private participation in ports, there was only mention of enterprise and efficiency. These would be achieved through the formation of partnerships with entrepreneurs to develop infrastructure and equipment, provide outsourced labor and develop land resources.[13] Five-year plans, too, made mention only of the prosperous future of public-private partnerships. The reality of the new forms of austerity capitalism were not visible in policy statements.

It is to the characteristics of this austerity capitalism that I turn next. As we will see, it produces insecure livelihoods and unstable forms of capital circulation. It proceeds through the devaluation of labor; decentralized speculative planning; and improvised low-tech investments. It radically alters the governance of labor, property, nature and technology.

Austerity Labor: Devaluing the Working Classes
and Impermanent Livelihoods

From the 1980s fiscal debts created a cyclical year-long crisis in the port trust. The question that entirely dominated the weekly board meetings was, How can we reduce our current deficit and head off the accumulation of further debts? A solution emerged early on that was returned to through subsequent decades, the reduction of manpower working on the river and in the docks. This always had two goals, a quick reduction in wage costs and a hollowing out of union activism. It also had a recurrent structure of circular argumentation. This was that the deficit in the port was caused by the politically active and unproductive working classes. It was through a restructuring of the port's relationships to its labor force that the problem of fiscal debt could be solved. In particular the solution was claimed to lie in the reduction of permanent employees and outsourcing of work. Similar efforts were not made to reduce the numbers of bureaucrats in the head office. The middle classes and working-class labor aristocracy of Kolkata began to struggle with each other over access to the state's diminishing resources.

This repetitive argument was first made in an influential report on the labor situation in Calcutta port prepared by a subcommittee of trustees in 1981.[14] This represented a turning point in which the "low productivity" of dock labor was first measured. Each month from this point on statistics were collected on traffic and delays to its flow through the port including measurements of labor productivity and strike action. This was not a Taylorist move aimed at increasing the efficiency of these labor forces. Instead it became an argument for the inherent lack of productivity of certain acts of labor; reducing labor forces; and turning work over to the private sector. Not all labor was equal in its production of value nor could it necessarily be made profitable.

In this report the trustees argued that

[t]he single biggest problem of Calcutta port is the poor labor relations, redundancy of labor resulting in low productivity and high cost. If this is solved on a war footing many other problems . . . would automatically get solved.

They added that it was the huge unutilized surplus labor force that created an atmosphere

which is ripe for trade union rivalry to flourish. A dozen major trade unions and some minor ones claim to represent the men. They have no stable known strength as the workers go on shifting their support or loyalties from time to time to whichever leadership they consider to be the highest bidder for increasing their salaries emoulments or agitating for their demands.

In addition they complained of protracted negotiations, which meant that

[in] each section of the Calcutta Port Trust endless discussions and arguments go on through the working hours at various levels between the officers of CPT and shop-floor representatives or their senior union leaders. As a result discipline and efficiency become a casualty . . . . Heads of departments reported that a major amount of their time was wasted on dealing with the above mentioned discussions and arguments and this retards the proper functioning.[15]

The reports of the strikes tell a different story from this one of an unproductive working class. They suggest an activist group of employees seeking rights to equal payment and permanent work. For example hydraulic power staff in Calcutta docks struck on 1 February 1981 because they wanted a payment by results scheme like that paid to the dock basin workmen. The berthing officers struck in August 1981 because they wanted the same weekly day off allowance as that given to dock masters. The coal handling workers struck on 30 September 1980 for confirmation in permanent service. On 1–2 February 1981 the unloading crews in Calcutta docks refused private forklift trucks access and operation. In addition, workers often struck in protest against work conditions. For example, the crew of the light vessel *Torch* refused to sail on 19 August 1979 because it was not fit for sailing. Sometimes these strikes ended in outright violence. For example, on 15 September 1979 the police opened fire in the docks and four workers were killed.[16] This was not a problem of lack of productivity but a battle between the working classes and middle-class bureaucrats on the Hooghly over shares of government resources.

As a solution for this conflict between officers and workers the committee recommended that the unions not be negotiated with. All discussion of pending demands would be discontinued and all of them would be placed before an industrial tribunal for adjudication. The labor force would be reduced by the application of a compulsory retirement scheme, and a strong message would be given that strikes do not pay.[17] Immediately in March 1981 the Central Industrial Security Force was introduced into the port to police the labor situation with four hundred men. The port implemented a combination of these recommended measures over the next ten years. In the subsequent decades, bureaucrats returned to a devaluation of labor both metaphorically and literally (the wages paid to contractual workers) to solve the financial problems of the port.

Relief from the problems of an activist working class eventually came from an unexpected quarter—union leaders. Faced by mounting deficits and promises of access to income for their members, unionists gradually converted to the logic of "productivity." In return for a wage settlement following an all-India strike in March 1984, the transport secretary, Prakash Narain, agreed with the representatives of the four major federations of port and dock workers to set up productivity committees in all ports.[18] These would meet four times a year to discuss with unions how to increase productivity and output, introduce financial reforms, use new technologies and create competitiveness with neighboring countries. A national productivity council was also set up that would issue centralized recommendations. The trustees on the Port Trust Board from the two largest unions, the Port Sromik and National Union of Waterfront Workers, recorded no opposition to this process. In 1985 the chairman of the port took these measures one step further using the deficit figures to argue that the port needed to take radical steps in line with the productivity council recommendations. They would close down uneconomic areas of operation, dispose of surplus and unusable assets and would create a total ban on fresh recruitment.[19] The walls were now closing around public-sector employment in the port in the wake of the deal made between union leaders and the central government. The working classes on the river now begin to be segmented between increasing numbers of contractual private-sector workers and a reducing number of unionized public-sector workers.[20] Union leaders capitulated in return for access to pay raises, faced with the fetish of fiscal deficit, and in the name of productivity. They conceded to the closing off of access to public-sector jobs and outcontracting.

Containerization at Calcutta Subhas Chandra Bose docks in 1990 added to the growing trend of manpower reduction and casualization. This placed increasing numbers of men in deunionized, temporary jobs managed by brokers on short-term, often day, contracts. Loading and unloading work was contracted out, as well as that of forklift truck drivers and crane operators. The contractual workers that had always existed alongside the port employees were now expanding as a group. By 1991 there was not only a ban on replacement recruitment in the port but also a complete hiring freeze and a voluntary retirement scheme to further reduce surplus manpower.[21] These measures turned the port into a closed gerontocracy with the lowest post in the line of command remaining unfilled when people retired.

By the early 1990s there was little remaining protest from the unions. In 1990 the very last attempt to stop the casualization of work came from the Port Sromik Janat Panchayat Union. They blockaded the Calcutta port from 26 July to 21 August protesting that coal unloading workers on contract and working as apprentices should be made permanent. The administration stuck firm to their position, and the union did not see its demands realized. Instead, the coal sheds at Calcutta were closed to traffic shortly afterward, and it was diverted to Haldia with its more mechanized systems of unloading.[22] In 1992 ship repairing and building work began to be regularly outcontracted from the port. By 1995 the outsourcing of marine labor to private contractors was uncontested by the unions.[23] In 1998 the Calcutta Dock Labor Board and Calcutta Port Trust were merged, further reducing the numbers of employees in the port. This move was resisted by the unions in the Calcutta Dock Labor Board but not by those in the port unions. In the period from 1981 to 2000 the permanent workforce reduced from 31,707 in Calcutta and 2,785 in Haldia to 11,514 employees in both places.[24]

In 2000, when the port's most severe fiscal crisis occurred, Hemlal Chatterjee, the union representative of the Port Sromik Union, asked the board why there was such a severe deficit, since the traffic had increased and the manpower had already been reduced so much. As had become a frequent pattern, the members of the board blamed the working classes. H. P. Nopany, representing the Shipping Corporation of India, suggested that "Calcutta Port Trust had inherited the legacy of the past in the form of bloated manpower."[25] Another board member, H. P. Kabra, argued that "dead and non-performing assets should be disposed of."[26] In response to the collapse of operating income, the chairman instituted a permanent hiring freeze at every level of the port, which continues to the present. He called for the reduction of port employees, removing "idle men" in particular from the Calcutta docks. The restructuring of the working classes on the river had by 2000 made permanent port employment into a privilege held by older men that was protected by their unions. Younger men joined the growing ranks of sporadically employed, deunionized contractual workers. They would bear the burden of insecurity created by the financialization of state debt. In the austerity capitalism that had emerged, the contribution of working-class labor to national prosperity was devalued, and impermanent livelihoods had increased. It was brought into being by alliances between middle-class bureaucrats and the unionized labor aristocracies of the Hooghly. They sought to maintain their access to dwindling state resources and thereby, paradoxically, helped to realize the new extractive forms of state institutions focused on deficit repayment.

Austerity Property: Speculative Planning,
Resource Grabs and Rentier Income

Pressed hard to generate revenues to repay central government debts, the Calcutta Port Trust started to treat its property differently from the mid-1980s. It looked for means to extract more value, more quickly. This led to forms of decentralized speculative planning and attempts to create public-private partnerships. Paradoxically, these did not result in a redeveloped waterfront, as predicted in government and Calcutta Port Trust plans. Instead, these policies generated resource grabs and, ultimately, an intensification of rentier income from temporary land use. Austerity property relations, as we shall see, rest on tributary payments and rights of use enforced through the networks of the informalized economy.

In 1984 the Calcutta Port Trust, looking for new sources of revenue, started to make ambitious plans for its property. It began by drawing up a commercial valuation of all its landholdings and a scheme for the use of the 3,326 acres of land it owned in Calcutta and its surroundings. The stretch from Cossipore to Hastings Bridge was intended for commercial and middle-class residential use with shopping malls, immersion ghats (jetties) and river recreation. The areas around the docks in Kidderpore would be used for employee housing, industry and warehousing, with a new housing and shopping complex in the boat canal area. East of the docks would continue as an industrial zone with the addition of warehousing and a container terminus. Along the waterfront in Howrah the port railway at Shalimar would be converted into a new south-eastern railway passenger terminus, and the growth of industries such as ship building would be encouraged.[27] These schemes lay dormant until 1991, as there were no monetary resources or mechanisms to fund them. In that year MOST gave support to public-private partnerships, so the Calcutta Port Trust began to try to actualize these through speculative planning. They began to widely publicize their plans in the press, presenting them as imminent in the hope of attracting business, public and political support for them.

However, these schemes only led to competitive attempts at resource grabs by other bureaucracies. Take, for example, the scheme for a public-private partnership to develop the boat canal area of the Calcutta jetties. This collapsed as the Calcutta Municipal Corporation (CMC) attempted to extract opaque benefits from the deal. In October 1991 the chairman reported hopefully that there were 74 acres of land available in the Calcutta jetties and boat canal area for development for commercial use. The India Road Construction Corporation, an enterprise unit controlled by MOST, had come forward with a proposal to develop the land for commercial purposes with the port. This could be done if slums in the Boat Canal Area were demolished and short term lease-holders were removed. MOST cleared the proposal, but now it was in the hands of the Calcutta Metropolitan Development Agency (CMDA) and the CMC.[28] In November 1992 MOST had agreed to the issuing of long-term, ninety-nine-year leases for this project, and the chairman wrote hopefully of a profit of 500 crores from it. The publicity department widely advertised the scheme, which was oversubscribed by members of the public who rushed to buy plots in the development. The CMDA had also agreed to the project.[29] But in January 1994 the project had to be abandoned because the CMC had repeatedly stalled the project by specifying impossible conditions and denying environmental clearances. Perhaps seeking to benefit politically or financially from the deal, the CMC produced an irresolvable stalemate. All the public subscriptions had to be returned.[30]

A similar stalemate caused by attempts to grab rights to port land (with a different resolution) occurred with the Calcutta Jetties in the heart of the city. In 1997 the port trust approached the West Bengal Government and CMC in order to discuss the conversion of this land to commercial use for housing and recreation.[31] Both of these agencies refused to grant permission for such use of the waterfront. Instead they suggested they should be turned into public parks and leisure facilities under their sole control. The CMC also dragged its feet on deploying the police to clear the land of the urban poor who had settled in the derelict warehouses. The influential politicians and bureaucrats associated with these organizations were most likely attempting to pressurize the port to hand over rights to the valuable property to them. A compromise emerged in 1999 when the land was divided up along the waterfront so that sections would be transferred on leases to the CMDA, CMC and a third section retained by the port. Once this agreement was signed, the CMC launched a drive with the police to demolish unauthorized structures and evict people living on the land. As the chairman put it, in his discussion of the agreement it had been signed so that they would get the "considerable administrative and police assistance from the government of West Bengal therefore we will sign the MOU to get this help."[32] This help enabled them to "beautify" the land along the river by making a recreation park and small gardens sandwiched between the circular railway and the river. The chairman justified the project by suggesting that beautification was one step toward eventually getting some commercial use out of the land.[33] "Beautification" was a compromise between the desire of the port trust to gain revenue to meet its annual debt liability and attempts by other bureaucracies to gain control of valuable public land. Such were the outcomes of the new forms of decentralized speculative planning characteristic of the new austerity capitalism.

These experiences ultimately led the port trust to an increasingly extractive and short-term approach to the land they leased out. From 1975 the port had leased out a small amount of unused land and buildings to private landlords and businesses. This rentier system combined commercial principles and temporariness in the rights of use. For example, leases would have only one option for renewal of thirty years, and the port could terminate the lease at any time should the land be required for port or public purposes.[34] A nested system of temporary leasing of small parcels of land between the port, tenants and subtenants developed as a source of revenue. As more port land had become vacant through the 1980s, this system of land-use expanded hugely. It was to an intensification of these tributary networks supported by the informalized economy that the Calcutta Port Trust turned after the failure of its speculative plans. By June 2000, out of the 3,326 acres of land owned by the Calcutta dock system, 1,956 acres were rented out on small leases.[35] To generate more revenue from leases the port appointed two more estate officers, a land manager and four junior inspectors who would collect dues by intensive personal contact. From 2003 the policy of maximizing revenue from existing lessees overtook completely. A brutal realism had set in that tenants had to be pressed hard for dues. I was informed that in spite of continuing public announcements of large-scale redevelopment along the waterfront, the policy of the land management department had shifted to one of pure revenue collection. The port had also started vigorously prosecuting rent defaulters. In 2008 the estate officer was given quasi-judicial powers so as to be able to pass a legal order of eviction without its going through a court of law. Beautification and long-term investment, even public-private investment, was now an obsolete dream. The Calcutta Port Trust simply aimed to speed up delivery of its dues through the chains of lessees and sublessees. This austerity property regime has a profound economic as well as physical effect on the lives of those living, working and running businesses on short-term leased parcels of port land. They live in this accelerating cycle of collection of dues without investment in infrastructure or long-term planning. The materialization of this is an increasingly decrepit waterfront managed by tiered fiscal and political brokering relationships.

Austerity Nature: Unstable Circulations and Dangerous Navigation

As public deficit increasingly shaped decision-making in the Calcutta Port Trust, the Hooghly was remade. New bars and islands were born from the effects of the new fiscal regime. An austerity nature emerged that made capital circulation unstable and navigation on the river increasingly dangerous.

In 1982 the hydrographic survey department presented a scheme to the Port Trust Board that it claimed would finally solve the problem of the falling depths near Haldia. Guide walls would be built on Nayachar Island along with bank protection works on the Hooghly and at the outfall of the River Haldia. Most important of all would be simultaneous capital dredging on the Balari bar, the trimming of Nayachar Island and the construction of a shore disposal terminal for silt. The chairman called for the central government to cover all the costs of this plan.[36] But MOST dragged its feet and would not agree to pay for it. Instead, in 1982 the government gave permission for a limited scheme in which a local private contractor would construct just the northern guide wall with less expensive materials. This make-shift wall started to collapse, so another private contractor rebuilt it in 1987. However, once this work was completed the situation became even more complicated. The new wall started to direct flood tide currents against the side of Nayachar Island. This resulted in the erosion of the island and siltation of the deposits within the Haldia channel, clogging the entrance to the docks. The failure of MOST to sanction the whole scheme was proving highly problematic. Its refusal to invest in large-scale works and the increasing reliance on private contractors was producing an unintended remaking of the Hooghly.

The hydrographic survey department found this development particularly disturbing because it threatened all their models developed over the previous twenty years.[37] These changes in the river would undermine all their previous plans for remaking the river unless they were stopped in their tracks. The solution— constructing spurs to prevent erosion along Nayachar Island and extensive dredging on the Balari bar and Jiggerkhali flat—was going to be an expensive proposition. As a compromise, spurs to stabilize Nayachar Island were built by private contractors. But the central government would still not provide funds for the ambitious dredging scheme on the Balari bar that would finally solve the problem.[38] The port continued to look for a solution through the 1990s, but whatever schemes it proposed, it was told by MOST that the costs would have to be met from internal port resources.[39] The technological dreams of the preliberalization period now died under the new liberalization regime of revenue extraction from public resources. Meanwhile the

Jiggerkhali flat and Nayachar Island continued to grow. These were born from the effects of public deficit on the complex vitality of the river.

The ordinary process of maintenance dredging also became increasingly problematic from the 1980s. In the 1980s the port had four working dredgers, which had been built with World Bank money. But two of them were increasingly decrepit and experienced frequent breakdowns.[40] Since there was no capital available from the central government or its internal funds to replace these, the port relied increasingly on hiring from the pool of Dredging Corporation of India (DCI) dredgers. By 1984 the port was almost entirely dependent on these to maintain navigable depths. In 1989 the chairman reported that there was a shortfall each year in the necessary dredging to keep the channels open as a result of a shortage of dredgers. Four years later, in 1993, the port only had one dredger, the Mahaganga, still operational and was using four dredgers from DCI to maintain depths, but these were often not available for all the required time necessary to remove enough silt, because there was competition for their use with other ports.[41] By 2008–10 there was a chronic shortage of dredgers. This threatened to close Haldia entirely to shipping and made all the channels on the river narrower and more dangerous. Pilots were forced to navigate container ships in increasingly difficult conditions with frequent accidents. Fiscal crisis had generated an unstable form of austerity nature that made the circulation of capital on the Hooghly increasingly uncertain.

Austerity Technologies: Short-termism and Low Technology

Through the 1990s and 2000s new kinds of technology began to be introduced by the port trust in order to overcome the escalating dangers of navigating the Hooghly. These were quite distinct from the technologies of the pre-liberalisation period, which were funded by long-term grants from the government and were large, durable infrastructures. They were funded by commercial loans or produced by cheap outcontracting in private businesses. They reduced the required amount of manning or were staffed by temporary low-cost contractual workers. They were often multipurpose and flexible. Increasingly they also involved low-tech improvisations. Overall they offered the promise of generating revenue for the port and private businesses in the short term with the least permanent investment of public resources.

The initial catalyst for the development of these technologies was an accident in November 1988. One of the three decrepit manned light vessels, the *Candle*, anchored in the high seas 46 nautical miles off Sagar Island, sank in a cyclone with forty men on board.[42] This event precipitated a decision to build three new un-manned light vessels, reducing staff costs. But it also led to protests from the newly reformed pilot association about their conditions of work. They considered these to be a death-trap because they were posted to the same stretch of the sea as the *Candle* in aging vessels. They would climb rope ladders from the vessels into small boats and be taken out to board the ships coming in. The solution they suggested was the introduction of a Vessel Traffic Management System (VTMS) and the set-ting up of a shore-based station for pilots at Sagar Island. This would mean that the pilots would not have to go out to the ships to guide them in over the rough seas, nor would they have to wait for ships in decrepit vessels at sea. Instead, the ships would be guided in using the VTMS, the pilots would board the ships closer to the western edge of Sagar Island and then take them on up to Haldia or Calcutta.

In December 1990 the chairman reported to the board that the VTMS and shore station would mean that "pilotage would be safer and it would remove all uncer-tainty on the journey particularly on Middleton bar. In addition accuracy would be increased . . . . There would be a reduction of lost time and a reduction of acci-dents."[43] Yet in the hands of the chairman and board of trustees the plan gradually grew into an even larger scheme in which the VTMS would cover the whole river. This, they argued, would help to eliminate the increasing uncertainty all along the river and lead to reduced manning by expensive river pilots.[44] In spite of this risk to their jobs the pilots pushed hard for the technology and shore-based station to be introduced, as they feared for their lives. In 1995 the pilots went on strike for twenty-two days in order to protest against their dangerous working conditions, to demand a shore-based station within two years and the introduction of the VTMS, but only to Haldia and Sagar Island. The plans for a larger extension were therefore dropped by the management and they agreed to the pilots' demands.[45] In return the pilots agreed not to strike for another five years.[46]

With their plans for cost-cutting through the replacement or reduction of pilots thwarted by their strike action, the chairman and board turned to other measures that would reduce the expenses of the marine department. In particular they be-gan outcontracting the construction and labor of marine technologies. They also looked for vessels that could be multipurpose and flexible. In 1992 the board began to give the construction work of smaller craft to private shipyards rather than to the large public-sector concerns along the Hooghly as a way of reducing costs. The first order was placed with a private shipyard for two river survey vessels. The board members were concerned by the lack of infrastructure in the yard, but the new vessel procurement officer reassured them that it would hire infrastructure as it was required.[47] When the decision was taken to install the VTMS, the marine department and board took outsourcing one step further. The old pilot vessel would be replaced by two fast pilot launches to be constructed by a private-sector shipyard that would move the pilots from or near Sagar station to the ships. The operations and maintenance of the vessels would also be entrusted to the same private shipyard, undercutting their own expensive marine employees.[48] In 1998 this shipyard also received the orders for two multipurpose seagoing river survey vessels to replace the three old river survey launches. The chairman argued and the board agreed that these vessels would be run with reduced manning.[49]

In an apotheosis of this trend in 2008 this private shipyard also built a new floating pilot station for the monsoon months, Ma Ganga. This vessel was necessary because it was found to be too dangerous to get from shore to land at Sagar Island during the monsoon. This vessel was fully manned by contractual staff and was problematic from the start. It was built for less money than required for a full pilot vessel as an adaptation of a barge so that it pitched heavily in the sea conditions. But it also was grandly fitted out with elaborate interior décor worthy of a five-star hotel because outside of the monsoon months it would be used by the chairman and other high-level staff for entertaining in Kolkata. It was a perfect flexible, inexpensive, public deficit generated vessel that did not serve the work needs of the pilots on the river.

Other low-tech solutions were also developed. In 1999 the port began its plans for an improvised deep water port.[50] This would be composed of a virtual jetty, a group of six giant buoys to which large mother ships would be anchored near Sagar Island. This would allow the offloading of bulk cargo into large barges at this location even during the rough weather from April to September. They would then go upriver and offload at Haldia, Baj Baj or Calcutta.[51] The buoys were built at a cost of Rs6 million by a private ship-building and repairing firm and installed off Sagar in 2004. But the whole project was problematic. It proved almost impossible to anchor the ships to the buoys in any but the calmest season and it was hard to find men in the mooring crew who would volunteer to work on them. This was because the work was so dangerous—they would have to balance on them in the rolling sea to catch the chains from the vessels. Working to anchor and offload the vessel in six hours before the tide turned and shifted its position proved almost impossible. The quest for low investment meant that the project was driven by fiscal constraints rather than knowledge of the conditions of the river itself.

Despite its failure this project did set a precedent for other similar schemes that would maximize revenue from the river using minimum investment in old technologies. In 2003 the government of India and the Kolkata Port Trust started to seek to revive inland water transport. The project was given the grand name of the Sagar Mala project.[52] In January 2004, at a meeting with the secretary of shipping, the chairman and barge operators agreed to turn two out of three jetties at the port into inland barge jetties. The chairman and secretary of shipping agreed that the Kolkata port was the only riverine major port in India that had the potential to develop as a hub for inland water transport because of its connections to the north and northeast states and to Bangladesh via the Sunderbans. The report to the trustees continued that the old jute mills might develop their sites for handling inland water cargo and private-sector participation could be brought to bear on the project.[53] But the export quotas of foodstuffs to Bangladesh proved unreliable for a constant and growing trade. Instead, the outcome from this project was the development of fly ash trade from the Calcutta Electrical Supply Corporation power station below Baj Baj and from a jetty at Shalimar brought by trucks from Kolaghat power station. Barges converted at low cost in Bangladesh from non-propelled barges moved into the water of the Hooghly. Fly ash trade was entirely developed by three private firms who took the fly ash to cement factories in Bangladesh. The vessels they used were so unreliable and the river so unpredictable that there was an epidemic of accidents of barges sinking in the river from 2004. The logic of fiscal deficit and its low-tech solutions to generating revenue had reached another limit. This was that of decrepit vessels overloaded with heavy ash sinking in the river blocking the narrow tracks for container traffic.

Yet the port trust still sought more low-technology and low-investment opportunities to generate revenue through 2002–6. In particular the chairman, A. K. Chandra, started to reduce port charges on goods in an attempt to draw container traffic back to Kolkata from other ports. But this was done with no investment at all in the infrastructure that had been developed many years before. As a result, container ships traveling from the high-tech ports of Singapore and Colombo upriver to Kolkata were met by disintegrating tugs, periodically nonoperational lock gates and ruins on the dock edge. Rates for smaller ships to carry out lighterage midstream and in the docks were reduced. Ships from China and Vietnam offloading imported hardwood logs into nonpropelled fifty-year-old barges appeared in the broad curve of Diamond Harbour, which had not been used for shipping since the nineteenth century. Here the port also started to plan to develop jetties for 7-meter-draft vessels (which were too large to enter the docks at Kolkata) to offload into barges. Barges would be used for the lighterage of bulk cargo and if the connectivity by road and rail were improved, containers could also be offloaded and iron ore taken on, especially for export to China.[54] Administrators continue to seize on the least-cost, fastest, low-technology solution. Short-term improvised austerity technologies predominate on the river.

Conclusion: State Debt, Liberalization and Austerity Capitalism

Since my fieldwork, the change of government in West Bengal and at the center has not resulted in any alterations to the forms of austerity: labor, property, technology and nature on the Hooghly. In 2011 when Mamata Banerjee and the Trinamul Congress swept to power ousting CPI(M) after thirty-four years of continuous control, she announced a beautification project for the banks of the Hooghly in Kolkata. Her aim was that it would become a second Thames, promising to build an equivalent to the London Eye.[55] Now a new path runs along the Kolkata waterfront between Millennium Park and Princep Ghat, but none of the divided municipal and port trust ownership of land has ended, nor has further, more ambitious development yet occurred. Since my fieldwork, various infrastructure developments for the trade on the Hooghly continue to be proposed. The twists and turns of these projects are characteristic of the fate of speculative infrastructure funded not from government funds but by public-private partnerships. Since 2005, vaulting plans have been mooted to turn Nayachar Island into a chemical hub funded by a consortium of Indonesian and Singaporean capital. Mamata Banerjee's government altered these plans to an ecotourism project, an industrial center and power plant and awarded a contract for these in 2011. Yet this scheme remains unanchored in any physical reality, although it has caused land speculation on the banks nearest the island where a bridge has also been proposed. Plans for a deep sea port for Sagar Island and a bridge from the mainland have been mooted from 2006. When Mamata Banerjee came to power, she announced that this project would definitely be built, bringing prosperity to Kolkata and the district of twenty-four Parganas.[56] In 2013 the Kolkata Port Trust announced that they were abandoning the scheme because no private capital could be found to support the project, and it was not viable in that location because of cyclones and shifting ground.[57] Yet by September 2013 it was being promoted again with announcements that construction would start on a Rs8000 crore port with eight berths for containers by 2015 to be completed in 2017.[58]

This development would reduce the Kolkata docks into a barge port, with container traffic coming by road or rail from Sagar.[59] This initiative continues the policies of the rentier austerity state, which support private profit and unregulated labor. Financing would come from the use of government and international development funds to attract private investors and guarantee their profits. Once constructed the port would be a landlord port. The Kolkata Port Trust would rent berths to private operators who could set their own work and pay conditions. The Sagar port would amplify the Hooghly's unequal speculative economy. In the meantime men on the Hooghly continue to live with the uncertain future of Haldia and Kolkata docks, working vast volumes of trade with decrepit infrastructure and in dangerous conditions. They are supported by larger numbers of informalized workers, whose situation will not be altered any of these plans even if they are realized. The informalized economy that they are part of is still organized by grass-roots political and union brokers, and river workers claim that these local figures have simply switched sides from CPI(M) to Trinamul. Most significantly, the technical mechanisms of state debt management and austerity public-sector drives have not altered in any degree.

Much work has focused on publicly announced state policies and the visible consequences of new private capital flows that have emerged since liberalization in India. In this chapter I have departed from this approach to trace a hidden history of changing quotidian practices of state debt. These have dramatically reshaped the governance of labor, property, nature and technology on the Hooghly without showing their agency. This is in part because of the amnesiac power of figures of public deficit. These hide their complex origins and effects. In recent years they have produced narrowly financial crises and short-term solutions. These numbers stop analysis and lead to action. Their deployment as part of austerity capitalism makes all of the various rhythms of society and nonhuman phenomena subject to their cyclical routines of repayment. Public deficit is the absent presence in our understanding of the liberalization Indian state.

The attribution of a fiscal urgency to public deficit has become widespread across the world during exactly the same period described here. This is not something unique to either the Kolkata Port Trust or India, as I argue in the Introduction and Conclusion. Austerity policies attempt to make every rhythm of time in society and every productive action subject to the central time of repayment. But these policies are, as we have seen throughout this chapter, increasingly uncontrollable in their effects. They produce disjunctures in productivity and capital circulation. The *res publica* of infrastructures are increasingly subject to extractive temporary relationships. The question that the rest of this book seeks to answer is, How is this shift in state debt policies experienced and acted upon by the people who work on the Hooghly? How do financial obligations transform and conflict with other responsibilities to citizens, fellow workers, family members, technologies and to the river itself? What forms of ethical life and politics can emerge? The ethnographic chapters that follow explore the conduct of productivity and speculation practiced by river bureaucrats and workers. It examines their attempts to conceptualize the fertility of capital, generate productivity and build obligations. Some of the same events and policies will reappear, but within distinct interpretive frames that offer different vistas of recent history. Now we begin our journey onto the Hooghly into the spaces of negotiation between fiscal policy and popular ethics of productivity. Along the route we can trace how ethics of regeneration, care, friendship and reciprocity intersect with the new market-state relations of austerity capitalism.

Section II

The New Public Good

SINCE THE 1980S new practices of the public good have emerged on the Hooghly. Austerity policy has eroded the political obligations of class and nation associated with an earlier era of state socialism. Yet, as this section will show, it has not produced a bureaucracy in which the public good is practiced solely as a financial project. Instead, workers, bureaucrats and entrepreneurs create productive forms on the river as part of a broader project of the conduct of life (Appadurai 2011; Bear and Mathur 2015; Du Gay 2008; Weber 1994). This conduct of productivity includes models of the public good, of destructive forces and productive powers in the world. Although there are divergent ethical projects on the Hooghly, they share certain characteristics. All of them are oriented towards overcoming waste and decay through regeneration. Importantly, these ethics are dystopian rather than utopian in form. Not all labor is equally productive, and distinctions are drawn between state and private labor. New managerial hierarchies and class inequalities are supported by these popular ethics of regeneration. Through an analysis of these we can explain the inequities of the present. Inequality is sustained not by a single "neoliberal" ethos or market rationale. It is generated from diverse popular attempts to account for, and regenerate, the ruins of austerity capitalism.

I was first led to reflect on ruins and regeneration by the men of the marine department. Although there are many industrial remains along the waterfront, they were fascinated by one site of decay and an annual ritual of regeneration held there. Both marine officers and crew were captivated by Ash Ghat inside the docks in Kidderpore. They suggested that if I really wanted to know about the river I should speak to the old mooring crew who used to work from there. They also talked of how at this place there was an annual celebration for Ma Ganga that I must attend. They described how they sought to maintain parts of it, primarily a Kali temple. Everyone conveyed the sense that this place, these people and the festival would be a source of significant truths that I should pursue. I was entirely drawn into this quest. I sought out old crew and worked on gaining permission to go beyond the security gate separating Ash Ghat from the city.

Once I started to frequent Ash Ghat I could see it was filled with the remnants of older socialist productivity. Huge beached metal buoys half the size of a launch slid into the muddy silt of the foreshore. Old hawser boats—once used by the mooring crew—rotted into the overgrown bank. Collapsed signs pointed to derelict staff quarters that had been won in a strike by the Port Sromik Union (PSU) in the 1950s. In 1980, within the living memory of workers, this place was filled daily with two hundred men. Chained to nearby buoys were up to forty-five bulk cargo ships from Southeast Asian, South Asian and European ports. But fiscal discipline and falling depths in the river led to the closing of the Calcutta moorings. By 2008 only the steel launches for hydrographic surveys and for delivering river pilots to the ships were tied up here. The marine office at the ghat that had once controlled fifteen hundred men now oversaw a hundred permanent employees. But as I discovered when the Ganga puja returned, it filled this place with renewed life and recollections.

The day for the Ganga puja arrived on 13 June. At Ash Ghat around a hundred marine crew watched the puja intently. The festival re-enacted the life-giving descent of the goddess, and the crowd received her life-force by eating food blessed by her. As the celebrations continued Captain Verma (whom I had accompanied to the Ash Ghat puja) and I were drawn into conversation by an elderly man, Pronay Das, a retired mooring hand. He insisted on taking us to see the Kali temple nearby. He explained that this had been built by the marine crew in the 1950s and that recent renewed support from the crew had led to its growth and refurbishment. We reached the temple—above the door it said in Bengali: "In the Administration of the Marine Worker Brothers."

As we walked away from the temple, Pranoy Das explained that the Ganga puja started because there was a terrible accident that killed many mooring crew here in 1959. Back at the pandal (marquee for the goddess) the crowd jostled Captain Verma, urging him to garland the concrete memorial to the dead men with flowers from the goddess, and everyone shouted "Ma Ganga Jay Jay" (Victory to Ma Ganga). He also garlanded a statue to B. C. Ray, the first chief minister of West Bengal, while everyone shouted, "B. C. Ray. Jay Jay!" (Victory to B. C. Ray). Pranoy explained that the minister had established the Inland Water Training Institute, where they had all apprenticed. The official became nervous as men crowded round, complaining to me about the decline of unions, the insecurity of their jobs and the decrepit buildings. This ritual has a structure of regeneration. It makes manifest permanent life-giving forces. As will become clear in the chapters that follow, it is one small part of the increasingly diverse and growing Hinduized conducts of productivity practiced on the Hooghly. These aim to re-create the public good by overcoming the waste of, and regenerating the ruins of, austerity capitalism. Yet ultimately they cannot, because it is out of them that the social relations on the river emerge.

Since the 1980s the waste created by capitalism has become an important topic of inquiry, as deindustrialization has become more visible to academics (Ferguson 1999). This research suggests that waste is inherent to capitalist production. This includes both the "waste" of reserve armies of labor and the polluting by-products of consumption and production (Alexander and Reno 2012). This work has drawn on the insight that zones of exclusion, or of necropolitics, have always accompanied formal citizenship and labor relations (McIntyre and Nast 2011; Mbembe 2003; Yates 2011). It has also begun to chart the representational politics of industrial ruins (Edensor 2005; Hell and Schonle 2010). My approach here expands these accounts further. It explores the ethics that people use to evaluate the destructive effects of capitalism. We can only understand the reproduction of inequality and populist politics among the working and middle classes in India, and elsewhere, if we examine these historically emergent ethics. These ethics are visceral and affective because they link the reality of processes of decay to the problem of regenerating productive life. As we will see, they emerge from acts of labor as senses of workmanship. It is not only philosophers who develop ethics that recognize the vitality of commodities, tools and technologies (Bennett 2001; Sennett 2009). As the chapters that follow show, workers, bureaucrats and entrepreneurs construct their own accounts of the relationships between material, imminent and transcendent powers. In this case these ethics draw on popular Hinduism and histories of labor on the Hooghly to reflect on the masculine productive potential of economic action.

Fig. 3. Ma Ganga puja at Kolkata docks

Chapter 2

Nationalist Melancholia and the Limits of Austerity Public-sector Unionism

IN THIS CHAPTER I explore the ethics of waste and regeneration among the marine crew in the Kolkata docks and its political entailments. The marine crew who worked from Ash Ghat were filled with melancholia for lost courage and masculinity. They associated this loss with the growth of private-sector labor, which undermined the vitality of their vessels and themselves. One member of the marine crew, Bolai Das, made this particularly clear as we talked through the months waiting for work becalmed at Ash Ghat. Bolai spoke bitterly of the scrapping of the old pilot ship and its replacement by the new privately constructed and manned floating barge named the Ma Ganga. The construction of this vessel had led to his demotion to work upriver ferrying marine officers in Kolkata at Ash Ghat. He explained: "We used to go to Sandheads at Sagar Island with so much rolling and danger." The new vessel, he thought, was, "not a proper ship. Just a platform with no steering wheel or *hater kaj* (work of the hands). Just electrics." One day he told me that the steering wheel on the launch itself was called the *sarang* (steerer)—the tool standing for the person who operated it in a complete identification of human and machine. Then he started to talk about the huge steering wheel on the old pilot vessel, adding with emotion, "The new ship is not like the old ship. It is just a station. The old vessel was a real ship," and he turned away with tears in his eyes. He regularly complained that he was stuck on an old decrepit launch, using its condition to reflect on his own mortality. He explained that he was denied the opportunity to work on the river in a ship or in tasks that would fully express his *komota,* or capability. The declining qualities of vessels manifested the private-sector forces of waste at work on the river that also eroded the strength of men.

Since the 1980s the public-sector working classes on the Hooghly have lived through a dramatic transformation in their position. Austerity labor policy has led to an erosion of their status, privileges and working conditions. Its devaluation of labor resulted in fierce battles between the middle and working classes on the river over diminishing state resources.[1] Their once powerful unions have largely joined forces with the Kolkata Port Trust and contractors. Yet in the present public-sector workers are in a relatively privileged position. As permanent, unionized state employees, their wages and pensions are subsidized by the less expensive labor of a much larger number of informalized sector workers. How then, do the public-sector working classes of the river evaluate the austerity capitalism of the present? How can attention to these judgments help to explain the limits of public-sector unionism on the Hooghly, which no longer seeks rights for informalized sector workers?

Like other situations of working-class insecurity, the ethics I will describe contain a melancholic populist nationalism that asserts long-term inalienable obligations and large-scale transcendent cosmopolitical forces (Holmes 2000; Kalb 2009; Kalb and Halmai 2011; Kideckel 2008). To understand this sense of workmanship, it is first necessary to turn to the history of unionism and labor among the marine crew. It is from this history that their common sense of solidarity and injustice has emerged (Kalb 2009). As we will see, their ethical evaluations, and the political limits of these, arise from specific experiences of historic and current time-spaces of labor.

From Nationalist Duty to Scarce Economic Resource: Unionism and Public-sector Labor in the Marine Crew, 1950–2011

Shortly after Independence, employment in the marine crew on the Hooghly became part of a project of nationalist renewal after partition.[2] Prior to Independence, marine work directly on the river was carried out largely by Muslims, usually with family origins in Khulna and Noakhali. There was a steady flow of lascars, inland water masters and apprentices from these regions. This movement for work was stopped by partition and Independence. Faced with reducing numbers of skilled river workers, the Congress state government and port bureaucrats began to employ East Bengali refugees preferentially on the river. From the 1950s to the 1970s the possession of a refugee certificate gave special access to training in the Inland Water Institute.[3] After six months of training men were placed in the port's marine department. So in the 1950s refugees worked as apprentices learning a new trade from the remaining Muslim *sarangs*. The first refugees after the 1948 riots were Hindu high-caste landowners and urban professionals (Chatterji 2007). Soon these refugees were working side by side in the marine crew with men of scheduled castes who had fled East Pakistan after the Khulna riots in 1950 and the riots over the Hazratbal shrine in 1964.

Tensions between the remaining Muslim and East Bengali refugee crewmen surfaced periodically. There were unusually large numbers of "voluntary resignations" in 1950 and fifty-one by Muslim crewmen and a slow attrition after that.[4] After a strike in 1957, one of the union demands accepted by the officers was for the removal of "Pakistani nationals" from the marine department.[5] In 1959 the port administration began to drill East Bengali members of the marine crew in a special territorial army unit so that they could take over the running of the port if foreign nationals working the trade on the river caused trouble.[6] This unit patrolled the docks in the 1964 riots in Kolkata and the 1965 war with Pakistan. In the 1971 war the unit was sent to East Pakistan. In the sixties and seventies the port continued special programs to recruit East Bengali refugees into key marine posts. Yet other port work not directly on the river, such as cargo-handling, continued to provide a large amount of employment for Indian Muslims. Kidderpore progressively became a predominantly Muslim neighborhood as a result of successive riots in other parts of the city leading to a concentration into ghettoes (ibid.). But work directly on the river in the marine crew had now become the domain of East Bengali refugees and their descendants, and remains so to this day. The majority of marine crew and dock officers are still men who left East Pakistan as children or are the sons of refugees.

The East Bengali marine crew were from early on associated with a strong unionism that demanded rights in return for their nationalist duty. They were central to union activity in the port, especially in the politically nonaffiliated and Congress unions. From the 1950s they provided the disciplined core of the PSU. They also were the main office holders in the PSU and later on in other unions. The PSU, along with the Congress-affiliated National Union of Waterfront Workers (NUWW) won the rights to shorter shift systems, rest days, pensions, food allowances, free education for children and housing allowances for all employees through the 1950s and 1960s.[7] At this time of high unionism coalitions of class overcame the separations between the Hindu marine crew and other groups working in the docks. Collaborations were forged with Muslim unions and other splinter groups. Through the 1960s and 1970s, breakaway groups formed from Muslim stevedores rejecting the new Hindu leadership of the NUWW, or who had been arrested and accused of communalism, forged alliances with the PSU (Bogaert 1970). In the early 1970s under the leadership of Makhan Chakrabarty this union had the largest number of members of all the unions in the port. Both the head of the NUWW and Makhan Chakrabarty sat on the board of the port trust and negotiated in Delhi with successive prime ministers and shipping ministers. But during the late 1970s into the 1980s, the communist-affiliated Calcutta Port and Dock Workers Union (CPDWU) gradually gained more members than either of these two unions. This reflected the rise of the CPI(M) and Left Front in West Bengal. This growth came from CPI(M)'s systematic techniques for building vote banks, which included spreading party cadres throughout industrial establishments.

Through the 1980s strikes were common in the docks, often bringing them to a standstill. As the new austerity regime was introduced in the 1980s, unions competed fiercely for the decreasing resources in the port and protested against the decrepit infrastructure. Unions were valued by members primarily because they acted as brokers with the administration and advocated for employees in disciplinary inquiries. The PSU and NUWW were in particular key brokers, accepted as such by the port bureaucrats. Their leaders were recognized as legitimate and central to the productivity of the port and served on the board of trustees. The newer marine crew recruited during this period also joined the nonaffiliated and Congress unions, following the pattern of the men who had taught them their trade on the launches. They and the older crew became skilled brokers in petty and large disputes.

In the latter part of the 1980s into the 1990s, the role of unions primarily as brokers for individual workers became even more important. During this period union leaders confronted by spiraling financial crises capitulated in the process of reducing staff and introducing contractual work. They limited strike calls to national level strikes that were bargaining chips with the central shipping ministry for pay increases and pension rights for permanent staff in the port. In the battle for scarce resources the port played factions off against each other. For example, they persuaded the port workers' unions not to protest when the Dock Labor Board that provided stevedores for offloading ships was dissolved or contractual coal shed workers were laid off. In this crisis atmosphere unions further split with the Calcutta Port Shore Mazdoor Union (CPSMU) [CPI(M) and CITU affiliated], the National Union of Waterworkers (Indira Gandhi) (affiliated to Trinamul Congress), the Port Sromik Janata Panchayat (affiliated to the socialist Hind Mazdoor Sabha) and the Bharatiya Mazdoor Sangh (affiliated to the Bharatiya Janata Party) all emerging.

The urgency of successive financial crises led to a progressive erosion of any remaining cooperative class vision among port workers. Unions competitively scrambled to protect the economic interests of their individual members. The leaders of the largest unions, which were now the PSU (affiliated to the HMS), the NUWW (affiliated to Indian National Trade Union Congress) and CPSMU [affiliated to Communist Party of India (Maoist) and Centre of Indian Trade Unions], were told in meetings with the chairman to fall in line with austerity measures or else the port would be in danger of closing. By 2000 this led to the paradox that the largest union, the CPSMU, had diversified its brokering activities into securing contractual work in the port solely for CPI(M) party activists and supporters. Other unions, such as the Port Sromik, faced drastically cut subscriptions as a result of the decline in manpower of the port. They were courted by contractors offering payoffs so they would not object to further privatization and outcontracting of work. Now dock workers could no longer be certain that unions would act to protect the rights to permanent work and benefits of their individual members.

The East Bengali marine crew were both agents and victims of this process. Their numbers had been drastically reduced, and skilled work had been taken away by contractors. Yet many of them were also the union officials and members who had attempted to win the brokering games for themselves at the expense of other workers in the 1980–90s. In their lifetime they had experienced dramatic changes in the rights and duties that their labor on the river for the state entitled them to. This work had started in the 1950s as a patriotic duty of building a new West Bengal. In the 1960s–70s work on the river had become an activity that guaranteed rights for a class of port workers thinly divided from each other by allegiances to various political parties and community groups. In the 1980s–90s work for the state became a scarce economic resource maintained by competitive brokering between unions. Long-term political rights and duties that previously had been associated with labor for the state on the river had been eroded as a result of austerity policy.

Since the 1980s daily routines of work had also changed dramatically. This altered how men encountered the Hooghly. The mooring crews with their daring labor of diving into the river and anchoring vessels had disappeared from Kolkata with only forty or so men remaining at Baj Baj. The marine crew had been slowly reduced, and their routines had become deskilled and pedestrian. Until the 1990s men had worked near the mouth of the river or on the sea at Sandheads near Sagar Island. There on dredgers and pilot vessels they followed the disciplined marine routines of watches, navigation and command. They had spent days away from home with generous allowances. Now they worked on small launches ferrying pilots and equipment in the narrow stretches of river near Kolkata. They were on twelve-hour shifts, increased ten years ago from eight, alternating nights and days every six days with one day off for rest. In the worst position on the launches were the *bhandari,* or cooks. These were young men who had all been promised permanent work and promotion in the port. Yet ten years after the hiring freeze and cut-backs of the late 1990s they still worked on contracts in a menial, apprentice role with no end in sight. In contrast to earlier skilled naval routines, men of the marine crew were becalmed on a narrow, predictable stretch of river. They also had to deal with increasingly decrepit equipment on the launches. Their engines juddered to a halt or their steering lurched in unpredictable directions. When this happened the port launches were replaced by private country launches manned by young men on contract, an event that the crew found humiliating. This was especially troubling because it was rumored that the chairman of the port wanted to replace all the port launches, which he claimed were beyond repair, with contracted vessels and employees.

But how did the marine crew ethically frame this history of public-sector labor and restructuring of the working classes in the docks? How did they represent the productive power of unionized labor? What were the forces that provided its antithesis that generate waste? Why were they so fascinated by the ruins of Ash Ghat and the mooring crew that used to work there? How did their ethics limit their critiques of austerity capitalism? It is to these questions that the chapter turns next.

The Productive Power of Unionized Public-sector Labor: Courage (*Shahosh*)

Melancholia for Courage (*Shahosh*)

For the marine crew the productive power of unionized public-sector labor was manifest in the quality of courage, or *shahosh*. This had been most present among the mooring crew and was commemorated by the ruins of Ash Ghat. This power of *shahosh* was associated with a now threatened nationalist project of East Bengali refugees rebuilding Bengal in return for patronage from the state. Although I spoke to many past and present marine crew members, I will most often refer to the accounts of two men who are key to both the celebration of Ganga puja and unionism in the docks. The first of these is Jagesh Gupta, a retired mooring hand who started work in the early 1950s as a trainee lascar. He was a founder of the Ganga puja. He had left from Noakhali in East Bengal in the late 1940s and searched for any manual work he could find until he was taken on in the Inland Water Training Institute. When I met him he had recently ended his lifetime of work as an official in one of the politically nonaffiliated dock unions. Reflecting the significance of union solidarities to him, Jagesh, a widower, lived with an old union friend on the northern outskirts of Kolkata. The second is the man whose words opened this chapter, Bolai Das, who is a *sarang* on a river launch. His family was from Jessore in Bangladesh. He started work in the late 1970s, had received his qualifications from the Inland Water Training Institute and was a high-ranking officer in a Congress-affiliated union. As was typical of many of the marine crew at Ash Ghat, he had been displaced from lucrative work on the pilot ship at Sagar Island because this had been taken over by outside contractors. His current work was very insecure because of the plans to replace the port launches with private ones. He was on the Ganga puja committee.

The men of the marine crew insisted that a special quality was required to create productivity on the river, *shahosh* or "courage." It was the waxing and waning of this power that they traced when they told the history of the previous fifty years on the river. *Shahosh* was a mental and physical masculine strength that made you able to survive the unpredictable force of the Hooghly. The river's power was described as manifest in the difficult tides on the river. The fullest realization of these was the bore tide, a four-foot-high wave of water that came up the river during the flood tide in certain seasons. The old mooring crew were fascinating because they most possessed *shahosh,* and Ash Ghat evoked these men. All the marine staff described how the mooring crew used to row out in wooden hawser boats to let down the anchor chain from the ships, detach the anchor and then swim carrying the shackles to attach them to four buoys. For example, Jagesh proudly spoke of how much *shahosh* you needed for this work. He also suggested that such hard work generated ties of solidarity that stretched to a mutual duty of care between friends beyond death:

This was always very hard work, but especially in bore tides or strong tides. Whoever was working with me I would call friends. One friend was in the dock at night drunk. He was the last man to board the launch. After some distance he fell from the launch, but no one saw when he went. The harbor master stopped all the work and they took 3 or 4 launches with hundreds of men. They were searching for the dead body. They would not stop looking.

Bolai too suggested that *shahosh* was the most important quality for survival and work on the river and that it was epitomized by the mooring crew. He said that when he first came to work on the launches there were so many ships on the moorings and the men were so full of *shahosh*. The river too mirrored their strength: "There was a much bigger depth and stronger current at Ash Ghat then." He then continued to explain:

I did all the work on the pilot vessel from being a sweeper up. My work was full of danger and risk. There were many problems with accidents. I saw one. There was so much rolling that the pilot fell into the boat and broke his legs. *Shahosh* was necessary. . . . I saw one ship sink in a great storm in May 1997.

He often pointed with disdain at the contractual security guards and men on nearby private launches saying, "What is the point of a useless person like that?" contrasting their qualities with the essential quality of *shahosh*. In these accounts the marine crew suggested that only true men, like the disappeared mooring crew, with the required amount of courage, could labor successfully on the river to make it productive. The river's power required men with equivalent strength to its force to make it generative.

This *shahosh,* or masculine power, was manifest in heat in the body that was amplified by certain foods. Both the work hierarchy and solidarity of the crew on port boats has long been created by the cooking and sharing of food. Everyone starts out as a *bhandari*, which is the first apprentice role in the marine crew. Apprentices make the food that is eaten together and that then fuels masculine collective work. As one of the *bhandari*, Nimai Laha put it:

Our work is very important. We have to give a lot of mutton and fish because the men on the boat need it to do their hard work on the river. It is not like usual canteen work because we have to make very clean (*poriskar*) food to eat.

The old marine crew were famed for the scale of their appetite and therefore for their *shahosh*. As Sanjoy Misra, a forty-year-old man who worked in the marine crew at Ash Ghat, put it:

When you are at sea it is very dangerous. There is rolling all the time. You have to take a lot of wine or else those who do not take wine take green chilies and dried chilies mixed together. You need *shahosh*. The river is so powerful that it can just pick people up and throw them into the waters of the Ganga at any time. The work is so hard that you have to eat a huge amount of mutton and rice. I saw in the docks old saucepans that could take so much rice because the men would eat so much, 7 or 8 kilograms at one meal easily.

Jagesh underlined that labor disputes in the past and the present would flare up if the usual *bhandari* did not turn up for work or the quality of the food went down— the crew would all refuse to work. Bolai, like other crewmembers, greatly resented the reduction of their rations and decline of the food since he moved from the pilot vessel to the launch. Making the river productive necessitated *shahosh,* and this quality could only be generated if men were sustained properly by their employer's provision of heating foods. It was this quality of *shahosh* that made productive labor on the forceful river possible. Men's descriptions of the act of labor joined together *shahosh*, heat and work. They explained that by singing collectively during work on the river the heat necessary for labor would start to rise in their bodies along with their courage. In these accounts, from a present where economic necessity is used to measure the power of men and the river, the marine crew asserted different kinds of obligations. They suggested that work was a productive, skillful act that had its own ethical necessities. The river too was not just a resource to be exploited, but was an unpredictable, dangerous agent. Ash Ghat and the old mooring crew were fascinating because they and their special qualities of *shahosh* suggested this counterpoint to the present.

These qualities of *shahosh* were not, however only associated with masculine solidarities of work. They were also part of the political solidarities of a Bengali nationalism. The marine crew described themselves as part of a patriotic history in which East Bengali refugees had taken on work on the river in spite of its polluting associations with Muslims and low-caste groups. Men revived heroic tales of B. C. Ray's recognition of the essential role of East Bengali refugees on the river. Jagesh remembered: "Actually at that time work in the port, *jahaj kaj* (ship work) . . . was rejected by the middle class people. A father would not marry your daughter to you." But Jagesh claimed that B. C. Ray had the foresight to see that it was a patriotic duty for East Bengali refugees to work on the river. He said that he had set up the Inland Water Training Institute for refugees because "he decided that these rivers were very important in our life, but they were maintained by foreign [Muslim] crews. If they all stopped work at the same time then my country will be stopped." He said that B. C. Ray's plans were well placed because he claimed that "when the war came with Pakistan all the Muslim crews resigned all together on one day." Other marine crew such as Bolai asserted that B. C. Ray had a special relationship to them, that as a result of his patronage refugees "could eat" and he was the *roopkar* (form-giver) to their future, as well as that of the river itself. B. C. Ray's acts were a sign that in the past the marine crew had received patronage from the state and the port trust in recognition of their essential national labor.

Marine crewmembers also asserted that the historic labor of the marine crew had returned the river to its Hindu origins. For example, Jagesh described how when refugees first arrived they had to be apprentices to Muslims on the boats, but their only thought was, "We were not ashamed of this. We said to each other to encourage ourselves, 'Keep working. Keep working.' Let us build something and show we can do this without them. We worked and worked so that we could take over." He continued:

We took our revenge on them, us Hindus working there. They used to take beef on the ship and everywhere. On the day of Id they would openly slaughter cows in the docks. We made a protest that we would not take the Muslim *bhandaris* to cook food for the crew members. It lasted for two or three months and then all the *bhandaris* left. A thousand Muslim river workers in the end left because of our protests.

Marine crewmembers described their life's work on the Hooghly in terms of a patriotic task of Hindu men.

Within this ethic the quality of *shahosh* was also associated with the solidarity of the working classes of the port. Collective union action was a coming together in which men mutually recognized and enacted their *shahosh*. Marine crew argued that in the past it was even possible for antagonistic Muslims and Hindus to unite in union action. This was because they were under the control of leaders with even greater *shahosh* than that of the men they commanded. Union protests at the Kolkata Port Trust head office by the PSU, both in the past and present, spectacularly displayed the physical presence of this *shahosh*. Men walk bare-chested, as the old mooring crew would work in the river, displaying their physiques and shouting slogans as loudly as possible. But this past in which masculine Hindu *shahosh* controlled the recalcitrant river; produced a balance of forces with Muslim strength; created collective union action and joined men in national productivity was now mourned as in decline.

The Waning of Shahosh: Decline, Waste and Pollution

The marine crew suggested that it was a loss of *shahosh* and its solidarities in the 1980s that had produced the corrosive antiproductivity of the present. Amoral forces of selfish individualism now generated decline and waste. These drove divisive party politics (*rajniti*), the outsourcing of work to contractors and the indifference of the state. Evidence of decline came in the ruins of Ash Ghat and the unbalanced power of Muslims. It was also visible in the weakening of machines, men and the force of the river.

All marine crew argued that decline had followed the splintering of unions during the 1980s. Many of them linked this to the loss of strong leadership caused by the early death of Makhan Chakrabarty. Jagesh stated, "He is the father to us. He is the *roopkar* of our marine department. He was such a man that he could create unity between all people. Everything was lost after his death." Then he described how the unions had competed with each other to outdo their demands "looting the Port." He suggested that now most of them had become the "only business you do not need to invest anything in to make money. So they have to be corrupt." They form alliances with contractors who are "all Muslim contractors, who are getting rich. If you have property that side [in Kidderpore] and you are a Hindu, all these rich Muslims will buy you out. They are buying all the Hindu people's houses over there." For the marine crew this amoral present without a proper balance of forces was symbolized by the ruined condition of Ash Ghat. Typically Jagesh suggested that it had become a place of death repossessed by its previous Muslim associations. He said that everything the unions had built up had become "a *khoborstan*"— a Muslim graveyard.

The marine crew also evaluated the present as a place where productive reciprocities between unions, the state and workers no longer existed. These had been eroded by amoral selfish alliances between political parties, contractors and an uncaring state. Bolai sadly described this situation to me as I sat with him over the months on the pilot launch at Ash Ghat. Bolai would grow animated as he described how when B. C. Ray was the governor of the state he had especially helped refugees find work in the port after partition and that it was from him that refugees "could get food." This he argued was in stark contrast to the present situation. His Congress-affiliated union existed

only to support the workers, but the port was only giving them number two work. The contractors have pushed us out of our work. Our union used to have seven hundred members, but now as the port has got rid of the people the courage of the union has got less. The work of the union was that the workers should stay well. Most love is in the union. Each and every one of us love each other and support each other if there is trouble in our job or an accident. If the workers are treated well, then the state will be treated well too and the port also.

This mutual reciprocity between workers, unions and the state had been broken by antiproductive forces. Bolai and other marine crew suggested that they were shut out from their proper work in the pilot vessel and elsewhere on the river. This was because, they claimed, the communist-affiliated union had agreed with contractors that only CPI(M) members would get this work. The rumor was also that this union had agreed with the port that only their members would be protected from dismissal.

These antiproductive forces were for the marine crew most present in private-sector work. This work was seen as essentially and morally different from public-sector work. Crew members attributed the decrepit nature of vessels directly to the failures of contractual work driven by profit. Bolai, and other marine crew, often connected the faulty steering and rusting hulks of their launches to the fact that they had been built by private contractors. Deshbondhu Boral (who joined the port in the early 1980s, whose father was a lascar from Jessore) commenting on the Ma Ganga summed up this kind of evaluation:

Look at the Ma Ganga. These things built by contractors. It was so expensive and it was only just built and look at it now. It is rusted already. It is not solid work. For the contractor it is profit and for the officers it is profit. They eat all our *paise* [money], but they do not do good work and they do not do solid work. These things will not turn out well.

In these accounts the qualities and capacities of men to realize their capacity, as Bolai's comments that opened the chapter reveal, was also declining. Along with this the river too was declining in its strength and purity. For example, Deshbondhu explained that there used to be a machine to keep the mooring basin in the Kidderpore docks clean by pumping out the water into the river. He claimed that as a result there wasn't any pollution at all. Now the equipment had broken down and hadn't been repaired. Instead the port used private dinghies on contract and people fished things out from the water by hand. Deshbondhu explained that now the Ganga was not being kept clean (*poriskar*) and as a result it was losing its strength. Marine crew as a group spoke of the greater force and purity of the river in the past that was now eroded by inadequate care for it.

In these evaluations the mutually sustaining reciprocal relationships between state, unions and workers no longer held. The marine crew asserted that these had been disrupted by selfish acts driven by profit. This amorality was most visible in the corrupt, shoddy practices of contractual work. It had led to the decay of the force of men, vessels and the river. It also returned the waterfront and the river to a Muslim past eroding the patriotic labor of Hindu men. How then did the marine crew regenerate the ruins of public-sector labor on the river? It was through the practices of the Ma Ganga puja and, the protection and rebuilding of the Kali temple at Ash Ghat that this was achieved. These restored the ideal life-giving reciprocities between men, the state and the river.

Regenerating the Ruins of Labor:
Ganga Puja and the Kali Temple at Ash Ghat

Goddesses as Mediators

In Bengali popular Hinduism, goddesses, such as Ma Ganga, act as mediating life-giving agents. During the twentieth century their powers became central to the iconography of nationalist political movements (Bhattacharya 2007; McDermott 2001, 2011; McDaniel 2004). In pre-Independence Bengal, *desh Bhakti* (devotion to the nation) was closely associated with the iconography and worship of the goddesses Durga and Kali (McDaniel 2004). For example Sarvajanin pujas "of all people" from 1918 involved men's athletic clubs organizing pujas in which "devotees made vows to the goddess to free the country with blood if necessary, patriotic speeches were made and there were exhibitions on the state of the nation and pictures of national heroes" (Sarma 1969, 583). Popular devotional songs to Kali and Durga were used from 1904 on as part of the Swadeshi and noncooperation movements. The partition of East and West Bengal was also depicted as a *bali*, immoral sacrifice by the British, that carved the goddess herself into pieces (McDermott 2001). Nazrul Islam's still hugely popular songs also made Kali and Durga into vehicles for nationalism and social reform. These uses of goddesses drew on the structure of ritual practice in which "the major contrast is heaven and earth but there is no dividing line. An overlapping area is governed by the goddess herself in her manifestations among gods and men" (Ostor 1980, 177). Every element of pujas to goddesses enables exchanges between various forms of life and domains of action revealing their interdependence and common essences. Importantly, the political and social uses of goddesses were not a bringing together of separate domains of the secular and the sacred or the material and the spiritual. Instead goddesses in Bengali popular Hinduism are mediators who move in an overlapping arena of the human and the divine. In their presence any distinctions between politics, economics, religion and of the material and spiritual no longer hold. All of these domains of action are instead shown to be unified and dependent on reciprocal life-giving exchanges.

It is often assumed that there has been a radical transformation in the role of goddesses since Independence with the growth of a separation between the "sacred" and "secular." This is attributed to the development of an individual piety more suited to democratic city life (McDaniel 2004). Or to the influence of CPI(M) political ideology, which has divided domains of economics and politics from ritual (Chakrabarti 1999; Ghosh 2000). But this work has not taken into account rituals associated with urban labor. As we will see, in the case of the marine crew (and in many of the uses of ritual along the Hooghly), such rituals to goddesses still make manifest the inherent unity of politics, economics and ritual. In addition they re-new the life-giving productive forces that unify material and immaterial worlds. These rituals are not associated with older forms of patronage and hierarchy. They are a celebration of egalitarian masculine community, the productive potential of the male body and inalienable rights to work.

Ma Ganga Puja: The Reciprocal Vitalities of Men, the State and the River

Ma Ganga, even more than other Bengali goddesses, is the manifestation of the animating foundational life of the universe. *Ganga jol* is used in ritual practice to bring life into the images that are worshipped (Ostor 1980). Ma Ganga and her *ganga jol* act as liquid mediums for the mediation between overlapping domains of existence, infusing them with life. Her fluidity links cosmos and society and she governs a medium that joins these with a single life force (ibid.). More specifically, Ma Ganga provides regenerating female *sakti,* or power, to a world filled with pol-luting death. In myths, she descends to earth to restore the life of the ancestral rela-tives of Bhagirath burned to death in anger by a *rishi* (sage) disturbed in his medita-tions. She is controlled by the male principle Siva, who catches her in his locks as she descends, because otherwise her unrestrained force would be destructive. Pujas to Ma Ganga (such as the one at Ash Ghat) re-enact the descent of the Ganga by the priests welcoming her, establishing life in her image, sacrificing to her and making offerings of food. The iconography of the statue shows the moment when Bhagi-rath called her to earth to renew life. Her representation, like Lakshmi and riding on the *mokur* (giant fish) associated with marriage, recalls the generative power of childbearing women. The life of the goddess regenerates and purifies the life of the community that eats her *prasad* (blessed food) together.

The puja to Ma Ganga at Ash Ghat is an adapted form of a ritual associated with low-caste rural fisherman and boatmen. The marine crew have since the 1960s used it in the very different setting of industrial state labor and mixed castes working together. In it idealized exchanges of life between the river, workers, tools and the state are enacted to assert permanent, inalienable relationships. Garlands from the goddess in the hands of a high-level marine officer are taken to the concrete plinth for marine crew lost on the river and to the statue of B. C. Ray. Breaking from the usual practice in which images are carried by men to a riverbank or body of water where they are immersed, the Ma Ganga statue is taken at the end of the puja on a port trust launch to the middle of the river. *Ganga jol* (Ganges water) is also put on the engines of the port launches. Both these acts allow the goddess to animate the tools of work. The regeneration that takes place of men, machines and the state is not associated as in other forms of Ganga puja with hierarchical patronage or a single caste group. The puja committee is composed of a democratic group: the head of the marine staff, two clerks from the mooring office, inland water masters from port launches, more minor crew members and crew who hold posts in various unions. Therefore rather than being hierarchical, the puja aims to materialize an idealized reciprocity between the state, workers, tools and the river built on flows of life between them. How, then, do marine crew interpret this ritual in the present in relation to their current ethics of productivity and regeneration?

Accounts of the origins of the puja make clear the importance of a Hinduized project of public-sector labor. Everyone attributed its development to an accident that occurred at Ash Ghat in the 1950s. For example, Jagesh explained that this had been caused by a Muslim launch master being overwhelmed by the current of the river:

There was a bore tide in the morning. The *sarang,* who was an East Bengali Muslim, was the master of the launch. The current was very strong. The force of the water smashed him down on a buoy and it went down—the vessel too. We lost eight friends that day. It was a terror to us. We Hindus thought because we were working on the River Ganga—for us it is a very pious and famous river. We made our bread and our life on this river. So we thought we should do some puja for this.

He continued straight on to link the event of the accident to the iconography of the puja:

Do you know that the Ganga Puja *thakur* is like Lakshmi and on her left is Bhagirath with a Shankar, blowing it? The Ganga came from Brahma. Her force was held by Mahadeb [Siva], was controlled by Siva. Bhagirath was praying to Siva to release the Ganga, to Mahadeb to release her from his hair. Every puja Siva is there. He is called in the invocations of the priest.

His account emphasized the uncontrollable feminine force of the river and the necessity of its careful restraint by Siva, the emblematic image of Bengali Hindu masculinity.[8] In such accounts the Ganga puja had restored productive relations between the Hooghly and public-sector port workers because it recognized the river's true nature as a Hindu goddess. The effect of the puja everyone said had been to prevent any other huge accident occurring on the river. The goddess's force was now contained by the productive agency of Hindu public-sector labor, just as Siva had controlled the descent of the Ganga. These origin stories suggested that the annual puja was a manifestation of the reciprocal life-giving relationships between public-sector workers and the river.

But what of the presence of the state in the form of B. C. Ray in the ritual, how did the marine crew explain this? Jagesh described how the marine crew had decided to erect the statue when B. C. Ray died in 1962. He explained:

I started with the Inland Water Training Institute and this was made by B. C. Ray only to feed the displaced persons from East Bengal. So we had a very strong feeling for B. C. Ray . . . . We told Makhan Chatterjee that we wanted to put a statue of B. C. Ray here . . . . We erected the statue at the time of Ganga puja. Makhan babu came and he also got the shipping minister to open it. There was a very big gathering, lots of Congress people too. We even proposed Bidhan ghat [B. C. Ray's first name] as the name to replace Ash Ghat.

Jagesh also described how the community that organized the puja shared egalitarian relationships. They formed a collectivity of workers beyond distinctions of politics, class or caste. Jagesh related how all the various unions would serve together on the committee:

There was no question of unions or cadres; all were the same. There was no bar. A peon can also be president of the committee. We were all like brothers in the same family working together. We had no other relations in Kolkata so these people we worked with were our relations.

The garland of flowers placed over the B. C. Ray sculpture by Captain Verma promised to the marine crew a regeneration of this patronage of the state to an idealized egalitarian community of men joined by labor. Younger marine crew also described the puja in similar terms. Bolai emphasized that the puja was not sponsored by one particular union:

In Ganga Puja everyone becomes equal. All the port staff take part all together with no separations at all. B. C. Ray is there because it was from him refugees could stay alive by their work on the river.

Men described the attendance of port officials at the Ash Ghat puja as a recognition of the essential reciprocal relationships between workers and these state officials.

Yet most important of all in marine crewmembers' accounts of the puja was the claim that it expressed an inalienable relationship between themselves and the river. For example, one day I was discussing the puja with Bolai and another leader of the crew, Pradip Kundu. Pradip explained: "We only worship Ma Ganga for our work. So in our mind we feel trust and peace (*bishash* and *shanti*)." Both he and Bolai then continued on to say that the goddess Ma Ganga was their mother and the mooring crew were all her sons, so it was a matter of filial sentiment to hold an annual puja. Through such statements the marine crew adapted the idiom usually used by boatmen castes in order to express their own unbreakable connection to the river (Doron 2008). Marine crew had recently placed a photograph of each year's Ma Ganga *thakur* on the launches next to the steering wheel. Every day when the crew started their shift they worshiped this photograph so that the effects of the puja continued through the year on the boats. This re-created the reciprocal productive relationship daily between Ma Ganga, the tools of work and their labor that was present during the puja. Overall, the men of the marine crew argued that the Ma Ganga puja manifested permanent life-giving collective obligations between public-sector labor, the state and the river. To them it promised the regeneration of the ruins of labor that had been produced by amoral, selfish individualism.

The Kali Temple: Conversions of Antiproductivity

Among the ruins of labor at Ash Ghat was one building that was growing fast, with a second story under construction. This was the marine crew's Kali temple. Kali in Bengali popular Hinduism is the necessary companion to goddesses such as Ma Ganga. She regenerates, but she does this by converting or deflecting destructive forces of death, impurity and anger. The particular form her image takes at Ash Ghat is of Nilasvaraswati Tara. Nilasvaraswati holds an animate sacrificial knife. She destroys uncontrollable emotions through knowledge produced from austerities and her worship (McDaniel 2004). Pujas to her are carried out in places of conflict and they ward off death, danger and violence. The iconography of Kali manifests antiproductive polluting forces in the universe, and her worship allows an overcoming of these. Importantly, if labor is represented as an act that is part of regenerative powers, as it is by the marine crew, then its negative effects and dangers can be explained only through the sudden antiproductive forces that Kali wards off.

The temple at Ash Ghat was recurrently described by the marine crew as a place where forces of antiproductivity and pollution were purified and converted.

In particular here, the purified bravery of a Hinduized marine crew was made from a past of Muslim impurity. This was particularly clear in Jagesh's descriptions of the origins of the temple:

One day some of the marine crew came with a small Kali statue and said that it had suddenly come up out of the river. They built a small shack there. That place is where the slaughtering of the Muslims was done there, that is the main reason the Bengali boys from Pakistan said if they can do it, then why can't we make our Kali temple there. Here they used to sacrifice their Bakr'Id cows, their slaughtering, so that is why we made our temple in this place. We would have our goddess of *shakti* so that *shahosh* will come. And all of this meant that the union-- the mental support [for it]was there . . . too. We had Ganga puja once a year but Kali worship for everyday work.

Nilasvaraswati Tara provided the appropriate vehicle for this transformation with her ability to overcome anger and to convert pollution, conflict and violence.

The thriving of the Kali temple at Ash Ghat was a source of great satisfaction and pride among the marine crew. In fact, they had recently come together to ensure not just its preservation but also continuing growth. After 9/11 the Kolkata Port Trust had to implement a strict cordoning off of the docks from its surroundings. At Ash Ghat the building of a security wall was met by strong protests and campaigns by the marine crew and nonaffiliated and Congress-affiliated union members. This was because it would cut off the community of worshippers from the Kali temple. The compromise that was reached was that in the morning and the evening worshippers would be allowed into the ghat, and for a December Kali puja. Sanjoy Misra explained:

The *mandir* was started by the mooring staff from East Bengal because at that time there was a lot of trouble between Hindus and Muslims. The Muslims used to do *namaz* in the port, so the Hindus had to make their own place. They built it on this uncultivated useless land where Muslims used to celebrate and made it clean for the temple. Each evening at *arati* time about a hundred people come each day. I, like all the marine juniors here, am on the puja and temple committee. The Port higher-ups would not support the practice of the worship here, so we formed a committee with the vessel masters, mooring masters, Ash Ghat *sarangs*, and juniors to organize the puja and the *mandir*.

For all the mooring crew I spoke to, the temple was an undeniable sign of the power of "*bishash*" or trust in the goddess. The marine crew had come together to preserve the temple, and their committee was now securing donations for the expansion of it. A long history of working-class labor activism was now commemorated by a growth of *bishash*, or trust in Kali, and a demand for the right to worship on the waterfront.

Conclusion: Austerity, Melancholia and Politics

Faced with a restructuring of class relations as a result of austerity policy, men in the marine crew attempted to reassert the value and rights of public-sector labor. This took the form of an ethical account of the present based on a melancholia for lost forms of work, nationalism and unionism (Blom Hansen 2012). Present social relations were seen from the perspective of a past in which unionized East Bengali refugees labored together on a Hindu river. Valued characteristics of *shahosh* had been uniquely manifest in their ideal form among the mooring crew, in old union activism and a patriotic project of solidarity. When the marine crew talked about the ruins of labor at Ash Ghat, in decrepit machinery and on the river, they mourned their decline as a wasting of their own masculine selfhood and capacity (Chopra et al.; Osella and Osella 2006). These ruins of labor and their own life-force were regenerated through forms of ritual practice and religious institutions. In these idealized long-term and large-scale productive reciprocities could be asserted that counteracted the amoral individualism of the present. The circles of reciprocity in these rituals did not extend to men who worked for the state on contracts. Contractual workers, their acts of work and the products of their labor were all manifestations of the amorality that generated the ruins and waste. This melancholic sense of workmanship produced a growing Hinduization of the Hooghly and its waterfront. This was most manifest in the mooring crew's collective preservation and refurbishment of the Kali temple. The ethics of the marine crew erased the traces of the complex history of work on the river, especially the past and present contributions of Muslim labor. They also made it difficult to build alliances with informalized workers in the private sector. They belonged to an amoral world apart from the solidarities of union action, and appeared essentially "other" to the collectivities of *shahosh*. Nevertheless, the melancholia of the marine crew was the result of experiences of insecurity and injustice created by the devaluing of labor in austerity policy. They ultimately aimed to re-create the ethical and political meanings of debts between citizens and the state.

In many postsocialist and postindustrial settings melancholies for socialist and Fordist modernity have emerged (Ferguson 1999; Steinmetz 2010). These are associated with new forms of right-wing populism, racism and nationalist politics

(Holmes 2000; Kalb and Halmai 2011). I traced a similar phenomenon among the marine crew affected by austerity policies. But my analysis has focused on how the act of labor is ethically framed within a universe of productive powers. As a result we can understand that growing forms of nationalism and populism are related to the experience of the erosion of long-term social obligations between workers, the state and private employers. Workers demand something more than a purely fiscal logic to determine their fate. They seek to infuse productivity and acts of labor with more than a calculative logic. Among the marine crew men have re-created long-term obligations through histories of patriotic nationalism and Hinduism, but these could also be asserted through transcendent links of kinship or race. Such ethics can lead to a disengagement from the fate of the growing groups of precarious, informalized contractual laborers for the state. Solidarities may, as in this case, exclude them because they are identified with the amorality of short-term fiscal ties. It is important that we explore emerging popular ethics of productivity more widely. It is only through attention to the changing meanings of acts of labor that we can fully understand the politics and inequalities of contemporary capitalism.

Fig. 4. State barges being converted into a pleasure cruiser

Chapter 3

Family Capital, State Pedigree and the Limits of Austerity Public Goods

SINCE THE 1990S bureaucrats and entrepreneurs on the Hooghly have been brought together in new relationships. Austerity policy has led to collaborations to produce low-cost technology. The outsourcing of vessel production and manning has led to other important ties with the informalized private sector.[1] The infrastructures on the Hooghly are now maintained through these public-private partnerships. Yet it was striking that in my conversations with both private entrepreneurs and bureaucrats on the Hooghly, they described their productive powers as entirely distinct. I began to reflect on this in particular from my encounters with the Jaiswal brothers, who ran one important private firm, Orient Ltd. Their accounts of the history of the firm interwove the quarrels and "adaptations" of the family with the changing patterns of industry on the Hooghly.[2] They understood their company history as a tale that linked the productivity of three generations of brothers in the paternal line to the fortunes of the river. Each brother would tell the story of the firm in a way that made this explicit. They would begin with their great-grandfather and his elder brother, who had a business together producing jute. But they explained that this trade was uncertain and the two brothers quarreled and separated. Their grandfather then bought his first barge for transporting jute. Their father gradually expanded this business with his three brothers and one cousin brother. When barge traffic declined in the 1980s, their branch of the family moved to the west coast of India to develop other transport trades. Their work in Kolkata was also being undercut by their father's middle brother, who had set up a rival business on the Hooghly. But this family feud healed in 1990 when they returned from western India to transport lash barges up the river. When their main client suddenly withdrew their contracts in 2000, the brothers explained how they had taken up new "high-tech" work on the river for the port and private clients. Entirely absent from this account was any sense that their opportunities were affected by state actions on the river. As Dilip Jaiswal, the eldest brother, put it, "That is the world of government offices and consultants and we cannot wait for them to make decisions." Their story was of a family seizing the fluid possibilities of capital. This quality of capital existed within objects. The family's task was to make the physical form of objects as malleable as this potential quality inside them. Likewise their family had to be as metamorphic as this force.

This chapter explores the divergent ways entrepreneurs and bureaucrats ethically evaluate the market and the state as they pursue new forms of the public good on the Hooghly. We have assumed that contemporary relations between the state and the market are legitimized primarily by an economization of the political (Power 1997; Harvey 2005). We have focused on the application of corporate models to bureaucrats that aim to make them entrepreneurial. Or we have shown how audit culture creates practices that hollow out the distinct characteristics of public institutions (Strathern 2000). Everything, it seems, is becoming "like" or "of" the market. This is often epitomized by the practices of public-private partnerships (Swyngedouw 2004). In contrast, this chapter will show that fiscal discipline and the pursuit of enterprise within bureaucracies does not produce a unified practice of market ethics (Barry 2002). Instead both bureaucrats and entrepreneurs engage in a much broader conduct of life that seeks to produce a public good (Bear and Mathur 2015). The financialization of state debt creates short-term fiscal imperatives, but the social relationships of austerity capitalism cannot be built from these alone. Bureaucrats and entrepreneurs legitimize their roles by claiming that they possess distinct qualities that release different kinds of long-term productive forces. Importantly, these ethics represent the state and the market as entirely different domains of generative productivity. It is this *separation* that leads to a misrecognition, and continuation, of austerity capitalism. Ironically, the more bureaucrats and entrepreneurs work together, the more divided in their essential productive qualities they appear to be. Ultimately, this chapter will argue that in all societies affected by austerity policy there will be such claims and counterclaims about who, and what, can produce the public good. The financialization of state debt does not create a unified pursuit of financial or market projects. Instead it generates diverse class claims for legitimacy that devalue some kinds of work as inherently unproductive. Once we look beyond formal market techniques, audit, and fiscal discipline, we uncover the various conducts of life that produce forms of accumulation.

This chapter explores these themes by focusing on marine officers and entrepreneurs who work with each other on the Hooghly. It is particularly important to analyze their conduct of life because these are the men who directly implement

central policy initiatives on the river. From their collaborations the new infrastructures and arrangements of outsourced work develop. To understand their ethics of
waste and regeneration we must first turn to the history of the marine department
on the river. It is in relation to experiences of historic and current time-spaces of
work that ethical evaluations of austerity capitalism have emerged.

From High Sea Mariners to Entrepreneurial Brokers: The Changing Public Good in the Marine Department

Unlike the Jaiswal brothers' account of the past, it is in the changing fortunes of
the marine department that we need to locate their entrepreneurial activities. Since
the 1980s marine department officers have lived through dramatic changes in their
status and roles. Before the 1980s marine officers were recruited from the Rajendra
Indian merchant navy training ship in Mumbai. They were selected through exams
held across India and often held high school qualifications. Their fathers were often
part of the labor aristocracy of the public services such as the railways. Their apprenticeship on the Rajendra led them to associate their work on the Hooghly with
naval and marine traditions. Relationships with captains and senior crew members
on the ships that docked in the port were close, especially as they stayed in port for
long periods of time to offload their cargo. On the other hand, relationships with
marine crew within the port were governed by the strict hierarchies of the navy
and differentials of education. Given this training and background a masculine
cosmopolitanism was cultivated among these officers. They were an elite group of
employees whose expertise, skill and necessity were rarely challenged. The Pilot's
Guild and the Port Officers Association rarely clashed with the port over hours, accidents or conditions of work. As men aged they rose through the ranks. They could
progress to the very top ranks of the marine department solely on the basis of their
skills of command and knowledge of the river.

During the 1980s several important changes occurred in the marine department. These led to a progressive erosion of the cosmopolitan marine traditions and
status of the service. As the value of real wages in the port declined in comparison
to wages on container ships it was no longer possible to recruit or retain men who
were fully qualified merchant seamen. So in 1988 the marine department decided
to build up a cadre of pilots, "so that they are capable of handling ships efficiently
but are not in a position to leave the port at their will."[3] From now on the port would
accept non–first class Rajendra graduates and college graduates in science subjects.
These recruits would be made to sign a bond to work for the port for at least five

years once they were trained.⁴ This decision created a mariner, nonmariner split within the service and an anxiety that the "BA boys" would not be of the same caliber, since the "safety of life at sea and of ships is always held uppermost by anyone or everyone who has had anything to do with a marine career for which . . . officers of right training, caliber and marine background are most essential."⁵ The uncertainty about this marine skill produced a harsh assertion of marine traditions of discipline on board the pilot ship where the new recruits were trained. This was especially because working-class men from diverse regional origins were often asserting authority over newly recruited Bengali lower-middle-class men. This recruitment also marked an erosion of the cosmopolitanism of the marine officer service, since new BSc recruits were more likely to be young Bengalis seeking to live and work near home.

The financial crises of the late 1980s and 1990s brought new onslaughts on the elite status of officers. As investment was no longer sustained, they worked with a declining infrastructure in the docks and on the river. It was only the new activism of the Pilot's Association that attenuated this process. After the wreck of the manned light vessel the *Candle* in 1988, the pilots decided to campaign for better pilot vessels, port equipment and for the new VTMS system and shore station. This campaign culminated in strikes that brought the port to a standstill in 1995. During this period the administration also began to discuss the possibility with marine officers of privatizing the pilot service. They also proposed cutting off the marine officers from their skilled navigational roots by placing pilots on shore in stations where they would guide ship captains up the river. The last remaining pilot vessels built in the UK were scrapped. New vessels and infrastructure were instead now made on the Hooghly by contractual workers. This process became acute in 2000, when the chairman instituted a permanent hiring freeze at every level of the port. All equipment, barges or vessels that could be sold off in the docks were auctioned. All new building or infrastructure replacement projects were discontinued. Repair of vessels and equipment in the port slowed almost to a halt, and the ship-repairing department was closed. Future new building or recruitment to the marine department would be carried out by contractual workers.

As these changes occurred, marine officers had to take on an entirely new role. They became the brokers for the outsourcing of work to private-sector companies. They also started to devise cheap technological solutions for the mounting problems on the river through relationships with private entrepreneurs. Central to this new work were the connections between marine officials and small family firms that expanded their activities to meet the outsourcing needs of the port. Who then were the private-sector entrepreneurs that marine department officers forged relationships with? These were men who were already moving through dock and waterfront offices because they were closely involved in port trade.

Typical of these companies is Orient, with its long relationship with the Kolkata Port Trust. Starting with jute transport in the 1950s and then expanding into the midstream unloading of ships into barges from 1960 to 1970 and then transport of lash barges from 1990 to 2000, its fortunes have waxed and waned with developments in port trade. In recent years Orient has become drawn into the new brokered projects of the marine department. They have, in particular, provided the port with low-cost solutions to the problems created by the lack of maintenance and investment. Using the resources, expertise and prestige gained from these projects Orient bought vessels from state agencies and adapted them to the needs of an ever-increasing range of clients.

One of the first schemes Orient carried out for the port was the laying of an underwater wall in a hydrographic scheme to reduce the silting of the channels near Haldia port. This area had become impassable for ships at particular times of the year because of a lack of dredging investment. For this project Orient took an old state-owned barge and converted it into a vessel with which they could build a spur in the river. This spur proved to be only a temporary measure that did not succeed in reducing silting, but it became the basis for further contracts for Orient. They reconverted the barge into four other vessels that were hired by a large global engineering company to construct a major river bridge.

In 2001, Orient also received a contract from the port for the construction of the virtual jetty. High-level port bureaucrats had conceived of this scheme as a low-cost substitute for building a deep water port. Its name was adopted because it suggested a high-tech solution equivalent to new knowledge technologies. But the form, eight giant buoys, mimicked the old practices of the laid-off mooring crew famed for their daring feats of diving and anchoring at Ash Ghat. The virtual jetty was intended to revive barge trade on the river and to act as a less expensive version of a deep sea port. As I described in Chapter 1, the results were not successful. This project has contributed to the further expansion of Orient Ltd. It now also works on contract for new private ports in Western India and large global companies. As is typical of such family firms along the Hooghly, their labor is informalized, works on day rates, has no benefits, is nonunionized and is recruited through labor brokers. The firm expands and contracts its workforce from around fifty to five hundred men according to projects, providing no permanent livelihood or long-term security for its employees. Importantly, it is from close personal and structural relationships with port officials that the prosperity of private companies such as Orient has emerged.

The growing connections between public and private enterprises on the river are obscured by two entirely distinct ethical accounts of the conduct of life and the public good. These evaluations propose different explanations for decline on the river and are based on contrary temporal structures. The account of marine officers emphasizes the necessity of continuing a legacy of marine skill, while that of entrepreneurs focuses on future-oriented innovations without any grounding in formal expertise. They are also founded on the agency of different deities, Ma Ganga and Hanuman and distinct claims about the vitality of technological objects. The river too appears with different kinds of agency. These divergent ethics contribute to the forms of the physical waterscape and to class inequalities on the Hooghly.

Regenerating the State: Pedigrees of Knowledge, Preservation and Ma Ganga

Marine officers claimed that they were uniquely capable of extracting productivity from the Hooghly. This was because they preserved with their actions, and in their persons, the specialized skills and tools of generations of river workers. This lineage, or "pedigree" (as they described it), had been transmitted in an unbroken continuity in the form of technical knowledge. Here, I will draw on the accounts of many officers, but central will be those of Captain Verma, a high-level controller of trade on the river whom we have already encountered in the openings of Section I and Section II. Like many of his fellow marine officers, he was a product of two generations of working-class state employment. He had grown up in railway colonies, where his father was an engineer in the state-run companies. He joined the port in the 1970s as a trainee pilot rising up the ranks gradually. His daily work was a calculation of how many risks he could take with the decaying infrastructure of reduced manning, decrepit tugs, rusting lock gates and declining depths in the river without any major accidents taking place. He often took to the river piloting ships to and from the sea because of the shortage of pilots. From 2000 he had also implemented the hiring freezes, cutbacks, sales of vessels and introduction of contractual work among the marine crew. He was now at the center of discussions about the possibility of privatizing the pilot service. He helped arrange contracts with private firms such as Orient and was friends with the Jaiswal brothers who ran it.

"River Castes": Nostalgia and Pedigrees of Knowledge

When marine officers reflected on the presence of decay in the Kolkata Port they began with a deep history of river work. They, like the marine crew, were fascinated by the mooring crew and Ash Ghat. But in their accounts the mooring crew were without a union history or nationalist significance. They were an apolitical community distinguished by their river knowledge. When their East Bengali origins were mentioned it was to assert that the mooring crew were from fishing and seafaring castes similar to those that had worked the river from time immemorial. In these accounts the physical presence of these men was lost, but their skills were alive in the present in the knowledge of marine officers. Captain Verma grew animated whenever he discussed the methods by which the mooring crew anchored the vessels to buoys even in the dragging current of the flood tide:

The mooring service was very skilled. They had screw-pile moorings shaped like a propeller that fitted deep into a rod. This was how they secured the ships. The mooring master serviced the moorings tightened them up, especially when they would come lose in the winter months due to contraction.

Once looking at an old photograph of Ash Ghat, Verma became so excited by their technical feat of mooring in the flood tide that he called in a group of fellow officers to admire the image. Like other marine officers he attributed these special abilities to the origins of the mooring crew in the fishing and seafaring castes of the riverine regions of East Bengal.

As Anil, a thirty-year-old berthing master, put it, the mooring crew were "people who had a link to the river and the sea, who knew the river well and the moods of the river with a seafarer's mindset." Captain Pandey, another high-level marine officer, who introduced me to Jagesh Gupta, saw him as one in a long line of tough people who would "live on small vessels in the water. They were totally dependent on the Ganga and it was a tough job living close to the river. So for that reason they had a Ganga Puja." There was no discontinuity in this historical lineage, for example of partition. This line started for the officers with the crews from Noakhali who manned the wooden pilot boats at Sandheads in the nineteenth century. For example, Pandey kept in his living room a reproduction of an old Victorian painting that showed a pilot and crew rowing in a storm to a sailing ship at Sandheads. This, he explained, demonstrated both the danger and the skill of their work, which produced "knowledge" that continued into the present. The mooring crew had been repositories of this. He explained that even a British pilot had written in his journal

when he came in the 1960s to the Calcutta jetties that he had never seen mooring men with such abilities. He added, "From this we have still been building our
knowledge up over history until now we know so much about the river." The past
skill of the mooring crew had flowed into an unbroken inherited stream of knowledge that the marine officers continued to preserve in their actions and persons.

It was common for the marine officers to describe this link through time as the
"pedigree" of the port. Captain Verma, for example, frequently argued that you had
to "know your pedigree in order to create a future" for the docks and river. This pedigree was understood as a projection of a lineage back in time founded originally on
a group of brothers, in the same way as officers calculated their own family history.
Captain Verma's collection of old photographs of the industrial Hooghly manifested
for him a visceral thrill of continuity that made this pedigree manifest. He had
made a special compilation of photographs on his work computer to underline this
deep history. For each old image of a technological feat on the river he had taken
a recent picture of the same place that exactly repeated the vista of the historical
one. He displayed these to visitors to the office one after the other, creating an effect that encouraged the viewer to project connections between the past and the
present. The marine officers shared a nostalgia for the past of the river claiming an
unbroken knowledge that linked them with this history of skilled technical labor.

Preservation and Historical Technologies

Technologies were treated by marine officers as a materialization of this unbroken history of knowledge of the river. Marine officers had strong affective relationships with the technologies of the port. A large number of men had archived them,
making collections in their homes of old photographs, objects and documents. For
example hydrographic surveyors would describe to me the minute differences between various kinds of obsolete tide gauges in all their technical detail. The most
active among the officers had enthusiastically sent unsolicited photographs of
technologies to the museum that the port trust was setting up. Captain Verma was
exemplary of this ethic. When I first met him in his office in the Kidderpore docks
he made it explicit. He began by explaining that he "loved the history" of the port
because he said without understanding the past you could make no future. He then
opened up a carefully curated file on his computer with photographs of the construction of the docks in the 1880s. We admired the feats of engineering. The images
jogged his memory of a group of British visitors in 1986 who had come to the dry
dock to see what was being repaired. Inside was an old launch from 1948. Captain

Verma said that they had been amazed by its beauty and age, and they had wanted to take it back to Britain to put in a museum. Captain Verma then laughed and said, "We couldn't let them because we were still using it for our work." His deep sense of a duty of care for the objects under his charge contained a mixture of frustration and pride. He often described the docks as a "living museum" and himself as a "keeper" of its objects. In a manner that was characteristic of all the middle-level marine department officers in the port, Captain Verma was passionate about the heritage of the docks that he saw as alive in old technologies. These evoked for him a living continuous link to old skills on the river. They were solidified skill that needed to be preserved. Most of all they manifested the unique and specialized workmanship that was necessary to carry out productive acts on the river. If they decayed, this essential knowledge would be lost as well.

The solidified pedigree within objects had also been activated to transfer what officers called the "marine spirit" to new recruits. In particular, when the port began to recruit university graduates rather than ship apprentices as pilots in the late 1980s, they set up training ships for them in Kolkata. These were two ancient paddle steamers on which were assembled old technologies of the port. The harbor master argued that these would transmit the right kind of marine spirit to the new recruits. When the financial crisis in the port in 2000 ended their upkeep, the marine officers did not abandon these floating museums. Instead they successfully campaigned against the port trust board's plans to scrap them. Their exhibits, as a result, were included in the shipping section of the newly built Science City.[6]

Marine officers in the hydrographic survey, such as Captain Kumar (with whom we first voyaged on the Hooghly in the Introduction), had a particularly acute sense of the necessity of preserving historical technologies and knowledges. They argued that it was only through such care that they could discern the complex reality of the river's agency and make it productive. Captain Kumar often returned to the topic of the silting of Haldia as a problem that was "killing us." According to Captain Kumar, what had gone wrong at Haldia was that:

Nature cannot go against nature and you have to take the help of it. At Haldia it [the river] has shoaled over for reasons . . . . We made a mistake at Haldia, the training wall was put in the wrong place at the wrong angle. This blocked the flow of the flood and ebb . . . We should have taken nature's help.

This kind of mistake could only be prevented through the retention of the minute historical knowledge of the river collected by successive generations. He continued:

What is very important is the transmission of knowledge about the river and the sea between older and junior officers. We will not understand how it is changing over time so we must listen to our seniors and talk to them.

Hydrographic officers were passionate about the maintenance of the historical technologies of the river. They were highly suspicious of the new electronic navigational charts that were being introduced. They resisted their sole use with fervor and meticulous revivals of old technologies. Captain Kumar and his colleagues grew animated as they discussed how they were preserving the old systems by digging out from the undergrowth the navigational columns that marked positions on the river. This effort he explained was because this knowledge would always be needed in a time of emergency. Similarly, hydrographic officers insisted that they must take their quintants out with them whenever they go on the river. Kumar explained, "These systems are our lifeline." This emphasis on old technologies and transmitted knowledges asserted a necessary and unbroken link between the current practices of state officials and those of river workers of the past. Marine officers suggested that without their careful preservation the Hooghly could not be made productive. Importantly, these deep lineages gave marine officers and their state labor on the Hooghly special, inalienable qualities. Only they could regenerate the river through their acts of preservation and knowledge. By implication, it was also only through the actions of a state bureaucracy with deep historical roots that it could be made productive.

This tender care for technologies made a virtue out of the experience of work among marine officers. Over the past ten years, as a result of the financialization of state debt, their daily routines included the preservation of aging infrastructure. For example, Captain Verma's work was built around the monitoring of repair and watching for decay. Take one of the days I was in the Subhas Chandra Bose docks with him. The docks were a stretch of barren ground dominated by a queue of trucks waiting to load containers, old yellow dock labor buildings empty of people and a vast ruined clock tower. As usual, new container ships from Singapore and Sri Lanka were being offloaded among the rust and decay. Captain Verma kept talking excitedly about "my docks," "my lock," "my dredger" as we walked toward the lock gates. Here a port dredger, the Subharnarekha, was stalled because the lock gates had jammed because of the rusting away of a pin. We walked across the lock gates dodging the holes worn in them through which you could see the water and mechanisms far below. The dredger crew sat bored and tired waiting for the problem to be solved. Verma spoke at length to the team put to work to fix the problem before the ships started arriving on the high tide at 4:30 in the afternoon. Captain Verma then made a point of taking me to the dry dock where a dredger was being repaired by contractual workers. He was overseeing this work and he explained this would be a long and painstaking job. He pointed out the markings on the plates where numbers had been written to indicate their thinness and whether they needed to be replaced. After some time Captain Verma took me along to his next project—the swing bridge into the Subhas Chandra Bose Docks, which he was repairing after years of disuse. A few men lifted mud from between the tracks, painted over rusting sections and repaired cracks with blow torches. Captain Verma became enthusiastic as he spoke of the men who had built this years ago and how he was reviving their work in the present.

Antiproductivity: The Market and Decadent, Nonutilitarian Technologies

But what were the forces of antiproductivity in this ethic? These were located in the unskilled practices of private firms that produced decadent, nonutilitarian technologies. These failures were epitomized for marine officers by the new *Ma Ganga* pilot vessel. This had recently been built by a private shipyard to replace the scrapped and much loved pilot ship. *Ma Ganga* was an example of the new multipurpose, flexible and least-cost technology that the high-level bureaucrats in the port desired. It was designed for the pilots to stay on in the monsoon months off Sagar Island before taking smaller vessels to board the incoming container vessels. The rest of the year it was used by the chairman as a pleasure cruiser and for parties. It was manned by a much smaller crew than the pilot ship, and they worked on short-term contracts. All the marine officers complained in similar terms about the *Ma Ganga* as the epitome of the decline of the present. Every description of the vessel was an ironic tale of how only the expertise of marine officers would lead to successful endeavors. Men swapped photos on their mobiles of its already rusted and pock-marked hull. Typically, Captain Verma complained that it was very unstable; it bounced on the waves because it did not have an engine; and it was built as a multipurpose vessel. He told me that the pilots couldn't relax in the elaborately decorated smoking room or sleep at night because the rhythms of the vessel meant that they suffered from severe sea-sickness. Echoing other pilots, he said that it was not practical at all but had been built as a vessel for pleasure—he called it a "pleasure platform." He contrasted it with the old pilot vessel, pausing in sadness before explaining that it had been scrapped. He added that he kept the bell and the commander's desk and chair from the old pilot ship at home in his bedroom. The decadence and excess of the *Ma Ganga* epitomized the antithesis of marine knowledge by its practical failures. It was a materialization of the waste produced by the private sector and the market. Marine officers found it ironic that the vessel was named after the goddess of the river when it was so unsuited to the Hooghly. The marine officers, as we will see, had begun to claim this goddess as their own.

Regenerating Lineages of Knowledge: Ma Ganga and the Marine Officers

Captain Verma and his fellow marine officers had recently connected their legitimizing ethic of preservation and knowledge to the Ma Ganga puja. In an unlikely innovation given their cosmopolitan marine past, they had started to practice their own version of this in 2007. The place the marine officers had chosen for the celebration of the puja connected it to their time-honed skills. It was the garden to the now unused quarters where they had all lived as trainee pilots learning their trade. On the day of the festival, many of the officers reminisced about their apprenticeship. They also talked about how wonderful it was to see the place filled with life again by the puja after so many years. They also waited with expectation and were exhilarated by the deputy chairman's brief patronage of the event. As the day progressed men grew more elated and expansive about the significance of the ritual. The puja, they said, showed their "respect" for the river as a dangerous force that had to be mastered by marine knowledge, just as Siva had mastered the Ganga's force as she fell to earth. They said the puja was being celebrated because there had been recent accidents on the river. These were attributed by them to the lack of marine training of the younger pilots. Conversations then circled around the inadequate knowledge of these younger river pilots, the hopeless plans of the chairman to recruit nonmariner staff as managers in the department and to hire private contract pilots. Each conversation would return eventually to Ma Ganga and the fact that she could only be mastered by the knowledge of experienced mariners like themselves.

Typical of this interpretation of the puja was Captain Verma's account. He explained that the river had such strong currents—in particular the bore tides—so it could be mastered only with deep knowledge of the river. He added that this was just like the story of the ritual by which "Bhagirath brought the Ganges to earth . . . . She was an uncontrollable river. She had to be caught in Siva's hair to stop her. Still she is like that." These series of analogies placed marine officers on the one hand in the role of Bhagirath. They, like Bhagirath, were initiating the appearance of regenerating life in the form of the Ganga by acts of ritual labor by sponsoring the puja. On the other hand, they were also like Siva; through their skilled work they controlled the river, as he had controlled her with his hair. In this ethics the ritual and professional labor of marine officers produced a regenerating, productive exchange between men and the river founded on the enactment of inherited knowledge. The deputy chairman's patronage of the puja, which officers emphasized so much, promised recognition of the centrality of the river and their special knowledge of it to the port.

Marine officers claimed that they were inheritors of the port's pedigree. Their acts of work were productive because they possessed special knowledge that only they, and the state bureaucracy, had preserved through time. In these ethical accounts there is no acknowledgment that the work of bureaucrats has changed. It was the marine officers who outsourced work, laid off marine crew and negotiated deals with private firms. Their nostalgias supported an ethical disengagement from their new brokering practices on the river. There was no acknowledgment of the fact that officers are now privileged agents within a new productive form that exploits informal sector workers. Instead, these ethics drew a line of separation between the public good practiced by state bureaucrats and the new forms of private enterprise on the Hooghly.

Regenerating the Market: Family Firms, Flexibility, Capital and Hanuman

Like all the family firms along the Hooghly, the prosperity of Orient Ltd has emerged directly from the brokering of marine department officials. Yet these connections with bureaucrats, and the state, do not appear in the ethical accounts of entrepreneurs. Instead their conduct of life is built around pursuits of family prosperity, flexibility and the release of capital from objects. Regenerating the market, and therefore the river, they suggest, can be achieved only through such actions.

Family Capital, Flexibility and the Potential of State Objects

In contrast to the technical knowledge ethic of bureaucrats, the Jaiswal brothers emphasized that they possessed an inherent family- and kinship-based creativity that did not rely on formal training, but on the ability to adapt. As I explained in the opening of this chapter, they always described their firm as a family enterprise apart from the state in which the quarrels and successes of their paternal line were expressed. The quality that Dilip Jaiswal said they had passed down from their "forefathers" was extensive relationship-building and adaptability. They were entirely oriented to future potential. In fact, historical, technical knowledge was represented as a disadvantage. It prevented one from being responsive enough to the fast-moving fluctuations in business on the Hooghly. The Jaiswal brothers claimed that their best workers shared these qualities of adaptability with them. It was precisely because workmen had learned their skills in their yard with no formal qualifications that they were able to convert vessels. This also meant that the men recruited through brokers could be paid on hourly rates, were nonunionized and could be laid off according to the availability of work. Dilip Jaiswal (the eldest of the brothers, in his fifties) expressed this sense of workmanship in the following manner:

The difference of our company is that not one of us is a qualified engineer. We have no master mariners or even anyone who has formal qualifications. Yet all these big companies like Reliance they all use us. This is because our father taught us that we should all be involved with the nitty-gritty of the business. Then we can't be fooled by anybody. This is what makes us different from the other companies. . . . We all have very good and family-like relations with the vendors, crew, workers, all people. This is a way of furthering our interests and their interests too. . . . Some companies have asked for permanent tie ups with our company, but we would rather be in the position of subcontractors. This is what gives us our specific advantage. We assemble what is needed just when the work starts.

Their workers were disposable elements in these assemblages. Dilip described how as projects were completed they would steadily reduce the numbers of workers to a minimum, since they were "surplus for requirements," calling them back again only if they needed them for another contract. In this entrepreneurial world the historical formation of technical skill is entirely devalued. Instead it is the flexibility of response in a temporal present and future to the needs of abstract capital that is sought.

This ethic of extensive connections, flexible adaptive skills and future potential had its materialization in the state objects the company stored and transformed into multiple reuses. The four brothers were fascinated by the potential of the vessels they bought at auctions from the port and elsewhere. From the first time I visited the Orient yard, I was struck by the Jaiswal brothers' enthusiasm for the limitless fluidity of the old state technologies they converted for projects. For example, one day, Dilip Jaiswal and I were sitting in the yard office made from the old wheel house of a barge and he explained with growing excitement how they had recently converted for the third time a state-owned barge:

We have to be creative in order to deliver on projects at a lower cost and in faster time than our competitors so we get the contracts. This is why we adapt existing barges into completely new forms in our boatyard. We can be faster and cheaper than the bigger companies that just start from scratch with a theoretical drawing made to the best mathematical principles.

The remodeled vessels were displayed proudly in the company brochure as a triumph of small business creativity. The company moored many of them in the center of Kolkata in a waterfront full of the detritus of the public sector, including decaying barges and tugs settled in by squatters. In contrast to this the vessels of Orient were painted a bright corporate red and they often carried spectacular high-tech objects such as giant reactors on their way to power stations in Assam.

The brothers repeatedly described the trajectory of two state objects in order to express their pride in their transformation of objects. The first was that of a pleasure boat they had recently made that had started out as a vessel sold off by the state-run Central Inland Water Transport Corporation. Dilip, for example, described its various forms:

Now we are building an air conditioned boat that will have a hall of 120 square feet. The French doors will open up to the deck where there will be a Jacuzzi and an artificial garden. It will be able to take 300 people on board. It will be used for corporate and private parties on the river. We will be converting the same barge that we used for replacing the spans on a railway bridge into this tourism boat. . . . We needed four dumb barges for the bridge job so we cut the two barges into four small dumb barges. One of these smaller barges will be used for this tourism venture.

Once the vessel was complete Dilip suggested that I film and interview him on it. It had no engine and was a floating island with hanging baskets of plastic flowers and artificial grass. It was painted the standard corporate red, and all the life-rings had its aspirational name emblazoned on them. There was no sign of the Jacuzzi or garden, as these would be added once it had generated some revenue. Orders for parties had been slow, and Dilip discussed the inaction of the state that caused this lack of tourism:

The government is doing nothing to beautify the banks . . . . They don't provide jetties either. We wanted to take over the Water Ghat jetty from the port but they were not giving it. We could take such good care of it and look at it now. We want to expand our tourism business and this would be the only way to do it . . . . The government won't even impose the regulations on people to paint their buildings and keep them in good upkeep along the banks . . . . Everywhere else there are tourists for the sacred Ganga, but not here because of the port.

Within this ethic the port trust, and state action more generally, were unequivocally a source of waste on the river that betrayed its sacred and monetary potential.

The brothers' focus on the inherent capital potential of objects was also expressed in their accounts of a steam tug that they stored on the river near their yard. Dilip described how this was the oldest vessel that they kept for reuse. It had, he said, been built in 1888 in Holland, had been used in the port and although it was "heritage" they were keeping it for when it could be reused in a new way. They converted it from steam to diesel to use in the Lash Barge trade upriver. But Dilip kept the old steering wheel hung on the wall of their office as a mascot. For him this emblem expressed an ethic of production that benefited the nation as a whole:

We are using the existing equipment available in the country by modifying it. . . . If you think on a country-level situation this is good. We are not creating things that are not required. We are creating cheaper solutions which is good for the country also.

The tug was not alone on the waterfront near their yard. Along the muddy bank Orient stored many rotting hulks that had not yet found a use expressing a hope in the future life of these objects that exceeded any rigid economic calculation. Among these were a small hydrofoil and a fiber glass pilot boat that Dilip hoped would one day be "converted into a small pleasure yacht that could be used for people to travel on the river. Now that we are in this entertainment business." For the entrepreneurs in Orient Ltd, consumption, pleasure and future-oriented flexibility would secure national prosperity.

Work routines and facilities in the yard reflected these ethics of flexibility, low investment and the metamorphosis of objects. The yard was a narrow, muddy stretch of ground joined to the waterfront by a platform welded together from remnants of vessels. Barges were tied up to this and converted on the river to reduce the area of land that had to be leased from the port. Minimum equipment was used for the remaking of the vessels—only welding torches and physical labor. Cut into the bank was a wide muddy ditch in which smaller vessels were repaired and transformed. This acted as a dry dock at low tide, but vessels could be floated off from here on the highest monthly tides. Moving back from the waterfront the yard was filled with small parts and mechanisms that were being renewed by workers stripping, filing and welding. In a large warehouse nearby was a huge stock of rusted chains, old life-rings, anchors, joints and handles waiting for the moment of revival. The yard office had been built so that it could be easily transported to another location should the lease of this piece of land ever prove too expensive.

Regenerating the Market: Hanuman and Service to Capital

For the Jaiswal brothers one deity explicitly signified their ethic—Hanuman. All their vessels contained lithographs of Hanuman wielding his mace. Each office had a medium-size icon of him that was worshipped in the morning and evening. A giant painting of Hanuman stared down from the corrugated roof of the covered area of the yard. This choice of deity was somewhat unlikely. Hanuman is not particularly important to the company's Bengali workers, who associated him with the practices of worship of migrant labor from outside West Bengal. Although the BJP, RSS and VHP have all since the 1980s promoted a revival of worship of Ram's loyal henchman, they were not active in the areas of Howrah where the yard is, nor were they supported by the Jaiswal brothers or their workers. The religious origins of the Jaiswal family also made such a choice of deity odd. But the Jaiswal brothers were unified in their assertion of the reason for Hanuman's presence. He represented the ensured future success that comes from a single-minded trust in and hierarchical service to a greater master. As Dilip put it:

Hanuman is a demigod in the Hindu religion and a symbol of service to his master. He saw Ram as his master and his everything. His whole life, his whole service, his whole thought was based in serving the master. If you look at it as . . . a worldly thing then whatever you do in life if you dedicate yourself to whatever you are doing, a job or a master . . . . If you dedicate your life, your thought, your mind to that job with a pure heart you *have* to have success.

Hanuman, an exemplar of dedicated service to a higher master, was worshipped in the hope that intentions could produce prosperity. His image in offices and vessels created a permanent, ubiquitous presence that existed beyond the short-term uses of men and materials in the company.

Unlike the state ethic of the marine officers this sense of workmanship erases the act of labor. It is will (in particular the will of entrepreneurs) that releases an essence that lies within the material world. Their dedication realizes the fluid potential of capital that always exists in things. Individuals live in a world where they engage with the imminent potential of capital. This ethic cuts obligations to informal workers who labor for you and to state institutions that generate work. Instead it focuses on serving the fluid omnipresent force of capital. The value of the act of labor disappears in this world shaped by correct thoughts. The river too disappears in its complex agency. It becomes a passive site for opportunity and a sacred river that can provide pleasures of consumption for pilgrims, tourists and party-goers. Importantly, although Orient's fortunes had been shaped by state officials and policies, the four Jaiswal brothers made these connections invisible. Kinship, flexibility and the force of capital were foregrounded as sources of regenerative power. In these ethics, family firms operating in the market appear entirely separate from the social relationships with, and flows of capital from, state institutions.

Conclusion: State and Market Separations: The Limits of the Public Good in Austerity

As capital and state objects move along the brokered connections generated by marine department officials, their essential nature appears to be converted. They come under the sway of different ethics and deities. The act of labor also takes on entirely distinct properties. It transforms from a technical bureaucratic intervention in a complex waterscape into a flexible response to the transcendent presence of capital. This movement across an ethical boundary denies the obligations of bureaucrats to informal workers and of entrepreneurs to the state. Entrepreneurship can only appear as a distinct form of productive action if these boundaries are present. State officials too can only make claims for their legitimacy if they distinguish their regenerative powers from those of private businesses. In liberalization, and austerity capitalism more generally, bureaucrats and entrepreneurs maintain ethical distinctions between their entangled actions. The financialization of state debt generates divergent claims for status and legitimacy within market and state institutions. The mechanisms and relations of state debt create a fiscal imperative, but new social relations and forms of accumulation emerge from the improvised conduct of life among bureaucrats and entrepreneurs. It is not enough to trace the economization of the state. To understand the present we also have to analyze how the public good is being practiced. In this case (and most likely in many others), the new forms of the public good support a disengagement from, and exploitation of, contractual and informalized, private-sector workers.

Throughout this section, we have seen that the identification of antiproductive forces is central to the meanings of labor in austerity capitalism. On the Hooghly processes of death, decay and waste have become key to the symbolism, and politics, of work. This is a development that is unanticipated by Marxist or Foucauldian theoretical approaches. These share an emphasis on how economists, corporations or state institutions are legitimated through claims to care for and preserve life. It is also different in kind from the utopian visions of corporate Taylorism or state socialism. These worked toward a horizon of increasing efficiency in order to harness more of the life-giving productivity of all acts of work. All workers and work processes could potentially be improved. But the ethics of austerity capitalism identify antiproductive forces. They designate acts of work that are negative or destructive of value. In this they are more similar to the hierarchical racialized ethics of colonial capitalism than to the projects of Taylorism, paternalism or socialism (Bear 2007). Their distinctions mean that not all labor is equal, even though it is all part of production and circulation. It is from such ethics that exclusions from equal rights to life and livelihood emerge.

Section III

Governing Speculation

On Speculation and Friendship: *Jogajog Kora*

This section focuses on the future-oriented individualistic relations between state and market institutions that are made invisible by the ethics of regeneration on the Hooghly. It explores how these are forged by bureaucrats and entrepreneurs through practices of speculation and friendship. My fieldwork on the Hooghly was shaped by a particular affective relationship of *jogajog kora*, or the creation of useful friendships. I did not understand how *jogajog kora* worked until I had spent several months moving along the arcs of these complicit relationships. These shaped my research, taking me outward from the port trust and the docks into private businesses on the Hooghly. Through these connections, state plans and revenue streams were linked to the projects of entrepreneurs and their informalized workers. Central to these practices were apparently minor marine department officials, such as Vikas Bose, who presided over a dilapidated waterfront office at Water Ghat. He was charged with the duties of licensing and inspecting vessels to protect public safety. His office stood in the stretch of the waterfront that was intended for middle-class use in the ambitious "beautification" plans that had been floated since the 1980s.[1] Instead, it was filled with the decaying ruins of old port jetties and people working in the informalized sector. In the tea stall next to Vikas's office were *majhi*s (boatmen), who man small "love boats," and the prostitutes who made a living in them, resting from the night before. Midstream, men in larger boats stood up to their necks in the water, lifting sand that would be used for construction in the new town rising on the eastern edge of the city. It was clear from my first visit that Vikas's office played an important role in these activities. Daily assembled in it were an unlikely collection of people from low-status *majhi*s and pimps to wealthy labor contractors, high-level officials and entrepreneurs. This open access had been recently introduced by Vikas. From the outset he encouraged me to shadow his work and join him on his inspection tours along the Hooghly. With me around he was able to claim a wide sphere of influence. He liked to say to his audience while I was there, "I don't have a passport and I don't need to as the whole world comes to my office." In this office people told me they came to *jogajog kora.*

Vikas did not completely draw me into complicity until an encounter two months into my research. As I arrived Vikas leaped from his chair exclaiming, "There have been some major developments here, Laura. I have decided to give logistical support to producing a *vajrao* for concerts on the river." We had spoken many times of the lost grandeur of these *zemindars'* (high-caste landlords) pleasure boats. Now he wanted to convert our shared enthusiasm into a scheme in which, with his help, I would run a business on the river. He continued:

The people who can build this in their shipyard by converting an old barge came in this morning. Then you came right afterward. Also the tourism board is encouraging this— here is their publicity leaflet. This must be the work of God because you came into my mind and then you are here.

Possibilities opening before my eyes, I started, in spite of myself, to plan the details of this project. I had come with my own agenda, since I wanted to ask Vikas's help in finding a wooden launch to use for filming on the river. When I mentioned this he abruptly switched to a threatening tone and listed all the agencies I would have to approach for permission to film without being arrested. But he added, he would help me navigate all of these. I felt a cold fear of regulations closing in, yet said with a new realization, "Your office is an amazing place." The disparate audience in the room nodded in agreement. A young contractor said, "See she understands this office is for *jogajog kora.*" Vikas smiled again and said, "Yes, I make information available, help people to meet and everyone benefits. What is the harm? The port from the end product benefits from business on the river." "This," he added, "is God's work. His reason for putting me here in this chair." His assistant, as if on cue, took the *prasad* (blessed food) from the Ganesh sculpture that sat on the desk and shared it between us all. Vikas's next gesture was to tell us some dramatic, confidential news. He said, "I am going to tell you a huge secret. They are going to close the Haldia Port." Everyone exclaimed in surprise.

On this day Vikas drew me fully under his influence through an improvised performance. He achieved this with a display of multiple sources of legitimacy for our relationship: divine destiny, state publicity leaflets, disclosure of state secrets and threats of punitive rules. This method is in fact the only technique he has to build influence and create income. There is nothing in his official role that would enable him to meet the demands of higher level officials that he should generate more revenue for the port through stimulating business on the Hooghly. His office is not simply a microcosm of such practices of *jogajog kora;* it is a vital node in the creation of new productive activity in a time of public austerity. Through a focus on the practices of Vikas and his clients, this section explores the increasing importance of *jogajog kora* to bureaucratic work. It will show that these friendships bring into being an entrepreneurial society on the river.

Governance, speculation and friendship have rarely been considered together. Yet, as I will show, a combination of Simmel's discussion of secrecy and ethnographies of friendship can help us to understand their connections. Simmel argued that friendship was founded in moments of revelation that create complicity between individuals. These disclosures produce a heightened, affective connection through the sharing of secrets, because "what is withheld from the many appears to have a special value."[2] Such disclosures evoke the possibility of a parallel second world alongside the obvious surface of relations. This world is seen as "essential and significant" and is heightened "by phantasy . . . [and] a degree of attention that published reality could not command."[3] The appearance of this parallel world beyond the obvious and reported surface also brings into being speculation. Speculation seeks to create profit by moving beyond the limits of the tangible and visible. It focuses on the incalculable future potential of an act, resource, institution or transaction. It aims to access opaque potencies and forces. Complicit friendships promise that it is possible to know the truth *beyond* and *behind* the public truth. It is these forms of speculation and friendship, as we will see, that are now central to governance and planning on the Hooghly.[4]

A rich ethnographic exploration of such complicit relationships exists in the anthropology of the Mediterranean from Pitt-Rivers and Campbell's discussions of instrumental friendship onward (1961, 1964, 1968). Much of this literature shows how such relationships are used to penetrate formal institutions and bend power in a favorable direction. It focuses more on "lop-sided friendship" or patronage than on the more equalized relationships between entrepreneurs and bureaucrats at work on the Hooghly. However, importantly, a recurrent finding emerges in this literature that we can build on to understand the importance of friendship. This is that friendship is a social relationship that is made in a border zone in which the rules of engagement are much more ethically fluid than in kinship and patronage (Campbell 1964, 1968). Loizos and Papataxiarchas (1991) show how friends are made not among kin or close community members, but with "others" with whom temporary market relationships are sought. Coleman (2010) has suggested that friendship is always used in liminal situations where other clearly defined ties, rights and obligations are temporarily suspended. Instead fluid connections can be built. This tradition of analysis culminates in Herzfeld's highly significant analysis (1997) of bureaucratic action and cultural intimacy, which shapes my approach here, although I am attempting to specifically trace forms of speculation that emerge from such interactions. Friendship then is characterized by nonobligatory improvised and individualistic ties across collective ethical boundaries. Recent state policy makes such friendship increasingly important to government action, since it emphasizes working with, and through, existing social networks of the market (Elyachar 2012a).[5] Through the pursuit of complicit friendship, bureaucrats and entrepreneurs can suspend their usual ethics and rules in a flexible, improvised pursuit of mutual speculation. Personal promises and state promises can combine creatively in this intermediary zone. The collective ethical separations between state and market described in Section 2 can be maintained, as bureaucratic and entrepreneurial classes draw closer together in individual relations.

This drawing together of state institutions to networks of instrumental friendship is problematic. In much of the world, where the urban poor work in the informalized sector, it involves bureaucrats in the direct creation of unprotected forms of work. Casual, deunionized and unregulated labor is predominant throughout India, where 83 percent of workers operate in the informalized sector (Harriss-White 2003; Shah and Corbridge 2013). Much research has explored how this workforce continues to exist because of the corruption or indifference of state bureaucrats. The situation of the working poor is often understood through the theory of "political society," which suggests that they exist in a zone beyond civil society attempting to negotiate temporary rights through patronage or community claims (Chatterjee 2004; Roy 2002; Roy and AlSayyad 2003). The practices of *jogajog kora* reveal a contemporary limit to this theory; bureaucrats and policy regimes in liberalization India seek to actively *harness* and amplify this informalized sector. I use the phrase "entrepreneurial society" to describe these emerging relationships.

What then are the changes in state practices that have made friendships so central on the Hooghly? Why is it that bureaucrats and entrepreneurs live the pursuit of *jogajog kora* with such enthusiasm? What are the possibilities and inequalities that emerge from these practices? What are their consequences for a political critique of policies of austerity and public-private partnership? These are the questions that the chapter that follows addresses.

Fig. 5. Majhis collecting "silver sand"

Chapter 4

Making a River of Gold: Speculation, Friendship and Entrepreneurial Society

Publicity and Speculative Planning

Before the middle of the 1980s, the Kolkata Port Trust shaped the waterscape according to detailed, precise and technically specific five-year plans authorized by the central government's Ministry of Surface Transport (MOST). The role of middle- to low-level bureaucrats was to apply the rules of the port, implement detailed plans that were centrally agreed, and to issue tenders to other state agencies. This situation changed slowly during the 1980s, accelerating in the 1990s. Five-year plans were still made but came to consist of general guidelines for creating revenue through public-private partnerships, the reduction of workforces, the selling of resources and the outsourcing of state work. The role of bureaucrats on the river had now become to stimulate such partnerships, extract revenue toward the center, and find cheap, fast ways of generating income for the state. This was a new form of speculative planning because its outcomes depended on responses among low-level bureaucrats, entrepreneurs, politicians and the middle-class citizens of Kolkata.[1]

It is highly significant that during the period in which these forms of planning accelerated in the Kolkata Port Trust, there was also a rapid growth in the Public Relations Department. The Public Relations Department was founded in 1991 in order to engage with the constituencies who had now become relevant to realizing the port's schemes. Its responsibilities multiplied. It started to organize public events, release future plans and organize share issues. It was the newspaper articles generated by it that I relied upon for my initial understanding of the port's redevelopment. It was these that the wider public of Kolkata read and on which they based their interpretations of the potential for the growth of circulation on the Hooghly. Importantly, the port publicity department did not only produce representations. It planted stories in the papers to advance the aims of high-level bureaucrats in their private negotiations with businessmen and ministers. It released speculative plans for prosperity-generating schemes in order to attract the interest of entrepreneurs. It was also rumored to hunt for the sources of unauthorized press stories within the administration to hold those people to account. By 2008, when I carried out my fieldwork, publicity had become vital for the sustenance of *jogajog kora* that made the economy on the Hooghly work.

I began to understand the importance of the Public Relations Department through the encounters I would have at the publicity events they mounted. Take, for example, an event that I attended to celebrate 138 years of the Kolkata Port Trust and honor the work of local shipping entrepreneurs. It was announced in the newspapers in a half-page advertisement showing a Victorian schooner pitching into the wind. Presiding over it would be a MOST minister from New Delhi. On the same page was an article revealing that Haldia dock would be forced to close completely in the next few days on account of silting caused by a shortage of dredgers. This theme of a resolute public service with deep historical roots that faced a natural crisis permeated the speeches at the event. A large auditorium had been hired in the center of the city. Its seats were filled with marine bureaucrats, key entrepreneurs and low-ranking employees who had been reluctantly bused in from port trust housing. Journalists scribbled in the front row. On the stage sat the assembled dignitaries, who were being fussed over by the head public relations officer. They included the chairman of the port, the secretary of the Ministry of Shipping, the consul general of Japan at Kolkata and the chairman of the beleaguered Haldia Port. An auspicious *diya* (ritual lamp) was lit by each of them in turn as a *sloka* (Sanskrit prayer) was intoned.

The chairman began his speech. He said that the port family had managed to live with grace and glory for such a long time. He proudly added it was such a distinguished port that it had provided three hundred years of service to the nation. He recalled that it used to be the dominant port and provided 44 percent of the trade in India. Then, he added regretfully, the problem of draft emerged because larger vessels were introduced into shipping lines. From that time, he said, the port has lived with the river and moved up and down with its tides. He insisted that it had continued only through the efforts of the port family, which had the strength to overcome any crisis. The chairman had presented an account of the decline of Kolkata Port that erased any details of the period since Independence. He offered an image of a resolute nationalist paternalism dependent on the natural phases of the river and international commerce.

Then it was the turn of the Japanese consul general. He said that the trade between Japan and India had a long history. In fact, he informed us that the first liner between Japan and India was in 1893, which J. N. Tata had arranged for the Japanese cotton business. He congratulated the port of Kolkata on being third in cargo handling in India for the past few years, and that in 2007 it achieved the highest net surplus of all the ports. But now, he admitted, it was running into the problem of the navigability of Haldia. Although, he added, Haldia should have a very great advantage over other ports, as it faces East Asia. It was this advantage he suggested that had led Mitsubishi chemicals to become the greatest investor at Haldia. He advised that in order to attract more Japanese investment the port should provide better service to users. If it is required, Japan would, he added, provide money to Kolkata Port to modernize from their overseas development aid scheme. This account overlaid the representation of nationalist paternalism, with an image of long-term private enterprise and international investment. This would continue as long as efficient customer service was pursued. The public-private and international partnerships of liberalization were given deep historical roots and promised as a continuous future.

The audience suddenly grew attentive and tense when the secretary of the Ministry of Shipping got up to speak. First he congratulated the port for being number two in total cargo handling in the past two years. But he reminded the audience that the river had the longest navigable channel in India, and now the problem of the draft in the channel was staring it in the face. He asserted that the ministry was solidly behind providing adequate facilities to deal with this. The auditorium erupted into clapping with this assurance. But then the secretary warned that the port must plan for the future by opening further dock systems at Diamond Harbour and farther south with fewer hazards and complications. This influential official presented the economic problems of the port as simply a matter of its natural features. Yet he promised the hope that the ministry would help benevolently to overcome these barriers to prosperity.

A high-level official, well known to me, then started to confide secrets about the proceedings. First he asked me if I had seen the announcement of the event and Haldia's closing in the paper. He was proud that it was he that had supplied the picture of the old schooner to represent the long heritage of the port. Then, as he always did, he began to reveal the negotiations beyond the publicity. He explained that the Haldia newspaper story had been planted by the Public Relations Department to create pressure on the MOST minister during the discussions that had been going on that day. But, in spite of public assertions, the government had not bowed under this pressure. They had, on the contrary, told the chairman that if he needed more dredgers he should pay for them himself. The official pointed out that this would make the whole port financially unviable.

I was left wondering who in the audience was for this performance of continuity, paternalist nationalism and collaborations between influential men. I glanced down at the journalists and then at the shipping entrepreneurs starting to receive their awards on the stage. They were representatives of two different kinds of public. One public was the citizenry of Kolkata, who would receive assurances in the next day's papers of the glorious past and prosperous future of the port. The other was that of entrepreneurs, state officials and politicians. They would soon be hearing confidences similar to those the official had just told me. Bound together through these exchanges they would then pursue the future prosperity promised in the speeches. These negotiations produce a reality quite different from that presented in the publicized plans.

Such forms of publicity have been analyzed as productive romances and performative utterances that bring into being neoliberal aesthetics and economic forms (Thrift 2001; Tsing 2005; Ghertner 2010). These arguments are very important, yet we also need to examine how such representations work as part of the practices of bureaucrats and entrepreneurs. On the Hooghly they are central to the play of concealment and disclosure that gets the work of the state done through complicit friendship. Publicity is a technique that generates a mesmerizing split between what is made clear and what might yet remain still opaque (Dean 2001; Barros-Grela and Liste-Noya 2011; Mazarella 2006). It is this compelling split that is deployed to forge relations of complicity that bring new social forms into being. This chapter follows how this split is used to forge an entrepreneurial society on the Hooghly marked by new relations of friendship or *jogajog kora* between bureaucrats and entrepreneurs.

The Growth of Entrepreneurial Society:
Friendship and Patronage

Bureaucrats practiced a combination of complicit friendship and state patronage in order to, as many of them put it, "make a river of gold." Their aim was to create prosperity by drawing informalized economies into the orbit of their influence. This was achieved through a deployment of friendship with equals and patronage toward the working poor. Let us return to Vikas Bose and his office as an example of these practices. He was a highly influential man and his office was also characteristic of the practices I saw in all the low-level port offices. Wherever I worked on the river, from the shipyards, dock offices, to conversion yards and sand boats, he would appear making deals.

Vikas described his current work as a continuation of long traditions of public service through new means. He was fifty-five when I met him and had spent all his life in the public sector. His father worked as a state clerk, but he had died when Vikas was young. So Vikas had left school and became an apprentice in the port in the 1970s in order to support his sisters and mother. There he had worked repairing the port vessels. In the 1990s he took his shipwright exam and then achieved his current position as the senior officer in the waterfront office in early 2000s. He lived with his two teenage children and wife in a cramped two bedroom rented flat in South Calcutta. Vikas hardly spent any time at home, leaving for weekends on long inspection or advisory trips. His cell rang every few minutes, even when he was at home.

Vikas did not relate his work to the commercial freedoms of liberalization. He associated it with an attempt to bring a paternalist nation-state closer to its citizens through new mechanisms. He was strongly influenced in this by the rhetoric of the 2005 Right to Information Act. This has been widely acclaimed by politicians and activists as the foundation of a new transparency in state-society relationships in India. It has given every citizen the right to access state documents and decisions. It also requires the computerization of all state records, a task being undertaken in office during the time I worked in it. This law also required all bureaucrats to disseminate information to citizens and make RTI rules accessible, in particular to disadvantaged communities. Vikas often spoke of this act and related it to the new open access that he had introduced. As he put it:

The only section that is large now is the Public Relations Department, but I do all the public relations in my office. I don't just enforce the rules. I make people understand the rules. They pay something and they have rights. We have to go close to them and explain the meaning of doing it or they will not do it. I could convert the river into a river of gold if they gave me the proper hands to do this.

Vikas's aim of producing a river of gold, like that of other bureaucrats, was also inflected by a specific Bengali popular nationalism. He rooted his actions in the precedent of the benevolent authority of the Bengali nineteenth-century nationalist heroine Rani Rashmoni. She was a wealthy *zemindar's* (high-caste landlord) widow, who was Ramkrishna's patron and built the Dakshineswar temple. When the British extended a water tax to fishermen, Vikas described how she had rescued them by placing a chain across the river that extended out from her waterfront property.

This had stopped the traffic to the port, leading to the capitulation of the British, who announced fishermen would never be taxed. Rani Rashmoni provided Vikas with a model for his own practice as a benign nationalist bureaucrat who entered sympathetically into the sufferings of river people:

I do this job because the human side of it is so rewarding. All the people on the river come to me to help them even if I am not the right person . . . . I do this because god helps those who help others.

He represented his role as the creation of access to the protection of the state. Rights would be guaranteed by a combination of new forms of transparency with an older patronage of the poor based on benevolent compassion. But how had he set about generating revenue for the port through more pragmatic forms of friendship and patronage?

State Fiscal Discipline and the Harnessing of Informality

Vikas's practical attempts to produce a river of gold aimed to bring private, informalized economic activity on the Hooghly into a direct relation with the port trust. His appointment in 2003 coincided with an austerity order from the chairman to all departments that they increase their revenues. Bureaucrats now had to intensify their extraction from the river. Vikas set about looking for means to gather this income by drawing boat-owners, *majhis* and other entrepreneurs into the orbit of the office. The previous superintendent had entirely ignored the illicit economy on the Hooghly. This linked together the river police, boat users, owners and the boat workers' union in a parallel world of predatory extraction. He had not enforced state licensing regulations and had run an office into which the "bad characters" on the river would not be admitted. Vikas altered this disengagement of the bureaucracy and instead began to intervene in these networks of informality.

First Vikas increased the number of inspections he carried out in the villages along the river. He used these visits as an opportunity to encourage boat-owners to register their rights with the state. Vikas also persuaded the head of the Marine Department that in order to increase the port's income he should petition MOST to change the rules so that when an unlicensed boat was seized by the river police it would only be released if it was first licensed. The ministry agreed, and the new law was put in place. Before this Vikas explained that the river police had made good business from "seizing the same boat over and over again." He undermined the last vestiges of influence from the local CPI(M) supported boatman union, which had already been weakened by the decline of barge trade on the river. Vikas claimed:

My office has got rid of the need for a union. Actually the union used to intervene in disputes and take money from both parties, but now they do not need the union they can just come straight to my office and talk to me directly.

Vikas also acted directly to undermine the illicit nexus between the union, river police and lack of licensing. Prior to 2003 in the Howrah area all the boats were unlicensed and the river police were reportedly making up to 4 lakhs per month from the 150 sand boats working on this stretch. The fees were collected by a *saddhu* (Hindu mendicant) who was the agent of the river police. One night Vikas conducted a raid on him with a journalist from a local paper and the police, but he escaped. After this all the sand boats started to be licensed. So Vikas had acted to draw informalized river labor into the revenue streams of his office in order to meet the intensified fiscal demands from the chairman. Through his measures the paternalist nation state would now extract income from these through increased collection of fees, rather than turning its back on an "unregulated" illicit sector.

Vikas went further than this; he drew entrepreneurs and boat-owners into his sphere of influence and aimed to increase their speculative activity. This he reasoned would regenerate the river and create more revenues for his office and the port. This is where practices of *jogajog kora* became central. What then were the forms of this complicit friendship and how was it forged?

Jogajog Kora: Soliciting Friendship

When entrepreneurs first came into contact with Vikas, he combined officializing and personalizing forms of address. And he drew on various sources of legitimacy. These included state documents, publicized plans, threats and growing intimacy. The improvised use of these created an atmosphere of hovering secrets and opaque influence. Vikas's incitement of connection was visible in his management of the construction sand trade. The owners of boats and *golabaris* (the middlemen who sell on the sand) sought help in Vikas's office. Owners rented boats to *majhis* (boatman), who recruit the crew. The *golabaris* give an interest free loan to the *majhis*. This is an advance on their labor that has to be returned in the form of sand. Vikas's official role was to inspect the boats during their annual survey and to renew the licenses of the *majhis* on the boats. But men came to him for advice on every aspect of this trade. When he was first approached, Vikas gave them counsel that established his role as a powerful potential friend (in a situation where he had little ability to enforce regulations).

When a novice *golabari* approached Vikas for guidance on starting his business on port land he advised him in an alternately authoritative and personal manner. He explained that to get permission he had to follow the government rules so that they would look on his specific company with favor. He then listed an overwhelming number of authorities he would have to approach for permission. The man seemed daunted. Vikas said he would help him through these. Then he asked him in a suddenly intimate tone if he had been feeling unwell. The man said he had, and had tried various ritual solutions since his mother died including wearing astrological stones on his fingers. Vikas admonished him that these would not help him, but only if he started to live and work with his brothers again and carry out the proper ritual observances would he become well. The man listened enthusiastically. Vikas added that he must take a *Ganga Snan* (ritual bathing in the Hooghly) for this business to be successful. The man left grateful for the multiple forms of help he had received and promised to come back when he had tried to advance his business a little more. The polytonal exchange confirmed Vikas's access to a parallel realm of state and ritual forces that existed alongside the surface of reality. In such a way the transactions of *jogajog kora* began. An intermediary zone of friendship was created. In this personal promises, state promises and all sorts of powers could intermingle for their mutual benefit.

As relationships with owners and *golabaris* developed further, Vikas began to help them in more direct ways. He had worked out creative techniques to use state documents and his inspection powers to this end. For example he did a lively trade in drawing up contracts between *majhis* and *golabaris* when they gave them loans. These documents had no legal force, but they mimicked the authority of state documents and Vikas witnessed their signing. He had turned official inspections into a negotiating site between different antagonistic parties on the river. In one instance, a boat-owner asked Vikas for his help. He had been forced to sell his boat at a lower than market rate to a gang of CPI(M) backed "anti-socials." But an inflated price was recorded in the title deed stored in Vikas's office. His own brother was now demanding a half cut of this false figure. So Vikas held an inspection of the boat to intimidate the party cadres into giving a little more money to the original owner so he could pay off his brother. He was inserting state tokens and his own authority into the practices of the informalized economy. His personal promises gave his friends access to a world of justice that ran parallel to official lines of procedure. The powers and documents of the state were dispersed within informalized networks.

Vikas forged connections through another means. He began to mimic the threats that are part of informal networks. One day a sand boat-owner arrived anxiously in the waterfront office. His boats had been seized by the river police when they were coming upriver for licensing at the office. He claimed that the police had asked for a huge bribe because the licenses were not on board. The boat-owner explained that he had brought all the licenses in the morning to Vikas's office in readiness for their renewal. Vikas assured the boat-owner he would phone up the river police to sort all of this out. But both I, the owner and the other clients were left wondering whether this event was an accident. None of us had any proof, but we were all aware that the distance between the river police and Vikas was not as great as he liked to suggest. The port itself paid the river police to go on their raids on the river, and Vikas had often accompanied them. It was unclear whether Vikas was party to the attempt to bribe the owner, or if he was simply using his connections to advance the owner's cause. Whatever the truth, our doubts greatly increased his authority over an arena of power parallel to official jurisdictions. This made his friendship a valuable, ambiguous resource that had to be carefully cultivated. Because friendship was spontaneously given, it could be just as quickly withdrawn, shutting down the intermediary zone of negotiation.

Once friendships had been made they became the medium for the speculative search for profits in government rules and publicized schemes. Entrepreneurs and bureaucrats on the river had come to understand government rules in a new way. They were not the distant actions of a legalistic authority (Hull 2003). Instead they were negotiable potential sources of private and public income—profitable rules. Vikas and his friends liked to discuss future uses of the rules. For example, a common topic of conversation was the pontoon jetties on the river and the ferries that plied from them. The ferry businesses had been entirely cornered by local CPI(M) party officials and were run by their supporters. Vikas and entrepreneurs often speculated together on how they could channel these profits back toward the port. State publicity and tender announcements were also common topics. Vikas often discussed the potential of the silver sand trade using articles from newspapers about future state infrastructure projects to support expectations. All of these, he suggested, would need good quality sand for cement, and this was available from the river. Through his forging of friendships Vikas was closely involved with the twenty companies operating up and down the river producing this sand and with the smaller scale sand boats. He also frequently spoke of how shipbuilding and re-pair was an endlessly expanding business especially as his old department in the port had shut down. He had become connected to several privately run shipyards as a "consultant." Sometimes he recounted schemes that combined elements of all these projects. He imagined a way for the port to raise revenues by outsourcing the raising of tolls to various groups on the river, who could then use the profits to dredge the sand from the river and sell it to the construction industry. These specu-lations were in fact much more than that. They were incitements among friends to make these things happen through *jogajog kora*. These conversations continued over long lunches and endless cell calls. Vikas enrolled his most prized friends in an NGO named the Association for Increasing Prosperity. They traveled together to eye camps and various other charitable activities. He was widely described by entrepre-neurs on the river as "a liquid man." Just as water would flow into any vessel and fill it, he would flow into your schemes and give them life.

Hidden Connections: State-generated Informality

These practices of *jogajog kora* promised access to an opaque zone of influ-ence and secrets that existed parallel to official regulations and publicity. They also generated growing inequalities. Vikas's friendships stimulated and harnessed the informalized economy in ways that benefited state revenues. Yet the connection be-tween the practices of bureaucrats and the growth of unregulated work was hidden. Such collaborations remained invisible as "only' personal, individual ties. This effect was most clear in Vikas's dual role as a broker of the continuing growth of informal-ized businesses and as an enforcer of public safety regulations on them. On one of my visits to the office I was surprised to meet the directors and booking agent of Ar-nav Ltd, a company involved in the infamous fly ash trade. These barges carried the poisonous waste from power stations across the border to Bangladesh, where it was used to manufacture cement. Arnav Ltd was problematic for the port, public safety and pollution because their vessels kept on sinking in the channels of the river. To cut costs their ships were hastily converted, poorly equipped and decrepit. The directors were seeking Vikas's advice on how to handle one of their barges that had run aground and split in two in an undredged part of the river. It was a state barge that the Bangladeshi government had leased out to a third party to use, who had then hired it on to them. The government wanted the barge repaired and returned, while the company wanted to sell the remains for scrap. The directors were seeking Vikas's advice on the legal document that they had drawn up for agreement about the fate of the barge with the Bangladeshi government. Vikas explained to me later that he had become closely connected to this firm because they sought his help in finding a private salvage operator for an earlier wreck. A private operator was necessary because the port no longer had the facilities or infrastructure to help them. When another barge went down, the director of the Marine Department suspended all the fly ash trade until safety measures were introduced for loading and operation of the vessels. Vikas was then made the inspector of the new safety measures on the fly ash barges. In all of these activities Vikas was acting in the interests of the port trust, by making sure that the barge was removed from the river, that the fly ash trade continued to raise revenues for the port and that barges were safe. Yet his direct cooperation with the problematic Arnav Ltd never entered the realm of the official acts of the state. Vikas became alternately friend/promoter and official inspector of this inherently dangerous chain of outsourced business that was an important source of revenue for the port.

Vikas also played a similar role in the small-scale shipbuilding trade. His job made him responsible for inspecting the construction and installation of pontoons and unpropelled craft on the river. However, his office was also central to the brokering of construction jobs to the yards along the Howrah bank. He had the role of both official inspector of and unofficial outsourcer of this work. Vikas acted to preserve public safety in his official role, while increasing dangers to other citizens with his friendships. To understand this let us consider the events around the state tendering of a pontoon barge. One day an engineer from a private firm arrived in the office. He showed Vikas the plan for a pontoon barge to see if he would be likely to approve it according to public safety rules. Vikas suggested to the man that he should outsource its construction to Vihaan shipyard. As soon as the man had left Vikas and I drove to Vihaan, carrying the man's plans. It was a stretch of open land with a river dammed to act as a makeshift dry-dock. The owner explained as we walked around the yard that Vikas had advised them to start their family business. He had also helped them get their first ever contract. Vikas flourished the plans for the barge in front of the owner said that this will be your next project. He contributed to the growth of the dangerous informalized economy in Vihaan shipyard, yet these actions took place in a zone of complicit friendship. Only his signature on the tender documents and inspections for public safety would be visible as state promises. All his other productive actions would exist within the realm of personal promises. Such are the opacities created by the operation of economic governance through friendship.

In Vikas's office the speculative plans of state agencies, out contracting of state work to informalized labor and the projects of entrepreneurs were connected. Here state tokens such as contracts, tenders, licenses or publicity were used to forge relationships between these various parties. *Jogajog kora* provided the unequal direction of movement of these state tokens and brought their power into transactions. A quite different sentiment of sympathy and relationship of patronage was directed at the urban poor.

Patronage and Hierarchies of Citizens

Although Vikas had represented himself as a public servant who brought a paternalist state closer to its citizens, his sympathy for the poor did not work in this manner. It was founded in a hierarchical model in which the laboring poor were morally inferior. This was clear in Vikas's treatment of the requests of *majhis*. He drew boat-owners and entrepreneurs into relationships of friendship using eloquent Bengali mixed with references in English to regulations. However a sharp line was drawn with *majhis* through his use of a domineering, aggressive Hindi. This was particularly striking, since most *majhis* were Bengali-speaking Muslims. Hindi is often associated in public offices in Kolkata with the force of command, often over low-status workers. Vikas berated *majhis* like an angry master to a servant. He and his entrepreneur friends also become complicit by discussing the comedy of *majhis* attempting to beat the official registration system. These conversations harnessed "certainties" about the immorality of low-caste groups and Muslims to create distance between the actions of *majhis* and those of the other clients negotiating the rules in the office. Entrepreneurs repeatedly spoke of the bad characters of *majhis*, the men who were the basis for their income, and sought Vikas's favors in order to discipline them. As soon as *majhis* entered the office Vikas switched demeanor. At one point, a love boat *majhi* and the love boat-owner arrived in the office. The *majhi* explained that he had been stopped by the police because a man had been taken ill on his boat, and the police had told him wrongly that his license had expired. The *majhi* complained that the police were just taking advantage of him to get money. Vikas replied bluntly with disgust, handing over a letter with his fingertips so he remained as distant from contact with the low-caste and low-class *majhi* as possible. "I have given this paper. Take it back to them again and say I am supporting the *majhi*." The other men in the room laughed uneasily and discussed the comedy of these two personifications of immorality complaining of an illegality practiced against them. The love boat *majhi* had asked for nothing more than most of the men assembled there—a personal favor from Vikas—but the problem was that access to his office was not as democratic as he claimed. River workers who generated the income for the boat-owners and entrepreneurs were a valuable source of revenue for the state, but their place was beyond the lines of friendship in an illicit, immoral space. The pragmatic practice of patronage and *jogajog kora* produced an unequal exchange. River workers gave the state a flow of revenue that their labor had generated and their loyalty to it as a source of permanent justice. Low-level bureaucrats gave little in return, save their sympathy and the promise that they might sometimes open up access to its rights and tokens.

So what were the new structural forms of entrepreneurial society that had emerged from these practices of friendship and patronage? Like all the other marine department officials I worked with, Vikas had lent the authority and documentary practices of the state to the informalized sector on the river. This had increased the power of *golabaris* and boat-owners over *majhis* and multiplied dangerous informalized trades. Most important of all, his office had become a central site for the negotiation of the affective ties linking informalized and state economies. Friendships created an intermediary site for negotiation and speculation. In this, personal and state promises about the future could intermingle. These relationships were generated through a play of complicity and a sense that a parallel world of powers and secrets hovered just beyond reach. Here many different kinds of actors sought to appropriate state tokens and to harness the strategies of the state to their own ends. These practices were not, as many middle-class commentators would assume, evidence for the "corruption, inefficiency and populist political venality" of a bureaucratic class that needs to be swept away by liberalization practices derived from the corporate sector (Chatterjee, 2008, 57). They were instead improvised in order to meet the fiscal demands and realize the decentralized planning characteristic of liberalization austerity policy. Vikas was well appreciated among the high ranks of the bureaucracy, attending meetings and making influential suggestions to the Marine Department. This reflected an overall flattening of the hierarchies of the Kolkata Port Trust bureaucracy as a whole. Any suggestions that could be made to raise income or increase business on the river in a time of austerity were accepted. But how, then, did the working poor experience this new entrepreneurial society on the Hooghly? Did they contribute in any way to its emergence?

Desiring Entrepreneurial Society:
Majhis, Informality and State Documents

Majhis working on the Hooghly are the descendants of three generations of in-formalized labor. Their forebears worked carrying loads for the port or brick and jute industries. Their current work continues an older pattern of adapting liveli-hoods to new economic activities on the river. Ethnographies of boatmen in nonin-dustrial settings such as Varanasi have shown that they claim rights from the state as a Nishad caste community strongly associated with the ritual and mythic history of the Ganga (Jassal 2001; Doron 2008). Such examples follow the pattern predicted in the influential literature on "political society" in which it is argued that the urban poor in India and elsewhere are excluded from civil society and exist within a zone of negotiated, community rights that they seek through patronage. In contrast to this, *majhis* in Kolkata understand rights as individual titles guaranteed by the state that they earn through their labor. In fact what is striking about their accounts is their refusal of the mythicohistory of the Hooghly and of patronage relationships proffered by officials and employers. These belong, they argue, to corrupt regimes that have destroyed the productivity of the river. It is their refusal of this world of patronage that makes them enthusiastic participants in the new entrepreneurial society on the Hooghly.

All *majhis* on the river were highly positive about their recent incorporation into the state's license regime. An uncertainty of rights and income is inherent to their livelihoods. Although my research also included sand boat *majhis*, here I will focus on the experiences of men in the "love boat" trade. This is because they oc-cupy a particularly marginal and paradoxical position in the entrepreneurial society on the Hooghly. They take part in the most illicit and low-paid labor on the river, yet they recently have been drawn under the jurisdiction of the state through the ac-tions of Vikas. Access to work on a jetty or in a stretch of the river entirely depends on relationships with the specific middleman who controls it. Income varies widely depending on seasonal patterns in the river and the whims of intermediaries, in-cluding boat-owners. Love boat *majhis* pay 60 percent of their daily earnings to an intermediary *majhi* who rents the boats from the boat-owner on the ghat (jetty). He passes on 50 percent of the ghat's income to the boat-owner. Out of the remaining 40 percent that the *majhi* retains, they pay a third to their apprentice helper. Police-men, and in the past union members, also extract revenue through sudden acts of intimidation. The only source of security of livelihood for *majhis* is the right to work on a particular boat that is registered in their licenses. This is acquired through long apprenticeship to and then succession from a *majhi*. Before Vikas began his drive to break the illicit networks along the river, this license had become entirely irrelevant. It is not surprising therefore that *majhi*s were universally supportive of the actions of Vikas, which they understood as an important inclusion in the state. They repeatedly told me, "We too are part of the state now."

Characteristic of this perspective were the conversations I had with Abu Talim. He was in his forties when I met him at Water Ghat. He, like most love boat *majhis*, was a migrant worker from the Twenty-Four Parganas district. His wife, two young daughters and adult son lived near Diamond Harbour, where they carried out agricultural labor. Abu had first left his village at the age of eight with a relative who had put him to work selling sweets in the Mohan Bagan football stadium. He sold these also along the Calcutta Jetties in the late 1970s, when ships from all over the world used to moor in the center of the city. The greatest sign of cosmopolitanism of that time for him was that there were what he called "*black sahebs*," who were sailors on the ships and that used to give him chocolate. Because he was regularly on the waterfront, he managed to get work as an apprentice on one of the boats that was still carrying loads at that time. Now he worked on the same boat as a *majhi*. He remembered the productive past of the river with nostalgia and looked on the present decay with bitterness, saying, "Now this is just a wasteland [*phaka*— useless, unproductive space]." It had become like this as a result of the acts of corrupt politicians, officials and unions. He described bitterly how the boatman union hadn't helped *majhi*s at all; they had just pocketed money from them. Politics. he said. he could not get involved in because he would simply get a bullet in his head, it had become so violent and corrupt. He attributed the most recent problems of the waterfront to the actions of the police from Lal Bazaar. Abu described how they used to arrest *majhi*s and take them off to jail so that they could be paid bribes. As a result, customers for the love boat trade stopped coming and the *majhi*'s fortunes declined even further. Abu's recurrent utopian solutions for these failures were redistribution and mutual recognition of equality. He insisted that there was no difference at all between him and myself or anyone else richer than he. It was just that one person wore fine clothes and the other wore rags. The important thing was that if someone had more than another person, they should give to that other. His central source of hope was that now, at last, due to the actions of Vikas, he possessed a license. This, he said, was on permanent record in the registration office and could not be denied by the police or anyone else. This, he said, would "secure my future."

Majhis such as Abu Talim sought release from patronage and negotiated rights. The new entrepreneurial society on the Hooghly had brought them one step closer to this through the revival of the license system. For them it offered the possibility of a more productive river and life for themselves. Yet it also contained new forms of inequality and class tensions. The urban poor now contributed part of the value of their labor directly to the revenue streams of the state. They were also subject to the outcomes of the negotiations through friendship between entrepreneurs and bureaucrats. They were promised individual rights, yet were dealt with through forms of distancing patronage. *Majhis* did not yet complain of these new practices. They were partial cocreators of the new authority of the state on the river. The predatory patronage and corruption of the previous regime had pushed them toward this position. For now the negotiations of friendship were invisible to them as a source of inequality.

Conclusion: Governing Speculation

Populist Secrecy

Here I have given an account that is different from many discussions of contemporary public sector economic policy. Debates have focused on growing practices of transparency, audit and accountability (Power 1997; Strathern 2000; Swyngedouw 2005). These accounts follow the effects of explicit policies of reform within institutions. The bureaucrats in the Kolkata Port Trust were also subject to such regimes through formal state tendering, the right to information act, computerization of records, fiscal targets and international I.S.O. certification. But their practices of *jogajog kora* show that our analysis of transparency will remain limited unless we also track new forms of secrecy and complicity. Secrecy has been discussed as a minor theme in the anthropology of bureaucracy solely in relation to issues of legitimacy. The secrecy I have described is not the same as the office secret that preserves the domain of professional expertise (Weber 1978 [1956]). Nor is it exactly parallel to the shared complicity of the knowledge of a gap between the official and unofficial state (Hertzfeld 2005; Taussig 1999). Nor is this the conjured world of conspiratorial secrets that creates an illusory image of an all-powerful state (Taussig 1997). It is most similar to the parallel world of spying that runs alongside public international policy and media disclosure (Shore 2011). Yet none of these approaches fully capture the qualities of *jogajog kora*. It is a pragmatic, passionate and populist secrecy through which state and personal promises are brought into relationship with each other. This activity becomes even more significant in contemporary forms of economic governance through public-private partnership. It is vitally important for us to examine populist secrecy, alongside transparency, if we are to understand these.

Speculative Planning

Economic planning always has unpredictable outcomes. Yet the forms of governance examined here produce a radical divergence between state promises and the reality generated by them. The content of policy becomes more loosely defined producing devolved planning. Diverse visions of what prosperity might be are included in the practices of bureaucracies. State tokens and schemes are dispersed through society. In contexts, such as India, where informalized work is widespread, this difference between state plans and outcomes increases further. Importantly, it is very difficult for a political critique of this kind of economic governance to emerge. This is because all that is visible in the public domain are plans for prosperity and the reality quite different from these. This gap is widely understood by the citizens of Kolkata as a product of corruption. They cannot see it as a result of the normal operation of liberalization policy. We need to examine further the political effects of the opacity produced by speculative, decentralized planning.

Public-private Boundaries

Practices of *jogajog kora* also reveal other growing aspects of bureaucratic work that have remained underanalyzed. Contemporary bureaucrats are Janus-like figures who stand on the boundary between public and private economies. They alternately suspend and generate boundaries between the state and the market. As this chapter has shown, *jogajog kora,* or practices of useful friendship, are the medium through which this is achieved. Through friendship individual affective ties are improvised that never appear in the public domain, but that re-create economic life. Their invisibility helps to sustain an illusion that is key to the politics of the "rebalancing" of public and private sectors. The state and the market appear as distinct spheres containing different kinds of collective ethics and productive powers. This separation between public and private economies is unlikely to disappear. This is in part because it supports a profitable division between state labor and a more precarious private sector. Yet, perhaps, the sense that *majhis* have that they are drawing closer to the state may lead to a political critique that could undermine this separation.

Speculation Machines

Finally, this chapter has revealed a characteristic of contemporary bureaucracies engaged in stimulating public-private partnerships. Their practices of publicity and decentralized planning turn them into speculation machines. This is an inversion of Weber's model of the emergence of bureaucracy in order to secure legal rights and mechanisms to make the market predictable. It is also entirely distinct from Foucauldian accounts of the liberal or biosocial state. Bureaucratic planning of the economy takes on the volatility of the market and of personal relationships. It amplifies the unstable effects of these. This is not the same problem as that of "corruption" or "patronage" for personal profit, which have long beset all levels of state institutions across the world. This is a not a diversion of state practices toward private gain. It is a transformation in the routines of the state.

Section IV

Contradictions in Time

Accidents, Austerity Time-spaces and Circulation

In this section I analyze the contradictions of austerity capitalism. These are fully revealed in the structures and experiences of timespaces of trade and production on the Hooghly, which are unstable and very difficult to govern or predict. The circulation and generation of capital within these timespaces is uncertain and even dangerous. River pilots and shipyard workers drew my attention to this through their accounts of accidents.

Accidents were frequent on the Hooghly. All river pilots had been involved in dangerous situations, and most men had narrowly survived cyclones. Some had permanent injuries that had resulted from these events. They had watched other ships sink in storms. Everyone had tales to tell of hitting jetties or going aground. Navigating down the river meant watching out for the remains of accidents. River pilots knew where wrecks from the nineteenth century were because these were dangerous areas that had to be avoided when following the narrow navigable tracks in the river. Most notorious was the James and Mary shoal just off Hooghly point, where the tide pulls ships onto the sandbars. All river pilots agreed, and my research in the port trust archive confirmed, that accidents had become more frequent in the past ten years. In fact, as we will see in Chapter 5, during my fieldwork the Pilot's Association focused its collective effort on preventing such events.

Accidents for private-sector shipyard workers in Venture Ltd were a daily experience and constant threat. Most workers had scars and all related stories of almost being sliced in two by sheets of steel that had dropped during lifting. Many small and a few large accidents occurred during my fieldwork. In 2007 the yard hired a doctor to wait in a cramped room in the slum outside the yard, ready to administer first aid. Each time I visited him he read to me from his ledger the accidents of the day and week. He saw about ten men a day. The majority of cases through the year were burns from acetylene torches. The worst accidents are electrocutions or falls.

He had joined the yard after a severe event in which a man had died when an electric cable had snapped and landed in a pool of tidal river water in the yard. He contrasted his work here with the twenty-four years he spent in a nearby public-sector yard—it had been much safer there. I asked if the workers could afford to go to the private hospitals he recommended serious cases to. He said only if they have health insurance provided by the company, which is just fifty among fifteen hundred men. Workers spoke often of their fears about potential medical expenses from accidents or the fate of their families if they were injured or killed. These events are warded off by daily household pujas to the goddess Kali, which workers called their "insurance." Workers described the dangerous conditions of the yard as created by "the burning of the stomach" and suggested that the company was growing large while the workers were dying. This individualistic, selfish hunger of the stomach is destructive. It is the opposite of the productive feeding of domestic and public pujas in which food is eaten with a collective sociable hunger once it has been blessed by a deity.

Through hearing such accounts and participating in these risky workplaces I began to investigate how these work conditions were generated out of austerity policy; why men continued to work in these environments; and how state- and private-sector accumulation was reproduced within such unstable, contradictory social forms. The two chapters that follow explore these questions.

Answering these questions has led me to rethink our existing accounts of credit, time and capital circulation. Taking credit first, following Marx, our models have focused on commercial credit (Marx 1991b). The expansion of financial market lending since the 1980s has been described as the advancing of overaccumulated capital within society so that primitive accumulation can continue. Here credit is understood to be a reallocation of capital that ensures circulation through a large-scale global spatio-temporal fix (Harvey 1989, 2000, 2005; Castree 2009). But this account leaves out the phenomenon of state debt. Since the 1980s credit has also been advanced from international organizations and financial markets to governments. This produces a drive to repayment and deficit reduction within public-sector institutions according to short-term commercial rhythms.[1] The social investment and redistributive aspects of rule are undermined. There is an intensified extraction of revenues and labor value within, and by, public institutions. Revenues are drawn in a tributary structure toward the central government and used to support financial market transactions. As a result bureaucrats dismantle public infrastructures, outsource work, seek quick sources of revenue and engage in speculation. State institutions become extractive from resources and labor in new ways. As I show in this section, these practices do not produce a spatiotemporal fix. Instead they lead to increasing contradictions in the structures and experiences of time-spaces of work. They generate unstable, short-term forms of austerity capitalism.

Turning now to time, there have been many claims that contemporary capitalism is characterized by time-space compression, cultures of speed or uncertainty (Castells 2000, Comaroff, Comaroff and Weller 2001; Harvey 1989; Hope 2006; Mains 2007; Tomlinson 2007). Futures are described as especially problematic, and as radically indeterminate or evacuated (Guyer 2007; Hell and Schonle 2010; Rosenberg and Harding 2005; Piot 2010; Wallman 1992). Yet there has been too little exploration of why the problem of time has become increasingly visible to our informants and ourselves. Nor has there been a full examination of how bureaucratic institutions currently attempt to govern timespaces or how our disconcerting experiences of time are related to their practices. Here I open up these arenas of inquiry with the aid of Thrift and May's approach to timespaces. They propose that our analysis of capitalist time should not focus on a single representation—for example, the abstract reckoning that is the basis for factory discipline or cultures of speed or uncertain futures. Instead, they suggest that we trace the intersections of four aspects of time within a social space (delimited by the analyst): representations, technologies, social disciplines and rhythms in time. In the following chapters I adopt such an approach, but further refine their arguments. I explore the full range of representations of time or time-maps with various relationships to human and nonhuman time at work within a single social field. These range from the representation of the cyclical return of ritual, generational kinship time, to predictive technologies that are more tightly linked to nonhuman rhythms. I also bring into view the act of labor in time-spaces that strains to reconcile diverse rhythms, representations and technologies of time in a coordination of human action toward their temporary unification. I reveal the many small acts of labor and their accompanying ethics that support forms of accumulation. My argument is that such labor is becoming more difficult and dangerous in austerity capitalism. Therefore time thickens with uncertainty and draws our attention.

Ultimately, these chapters show that the circulation of capital is not the large-scale generative process imagined in Marxist theories. Instead, it is a small-scale temporary arrangement that is contingent on the solutions that surface within time-spaces of work. Importantly, these solutions are always ethical in character and cannot be understood as global spatiotemporal fixes that conform to a single capitalist logic or representation of time. We will now enter two timespaces where the contradictions of austerity capitalism have become acute. The first of these is the navigation of container ships by river pilots on the Hooghly. The second is the private shipyard Venture Ltd, where a new form of short-term capitalism has emerged from the outsourcing and property regimes of the port.

Fig. 6. Racing the tide

Chapter 5

Ajeet's Accident: Timespaces of Global Trade and Ethical Fixes in Circulation

AUSTERITIY POLICY on the Hooghly has made the bureaucratic management of timespaces in the Kolkata Port Trust problematic. Decaying infrastructure and an undredged river unpredictably impede the flow of trade.[1] Bureaucrats and workers of the marine department find it more difficult to use predictive technologies to bring into relationship the rhythms of international trade and the seasonal tides and patterns of the river. During my research these problems came to the fore as a result of the increasing number of accidents on the river. Most significant among these was a spectacular event that was named after the pilot in charge on the ship as Ajeet's accident.

Four months into my research a container ship had sliced through a jetty and was left beached on the silt bank precariously balanced on its keel. Suddenly my conversations with river pilots and marine officers converged toward this event. Everyone speculated on its causes and consequences. It was when Tapan, a thirty-year-old pilot, took me to see his friend Ajeet, who had had the accident, that the full significance of the event began to emerge. Ajeet had been reverted back to harbor work. The stigma of this, Tapan said, meant that he had become "mentally destroyed and his immune system has collapsed. The whole of his arms have frozen up." Ajeet lived in pilot's quarters that vibrated with the noise of container trucks crawling out of the dock gates. The concrete blocks built in the 1970s were decrepit, with unkempt gardens dominated by a huge mobile phone mast built on port land recently sold off to a private company. Inside the small flat, Ajeet moved like an old man, slowly lowering himself into one of the arm chairs.

Ajeet launched into an account of his accidents. He portrayed these as a sequence of mishaps culminating in a single uncontrollable event. He would locate a proximate cause: the captain's lying about the faulty steering on the ship, the failure of a warning light or the two narrow tracks at that point in the river. Yet he would then move on to another one, unable to find a single explanation. Abandoning his effort, Ajeet exclaimed, "Nature and everything worked against me. My job is one that tests every person's limits—that is the kind of work it is." Tapan agreed, and said, "You are only dealing with the consequences of things that are destined to happen already before you start to do things." Ajeet added, "That is right. All the things that happened to me had already started to happen before I was there in the middle of them. God had made them." Ajeet's and Tapan's explanations moved between local proximate causes and a transcendent controlling force. They then bitterly complained that the officers had blamed Ajeet for the accident. Tapan began to comfort Ajeet by holding out the hope that technology could prevent such accidents in the future by solving a problem of time:

If we had the electronic charts with laptops, then it would help in difficult situations like this. Instead of planning on the chart then deciding what to do then, you would already look at the computer and know your position. This would save your time in situations where any time delay would create a greater problem.

Ajeet replied enthusiastically, saying, "Yes! In our work you have to use your own full concentration. You have to time manage yourself and follow what is happening now." Tapan then joked that if the river pilots succeeded in producing the electronic charts, Ajeet should bring a goat from his village. This wouldn't be sacrificed to the goddess Kali, but, Tapan explained, should be cooked in a feast to give to his fellow river pilots since they, not the goddess, would have warded off future accidents.

In this and many other conversations, the contradictions of the austerity timespace of the Hooghly that led to accidents were represented and experienced in a particular way. They were depicted as the effect of transcendent, opaque forces. They were felt as a problem of agency in managing acts of labor in time. In the months that followed, the Pilots' Association worked to get the electronic charts up and running in a collective response to Ajeet's accident. Instead of directly challenging their working conditions or the austerity policies of liberalization, river pilots focused on solving a problem of time through technological means in an ethical act of care for each other.

This chapter explores the everyday life of accidents in relation to the work-processes, predictive devices and ethics of workplaces. I call this the "everyday life" of accidents for several reasons. First, like Perrow's discussions of "normal accidents," I trace how accidents emerge from regular work processes (1984). The same combination of commercial pressures, authoritarian command structures, weak insurance laws, multiple commercial ownership and decentralized agencies for legal sanctions that Perrow traced in the 1980s without doubt contribute to the accidents on the Hooghly. However, now added to this are the effects of austerity on public infrastructures. These lead to greater risks. Secondly, I add a further element to Perrow's approach, a focus on the dangers created by the partial and incomplete predictive devices used in regulating navigation and trade. These heuristic devices that daily open up the future for bureaucracies can generate dangers too. This is because they are shaped not just by technical but also by commercial concerns. Thirdly, and most important (again departing from Perrow), I trace how accidents are not only "normal," but how they are normalized through quotidian workplace ethics. I show how the conduct of productivity supports the continuation of dangerous work practices; allows people to maintain faith in the utility of predictive devices; and is used to explain accidents. Ultimately I demonstrate that the contradictions of austerity capitalism are temporarily "fixed" not through large-scale processes but through small, piecemeal ethical solutions that allow circulation to continue.

It is striking that we have rarely considered accidents from this perspective—their everyday life as part of the ethics of workplaces. Instead they have often been analyzed as spectacular events in the public sphere (Sizek 1999; Schivelbusch 1987). The few accounts that do connect work processes, accidents and ethics assume that values remain implicit and pragmatic among workers. It has been argued that unlike the moral dramas of accident inquiries, the workplace involves an unreflective "tinkering towards the good" that makes urban systems work (Law and Mol 2001; Graham and Thrift 2007).[2] Absent from these discussions are the explicit struggles between divergent projects of "tinkering towards the good," and the wide-ranging ethical responses within workplaces to accidents.

Contradictory Timespaces, Bureaucratic Predictions and Hierarchies of Skill

Unsafe Predictions

The techniques of navigation and prediction used in the Marine Department are unlike those described by Hutchins in his influential account of US Navy warships. These are designed to answer the pragmatic, technical question, "Where am I?" (1995).[3] Most forms of navigation cannot be understood by a sole focus on technical skill and utility. This is because they are embedded in predictive technologies that seek to generate capital from movement. They are shaped by two questions, "Where am I?" and "How can I make a profit in the shortest amount of time?" This coupling of separate goals of navigation and profit generation characterizes the predictive technologies of the Marine Department. As we will see, this mixed aim of technologies on the Hooghly exacerbates instability in the work process of navigation. In addition, what will not or cannot be predicted is deferred from consideration. This is achieved through ethical attributions in workplaces. These attributions are an important social concomitant of heuristic devices that are also left out of Hutchin's approach, which focuses only on the utility of predictive techniques. The contradictory goals, omissions and ethical attributions of predictive techniques have increased under austerity policy in the port. These unsafe predictions and ethics have contributed to a rise in accidents on the Hooghly.

Each member of the Marine Department lives according to the unrelated temporal rhythms of the river, international trade and bureaucratic decisions. To carry out their work, they must rely on the calculations of multiple predictive technologies. Central to these are the imaginary track lines that mark safe paths across the fifteen sandbars that lie between Kolkata Port and the Bay of Bengal at Sagar Island. Charts of the river divide it into 1,200-meter sections named after the governing or highest bars in those segments. Every 500 meters on the charts are depth readings stretching horizontally across the river. But along the track lines that stretch vertically down the charts there are depth readings every meter. Unstable parts of the river and governing bars are measured daily by hydrographic launches and larger survey vessels nearer the sea. The charts give the depths at the minimum low tide recorded, but actual depths will vary according to the rise and fall of the tide. The charts are also marked with longitude and latitude positions so that they can be used on the river itself for navigation. The charts are updated every twelve days, but track reports—excel spreadsheets of the depths on each track down the river—are issued each evening for the next day. The predictive track lines are made from a 110-year history of repeated measuring creating a specific map of the river that is officially secret knowledge. These tracks and daily depth readings form the basis for the calculations that are given the most importance in the bureaucratic planning of work on the river—the draft prediction and the allocation of ships to pilots.

The draft prediction brings the rhythms of international trade in relation to the cycles of the Hooghly. The minimum depths for the tracks each month are predicted a month in advance. On the basis of this, the port issues a maximum draft (underwater depth of a ship, distance from the lowest part of the keel to the waterline at which the vessel is floating—that is, how large, or how heavily loaded, a ship can travel upriver) allowable in the river for each month on the basis of which shippers in India and abroad in Sri Lanka, Singapore, China and Vietnam book cargos in and out of the port. This figure entirely determines the size, type and loading of ships that are sent up the Hooghly. It is calculated by adding the current depths of the river from the track reports to the height of the tide predicted from the Central Survey of India data published in the port's tide table. These tidal heights are based on harmonic analysis of actual observations at stations along the river during discontinuous periods and at different years for different stations between 1975 and 1984. But this probability prediction is in fact merely a partial estimate of the behavior of the river, since actual tidal behavior and the silting of track marks is highly unpredictable, depending on weather patterns and unforeseen patterns of shoaling. There always has been and always will be a hidden uncertainty produced by these calculations that has to be negotiated by the labor of river pilots as they navigate the ships on the Hooghly.

The draft prediction brings the incommensurable, and potentially contradictory, rhythms of commerce and the river into relation through the calculation of tides and virtual tracks in the river. This occluded uncertainty and contradiction has recently increased. Since 2002 the predicted drafts have improved, apparently showing that the river has deeper depths for more months of the year. This enables shippers to make greater profits by sending more cargo upriver on fewer larger and more heavily loaded ships. The river seems to have fallen in line with the rhythms of capital and trade through an increase in "time economy," or a shorter time between investments and return. But a probability calculation on the basis of historical data has in fact taken on a new form. It has acquired a greater virtuality or distance from the actual dangers of navigation as a result of attempts to serve the rhythms of capital accumulation with an infrastructure produced from deficit. Frustrated by the lack of central government investment in dredging infrastructure or resources for river training and the falling traffic at the port resulting from falling depths the draft prediction is now made on a different basis. The required underkeel clearance between the base of a ship and the bed of the river has been reduced. Ships require a certain amount beneath them that will compensate for the bilging of vessels if they tip sideways as a result of strong tides or waves or for the effect of squatting on the bars (if you increase the velocity of a ship, you lower the pressure on its hull and so the ship sinks down in the water). But this maneuverable distance that prevents potential accidents and error has been cut drastically, hiding in the calculation of margins of risk a new danger. The illusion of predictive control and planning has become more illusory. Now, at some stretches on the river pilots say they work with less than 10cm clearance between the base of the ship and the bed of the river.

Hierarchies of Skill and the Hearts of Pilots

The other core element of planning of work on the river is the routing of traffic up and down the river. There is always pressure from shippers to get their specific ship into or out of the port before any of the others, because only a certain number of vessels can make it up or down the river in one tide (usually four from Kolkata, five from Sandheads to Kolkata and five from Haldia to the sea). Shippers always aim for greater speed of journey to maximize their profits by cutting the cost of payment for crews, berth hire space and storage space in the port. The riverine tides and depths in the Hooghly determine the assignment of traffic through the Kolkata port system and the rhythms of trade to and from eastern India and Nepal in the ports of Colombo and Singapore. Yet within these constraints there is much negotiation with shipping agents over the timing of the allocation of berths and pilots to their vessels. A day before, sailing pilots are assigned to ships by marine officers. More experienced pilots are always given longer vessels. In fact, the rank of a pilot—first, second or third grade—determines the size of vessel he is permitted to navigate.[4] Similarly, first-grade pilots are given vessels with deeper drafts, with anything above 6.9 meters always piloted by them. It is a matter of prestige if you are given a deep-drafted or large vessel. The orders are issued to specific pilots the afternoon before sailing.

Yet the allocation of ships can be a point of dispute, because in the interests of the realization of profit it contains omissions in its calculation of danger and difficulty. The hull shape and the engine power of ships are not considered. These factors greatly affect how ships can be handled in the river, and whether they can be brought safely up or down river in different tidal strengths and weather conditions. Yet these measurements are not part of calculations of when and how ships should be timed for sailings. Instead, officers turn to a qualitative ethical attribution of "skill" in the bodies and minds of pilots. Officers allocate ships according to the skill and "strength of heart" of pilots—fitting the character of the ship to the characters of men. Officers claim that in their calculations they take into account, as one put it, that "every pilot is an individual with particular skills. You have to know how to convince people to do a particular job. Some have a strong heart, some have a weak heart."

River pilots do not always accept this deflection of a quantitative omission into a qualitative measure. They try to refuse ships in order to preserve themselves from dangerous situations. As one pilot put it:

When we get our draft forecast we put a cross mark on the right hand side of the days with a strong tide in our tide tables so that when we get our orders . . . if the ship is below 7 and a half knots we know it will be impossible to take it. A larger than 160-meter vessel, for example, with an engine of less than 7 and a half knots, if it is coming on a perigee spring tide you would have to cancel the ship and wait for a less strong tide. But there is pressure on us to take these ships from the office. They want to show that they are putting more business through the port, so the more ships they can get through in the shortest time the better. They are just interested in showing a good report to the chairman. Because of this, accidents happen. A ship broke a jetty at Baj Baj recently: the pilot turned the vessel early on the tide but could not correct it because of the power of the engine. The office should not have taken the booking for this vessel. They just care what the draft and length are, not the speed. These are the reasons we refuse vessels, but the people in the office are only interested in taking bookings.

When negotiations over refusals fail, officers themselves take the controversial ships or loads themselves (all marine officers started out as trainee pilots). They are proud of this work, suggesting, as one senior officer put it, that "only we are capable of taking the risk." They describe with great joy and excitement the precise details of the narrow margins they work within on these jobs. One officer described how he brought a low-powered barge upriver with a heavy, unwieldy load of equipment for the port that had been refused by the pilots as unsafe:

I agreed because the chairman said the ships are suffering and it was an interesting thing to do; there was a satisfaction in doing it.

This invocation of skill, individuality and the excitement of danger is a consistent pattern in the Marine Department. Skill is another name for the ability of a pilot to overcome the omissions and contradictions created by predictive technologies and work practices that tie together the conflicting rhythms of trade and capital generation with those of the recalcitrant river. It is a hierarchical measure that automatically gives authority to Marine Department officers with their "experience."

Within this ethics the generational split between the younger pilots, the "BA boys," and the marine officers provides a compelling personified reason for accidents. From the 1980s, the port recruited a new type of person as river pilot—university graduates who could be bonded to service (see Chapter 3). In the past, men with marine training on the Rajendra pilot ship had been engaged. As Captain Reddy, a marine official, typically put it, "They don't have the right training"; they

"couldn't go to sea without gadgets and they are forgetting their navigational skills."
Officers told stories of older pilots who were emblematic of the mariner's exceptional organic sensory skills. For example, Captain Verma spoke of A. L. Soares:

Now in the fog months you can go up the river with GPS and below Diamond Harbour
you can get the help of the radar and go. Even in those days in the river when AL Soares
was working there was radar there, but he never trusted the radar. We could see nothing
outside on the river and Soares turned and said to me, "Look outside, we are going past a
buoy." I looked out and there the buoy was. I could not understand how he knew it was
going to be there. He could tell the exact point we were at without looking even. I said to
him, "How did you know the buoy was there? He said if you knew that you would also be
a branch pilot. He even taught us to use smells to locate our position. He said to me you
know when you are passing the Bata factory you can make out the leather smell so you can
tell your position and know where to anchor.

The living representative of this mariner organic pilotage sense for all pilots and officers was Captain Wadia, an eighty-four-year-old retired pilot who still worked on
ships at anchor offloading their bulk cargo at Diamond Harbour. He was renowned,
as everyone said, for "loving the river." He also coached most of the pilots, including
the younger ones, when they were preparing for their pilotage exams. Whenever accidents occurred and the pilot was a "BA boy," marine officers attributed the event
to this qualitative, ethical difference in skills and age of pilots. This contributed to
the prevention of any broader official questions rippling outward from accidents
on the river.

Accident Inquiries: Failures of Individual Agency

When accidents occur, formal internal inquiries confine themselves to three
questions: the behavior of the pilot, the condition of the ship and the tidal and
weather conditions on the river. The aim of the inquiries is to determine whether
the pilot was at fault. As a result, accidents are only investigated as a question of
individual differences of skill. Inquiries have consequences only for the pilot concerned, whose career may be affected through demotion to harbor work or, in severe cases, dismissal. The pilot and the crew of the ship are called to give statements
before high-level marine officers who decide the case. There is no attribution of legal or financial responsibility, since the port and the pilot have no insurance liability to the ship owners. The international marine insurance taken out on vessels will

cover shipwrecks whatever the cause or location of an accident. Official inquiries limit the frame of interpretation of accidents to the failure of agency of individual pilots. They never consider port investment policies, working practices or predictive technologies as a source of accidents. The rare, more wide-ranging inquiries that have occurred have been in relation to the financial liabilities of owners in the case of accidents. For example, after the sinking of the *Green Opal* at Moyapur in 1997, there were extensive inquiries into how to force insurers to pay for and remove wrecked vessels. The sinking of the *Fortune Carrier* in 2003 provoked an inquiry in 2004 into the possibility that ships at the end of their working lives were being deliberately wrecked in the river on the instructions of their owners. Despite the obvious dangers to pilots of such decrepit ships being under their charge, this led only to a change in regulations about the reporting of the age, condition and insurance coverage of vessels *once they had been brought into the port*. It is striking that regular official inquiries limit questions to issues of individual pilot skill. This entirely prevents the consideration of the contribution of port policies, predictive technologies and working practices to accidents. This is compounded by the fact that port inquiries are internal and are never reported in the media as a matter of public concern.

Interconnections: Bureaucratic Prediction and Ethics

The predictive technologies of the Marine Department open up the rhythms of the river to capital generation. Yet, as we have seen, they are filled with elisions that create unsafe practices as normal practices. These unsafe practices are intensifying in the context of austerity policies. The qualitative measures of men and form of accident inquiries deflect attention from the instabilities of predictive technologies and the escalating dangers of working the river. Importantly heuristic, predictive devices never exist apart from the contradictions they generate or ethical accounts. As part of work processes, they do not make reality within their own technocratic image. Instead, their elisions and failures lead to attributions of the moral qualities of people. Their appearance as neutral technical devices that open up the future is dependent on these attributions.

Turning away from bureaucratic calculations, how do river pilots experience their work process? What kind of timespace does their work take them through? What ethics emerge from their labor in this timescape? How do their responses to accidents relate to this ethics? Why do they understand accidents to be a problem of time that can be solved through technology?

The Ethics of River Pilots: Heroic Agency

The Labor of Circulation and the Problem of Time

From the work routines of river pilots we can begin to understand how complex realizing the labor of circulation is. The work of river pilots is a negotiation of the gaps between the predicted, planned and actual river. They also tie together with their acts the divergent temporalities of commerce and of the river. Ultimately, a completed journey means that the pilot has successfully adjusted his actions to the river and a specific ship in the conditions of that day. These negotiations begin the night before sailing, when pilots receive copies of the latest paper and electronic charts, their vessel assignments, the movement of ships in the river for the day of sailing and the water report. Pilots first use the depths recorded in the water report to choose the best tracks to take on different sections of the river. They also check the speed and draft of their vessels in relation to the next day's strength of tide. They calculate this from the lunar month and whether the moon is moving on its elliptical orbit close to the earth (perigee) or farther from the earth (apogee tide). Once the tracks and tidal estimates are prepared, if a pilot is sailing out from Kolkata, he waits for the next day's sailing.

Sailings can occur only in one five-hour segment of time in the duration between the last hour of the ebb tide and the end of the four hours of flood tide. Because of the critical and declining depths over the bars, it is only on the flood tide that many bars are passable. Critical to the success and safety of a journey along the river is a pacing of speed, which controls the time at which a ship is taken across a particular bar in the river. This speed and the ability to precisely maneuver a ship are the only forces that are under the pilot's control in the attempt to match the rhythms of commerce to those of the river. Here, because it is most familiar to me, I will describe the progress of a journey from Kolkata docks downriver to the sea.

Boarding at Kidderpore, the pilots are taken in a launch to their assigned ships. The pilots climb up ladders the full vertical height of the hull, feeling a familiar fear and the vastness of the ship. They are greeted with formality and taken to the wheelhouse, where the captain and first officer will also remain for the journey. If the ship is a regular in the port, they will greet each other warmly. But most often the pilots see their job at this point as a difficult one of inspiring confidence in a suspicious and often hostile captain. Being inside the wheelhouse is like looking down from a tall building, and the ship feels entirely out of scale in the narrow river. The pilot is now in effect captain of this ship and gives the orders for engines, anchors, speed and headings. He lays out his paper charts in a successive sequence on the chart table and, more recently, since November 2009, plugs in his electronic chart laptop into the ship's GPS. Although officially he is supposed to turn on the echo-sounder for depth readings, pilots never do this. That is because they say the depths are so tight that to do so would scare the captain and crew before they have even begun the journey.

After turning the ship so it is facing downriver using the force of the tide, the pilot starts to give the headings for the tracks. In the first 30 miles of the river until Kukrahati, the pilots rely entirely on the physical track marks on the banks. They watch from the windows of the wheelhouse to check that the ship is on the transit line. They use these physical markers because the GPS and the speed of charting are too slow and inaccurate for the finely measured heading commands that will keep the ship on the track lines. The pilot constantly has to adjust the headings, since the ship drifts off course. It is affected from moment to moment by the strength of the tide, the specific power and behavior of the engines and the curvature in the movement of the propellers. As a result, there is no fixed timing for when heading commands will be given. These must be judged entirely by the pilot's estimate of how and when to alter them. Junior pilots respect more senior pilots for their ability to pick up the "feeling of a ship"—how it will behave after giving a few helm commands. Because of the varying difficulties of navigating different sections, there is no standard interval for taking the time of a heading. When and how to change the headings depends on the personalized skill of a pilot. Some pilots are so skilled that they can just give one heading steady and will stay on course; others have to keep changing the heading to keep on the track.

Apart from these minute adjustments of direction, uppermost in the pilot's planning is clearing Hooghly point before darkness. That is because there is no safe anchorage for ships until past Hooghly point, and night navigation is no longer permitted because of the greater risk. There is a constant balance of speeding up to make Hooghly point and slowing down so as not to meet the bar at Moyapur too soon, before the flood tide has risen enough. The moments that pilots choose to speed up or slow down the ship are a complex triangulation between risk, the rise of the tide and the current position on the river. The rise of the tide is updated over the VHS radio from actual measurements on the river at Garden Reach, Hooghly point and Moyapur. The rise is affected by weather and wind, so it remains unpredictable in spite of the calculations the night before. The risk of speeding up too much on the river results from the fact that, as the ship moves into Panchpara, the tracks take the vessel right up next to the bank, and the pilot has to head straight for the bank at many points. Any slight misjudgment of helm commands would swiftly lead to a collision.

After Hooghly point and Diamond Harbour, the river broadens out and the pilot can relax somewhat. From here onward the pilot asks the chief officer for the GPS readings and then maps them on his charts to physically check his heading. Since electronic charts were introduced in November 2009, these have been used in this segment of the river. They give the position, course, speed and GPS updates every three seconds, so decisions don't have to be delayed by the process of manual mapping on the charts. Once the pilot brings the ship to Sandheads, he leaves the vessel via a small pilot speedboat and is taken to land or the pilot vessel, to wait for a ship to take him upriver the next day. In spite of the new technologies of bore thrusters, powerful engines, GPS and electronic charts, this journey has ever narrowing margins. That is because of the increasing decrepitude, larger size and greater number of ships that visit the port, and the diminishing underkeel clearance in the river. Given all of these variables and the constant necessity of a minute pacing of speed, the pilot's work on the river is never routine or without a sense of imminent hazard. Importantly, all the contradictions of the timespace of the river generated by austerity, unsafe predictions and ethical attributions are experienced by the river pilots as a problem of *timing*. It is in the thickening of the dimension of time as a vital resource and medium for pacing action that occurs.

The Ethics of River Pilots: Heroic Agency, Immediacy and Transcendent Powers

The ethics emergent from this timespace of labor emphasize the heroic, individual agency of river pilots. Ideally, pilots should overcome the problems of timing by achieving an immediate fusion with the ship and the forces of wind, waves, current and tide on the river. Social obligations and the constraints of the port bureaucracy should drop away in an unmediated encounter with nonhuman forces. One's own agency is amplified through this fusion. For example, Sudhir, one of the BA boys who joined in the late 1990s, described why he continued working in the port in spite of the dangers:

It is the autonomy and freedom of the work. When I am in charge of a ship, I don't give a damn about anyone else, not the harbor master, not the chairman, not anybody—nobody is over you at all. I am totally in charge of a 170 lakh machine. I take the decisions then, and if something happens then I am responsible and I know I have done the right thing. No one else commands you at all.

Another pilot, Abhilash, spoke of piloting in the following terms:

You pilot with something inside you, with your strength, and the ship becomes part of your limbs, part of yourself, when you are in charge of it. You are no longer a malleable, weak creature.

Captain Wadia spoke of why he had enjoyed working the river from the first moment he embarked on it in the 1940s: "It is the ship handling. You are an insignificant pilot on the bridge, but you are handling thousands of tons of machinery and this thrilled me."

Wadia's accounts of ship handling have shaped the majority of the pilots' interpretations of the work process, since he trained them for their exams. When I asked him to give me his famous ship handling lesson, he made the schema explicit. The pilot's universe on the river is divided into forces that are under degrees of individual control. Under direct control are the engines, propeller, rudder, anchors, moorings and the ship's inertia. Not under your control are the wind, the waves, the current/tide and the depth. The work of ship handling is to open yourself to these forces in order to, as instantly as possible, adjust your actions to them. That is why pilots aim to achieve an intuitive fusion within them of the "feeling of the ship" and the "feeling of the river." Tapan expressed this in the following terms:

The best pilot after two or three helm commands will have the feeling of the ship. The software that the dredgers have is point to point navigation, but on these there is no allowing for the curvature in the movement of the vessel. The best pilots have this curvature in their brain. The curvature depends on the tidal strength and anticipating the behavior of the ship. It will vary from ship to ship; you can anticipate this better when you become a better pilot . . . . Ninety-nine percent of the accidents happen on the river because the person has lost his feeling and is disrespecting the river. It is a learned feeling but also a god-given feeling.

The most admired pilots were described as having turned their feeling for the river into a love for the river. Captain Wadia was emblematic of this emotion. It was clearly demonstrated by his refusal to retire and work on ships at anchor in Diamond Harbour in his eighties. Captain Wadia's wife described his relation with the river in the following terms—a story that was well known among the other pilots:

He loves the river more than anything else. When we got married he told me when he came here from Bombay that I better get used to the city because he would never live anywhere else as long as the Hooghly flowed through it. He wouldn't leave the river.

This ethic among pilots included a sense that the forces they experienced on the Hooghly were an expression of a transcendent power. For example Captain Wadia had since the 1940s visited the priests at the Ramkrishna mission at Belur Math. He had read all the works of Vivekananda and his interpretation of his teachings took the following form:

Vivekananda explains that there is actually an impersonal god and god is in everything. Everything animate and inanimate is part of God, so the way you treat other people that way you are treating god also. This is what made me love the river: it was part of god. And ships too are part of god, and I always considered them alive.

Although this is a particular framing, this sensibility is characteristic of all the river pilots I met. Ships and the river were attributed a life that the pilot had to fuse with in an amplification of their individual agency. This life was ultimately the expression of a transcendent vital force that was the cause of events on the river.

Given this ethic, what most excited river pilots about navigational technology was the possibility that it would bring them into a closer, immediate relation with the forces on the river. The technologies they had most enthusiasm for were those that centered calculation entirely within the physicality of the body. As pilots enacted these technologies, they danced angles and planes with their arms projecting outward from their body as the pivotal core point. This enthusiasm was shared equally by young and old river pilots. Wadia grew animated as he explained how he had discovered the radiant rule for judging the distance that a vessel lay from one's own position, which he had then taught to all the other pilots. The radiant rule is that:

Twenty degrees of circumference is equal to a third of the radius. Now it is a magical thing that your arm and the span of your fingers is three times the length of your arm and your span therefore represents 20 degrees of circumference in front of you. So if you use your hand's span to measure the length of a ship traveling on the river and you know the length of that ship you can then calculate what distance you are from it.

As he enacted the calculation he sought to communicate the joy of the simplicity of the technique, which relied on no mediation. Similarly, Tapan was an enthusiast for obsolete forms of star navigation. One evening he began to explain this in the following terms. First he asserted that all navigation depends on the assumption that the ship you are traveling on is a fixed, nonmoving point. He then began to explain how to calculate direction from the position and curve of the moon using only your hands. He said that he had learned this from a friend during the time they were taking their navigation papers. It had helped him to remember and understand his navigation even now. He also explained the angles of the pole star and how just by judging these by lining up your arms with it you could calculate direction. River pilots enjoyed these navigational technologies because they fused in an unmediated fashion the body of the pilot, the forces of the river and the forms of the universe. They also made the pilot the heroic center of these forces and forms.

Accidents and the Terror of Loss of Agency

Within these ethics accidents are a terrifying collapse of agency. All pilots young and old, like Ajeet, described accidents as a loss of their own power, as a result of a cascade of uncontrollable circumstances. They left pilots experiencing personal crises expressed in uncontrollable bodily responses. Wadia, for example, described his first accident in 1964:

I had a collision at Moyapur and an accident there also. In the accident the ship had got stranded on the sand because the tide was falling and I was letting the anchor down. The anchor motor was so old it hit the side of the boat. An apprentice came running and took me down and I could see water pouring in the side of the ship. I stayed on the ship for two days. As the tide moved the ship tilted left then right. I was shaking when I finally got off the boat. I stayed on it to try and do something to rescue it. But the tide scoured the sand away from the ends and she broke her back. When I fell asleep in my bed, in my sleep I was turning and holding one side of the bed after the other like I was moving on the ship as she tilted in the tide. Ana (his wife) said, "What are you doing wake up." It is very difficult to get over this for a pilot and to do pilotage again. For two years there was an investigation.

Ana added that she had to sing Captain Wadia to sleep to help him get over it. Tapan also spoke in these terms, describing hitting a jetty at Haldia:

It is a shock to the system when you have an accident . . . . I remember when I was training with a senior pilot who had an accident at a certain point where he had collided with a jetty. Whenever we got to that point the pilot would say to me, "You take over here," and he could not even look. When I was first working I hit a jetty at Haldia. I would see it again at night in my dreams. My wife said I would call out in my sleep, "Astern, starboard."

For all pilots these traumatic failures can be overcome only by rebuilding heroic agency, by making accidents productive. They must be used to generate new powerful skills in oneself that can be passed on to other pilots. As Tapan and Ajeet put it:

"Accidents are good," said Tapan.

"Yes," Ajeet said. "Accidents give you the knowledge to pilot. Accidents give you practical knowledge of the river."

"Yes," Tapan said. "When you are a branch pilot and testing the young pilots, in a few years' time you will be able to ask them the most difficult questions!"

At the most quotidian level, accidents are reworked as transmissible knowledge in the telling of stories to fellow or junior pilots. Whenever I asked pilots to explain their work to me, they would always gravitate toward a discussion of accidents that they had experienced. They would also swap stories with each other. Very often I realized that as people started to describe accidents to me in general terms, I had heard the story told exactly the same way by the person that had had the accident. Stories of accidents circulated as general knowledge among the pilots. When Captain Wadia gave me his ship-handling lesson, it was structured around his recounting of his various accidents as illustrations of general principles. These practices restore heroic agency by turning traumatic events into skilled knowledge. However, they also prevent any broader scrutiny of the bureaucratic decisions, predictive technologies and work process that have contributed to accidents.

This practice of reworking accidents into productive knowledge in order to rebuild forms of heroic agency is long-standing and quotidian for pilots. Yet sometimes accidents result in their pushing for new technological interventions. How are these innovations a technological version of the pilot's ethics and mutual duty of care? Why do these technologies take a particular form focused on solving a problem in and of time? What do they reveal about the ethical fixes that reproduce contemporary austerity capitalism? Let's explore these questions as we turn to a discussion of the electronic charts that were introduced in the wake of Ajeet's accident.

Ethical Technologies: Traditional Electronic Charts

Why did a more wide ranging protest about working conditions and policies not develop among river pilots in the wake of Ajeet's accident? Why did electronic charts emerge as the solution for it? Why were river pilots so focused on solving a problem of time and timing—or, in other words, why did they concentrate their efforts on generating more immediacy in navigation? The answers to these questions can be found in the complex interdependent effects of ethical attributions among marine officers, the form of accident inquiries, pilots' lack of union radicalism and their ethics of heroic agency and immediacy.

The most conservative response to Ajeet's accident came from marine officers who simply assimilated it to the hierarchies of skill between BA boys and the older generation of working-class marine officers. They wanted nothing to change at all as a result of the event. They even tried to prevent the pilots from making electronic charts of the river. Characteristic of this response was that of a high-level marine officer, Mr. Sharma. One day he began unprompted to talk about what must have been on his mind—the electronic charts and Ajeet's accident. First he argued that you could not rely on technology to navigate the river. This was because no amount of computer screens or charts would allow you to pilot well. He suggested that if you used them, you would just spend all your time staring at the screen in a narrow way and you would not look at the river at all. Sharma then suggested that Captain Wadia was the person most skilled at the old forms of navigation. He talked about Captain Wadia with admiration, saying that he still insists on working the river and that he wants to die on the river. Sharma continued, suggesting that if electronic charts were introduced, the young pilots would become dependent on the screen and they would not know the river at all. He added that he feared what would happen if the equipment failed—then the young pilots would be helpless. He asserted that technology was no substitute at all for the experience of making journeys up and down the river through the years. He confided that an experienced pilot would know as soon as they got on a ship that there was a problem from the vibrations from the engine, but inexperienced pilots would not. Sharma also suggested that the young pilots do not have the mental strength to withstand the pressures of the job and become ill after accidents. The accident inquiry supported this official schema of individual failings. Ajeet was found to be at fault (although he claimed the steering had failed), and he was demoted to harbor work.

Yet it was the *combination* of this ad hominem attribution among officers with the pilots lack of union radicalism and own ethics that made electronic charts appear as a solution. From 1985 to the late 1990s, the Pilot's Association had been quite a radical organization. It focused solely on protecting the rights of its members and was not politically affiliated. In 1995 and 1997 it took part in two highly acrimonious strikes over pay and working conditions. However, in 2000 the leaders were voted out because pilots feared they had become too controversial. A new conservatism developed among the pilots because the deficit crisis in the port had become acute. In 2000 the Kolkata Port Trust had its most severe financial crisis, with a collapse of its operating revenue. As a result, a permanent hiring freeze was introduced at every level of the port, which still continued through my period of fieldwork. Soon after this rumors began to circulate that the Kidderpore Docks would be turned into a barge port, removing the need for river pilots entirely. Successive chairmen floated prospective schemes that would allow them to replace the pilots with less expensive contractual labor or various technologies. In this crisis atmosphere accommodation and negotiation rather than confrontation appeared to be the best strategy for river pilots.

Electronic charts suited this new conservative mood, as they were a solution that would allow pilots to "adjust" to the declining work conditions in the port rather than challenging them. And the specific technological form of the charts was highly attractive to river pilots. They promised to overcome their experience of problems of time and timing in the work process, which was the end product of austerity policies on the river. They also fitted within the pilots' ethics of heroic agency, immediacy and productive accidents. Although all of these points became clear from discussions with many river pilots, here I draw on conversations with Captain Kocchar, a key member of the Pilot's Association. Captain Kocchar was widely admired for his "feeling" for the river. When I met him he was on leave, suffering from great pain from a long undiagnosed injury from an accident on the river. In a personal commitment to prevent further accidents, he was using the time to work on the electronic chart system. A group of pilots, including Captain Kocchar, had been testing them on the river, and he was contributing to a report to the administration on them. For Kocchar (and other river pilots), the new electronic charts were inseparable from the ethics of the pilots and their association. This association was understood to be a guild, not a union. Kocchar explained its role in the following way:

We are a close knit family. If any one of us is having a personal problem we extend help to each other. If any one person has a problem like an accident, I feel that I did something wrong when I was training them. We are not a union. We also pass on secret knowledge to each other, so that way we are a guild too. If one member has a problem, then there is a problem among all the members. Recently one member [Ajeet] became very ill, and I personally went to the chairman to ask for the money for treatment, and we all supported him and his family together.

This guild was primarily described as a vehicle for the transfer of knowledge between generations. As Captain Kocchar put it:

In our training we transfer our values like a father to a son. No one has been able to write a manual in how to navigate this river. I have seen people try to write it down. No book can be right because the channel is always shifting and you learn from your superiors. You can't write our knowledge down.

Captain Kocchar suggested that this inheritance of knowledge was vital for preventing accidents. He stated that it was their "collective responsibility as seniors" to convey it to younger generations, because it would help them in tightly timed situations on the river. The new electronic charts were just the extension of this ethic and concept of the guild into a contemporary medium. Captain Kocchar explained this by first describing the inalienable genealogical relationship between the river, pilots and charts: "Most of the places in the river were discovered by pilots. The charts and our training are marked by their names." Then he explained he had once been sailing with an English captain named Harwood, who was the grandson of a Bengal pilot. Kocchar added, "I showed him the chart and said, 'Look, here is your grandfather's name here on Harwood point.' His grandfather's name remains on the river." Kocchar immediately pointed to the electronic charts on his laptop and added:

Look at the electronic chart. Look at all these pilots' names: Preston tower, Black's point. They named these places so their grandsons could remember them and they could continue in their minds that way. See Sidney point, Edward's creek. Here are the fathers of the service.

He projected a patrilineal line that fused the organic life of pilots to the technology of charts and the vitality of the river itself. Electronic charts were just a further manifestation of this knowledge and inheritance. His ethics here drew explicitly on Hindu practices in relation to the river too. Captain Kocchar described how for fifteen days before Mahalaya (the arrival of Durga during the puja):

I go to the ghat and I think of my forefathers and offer to the Ganga. I remember seven generations of ancestors at that time. It is a good time to remember my legacy and inheritance. I ask them to bless me so I will do my duties. I remember each of them by name and think of them all individually.

It was this same imagery of legacy and the river that Kocchar projected onto the charts, making them a sign of inalienable, organic connections between pilots and the river. This emphasis on electronic charts as the natural consequence of the pilots' legacy and as the correct solution for Ajeet's accident limited the implications of the event. As Kocchar and other pilots too explained, the new technology would mean that:

you can work with a lesser width of channel because you can have a very high accuracy of location. This will help with time management on the river too. We can reduce the channel to 1,000 feet width from 1,500 feet for 120 miles of the river, so we will have to dredge a smaller space in the river. This will mean an increase in drafts and less of the channel to dredge, so it will save money too. The chairman told me posterity will remember you for what you have done for the port.

This was a technical intervention that would place pilots in tighter navigational situations. It would allow them as heroic agents to "adjust to" rather than challenge the contradictions of bureaucratic planning technologies in the port. It would bring them into more immediate relation with the forces on the river so that they could manage the problem of time. Ultimately it deflected from a discussion of working conditions and it supported a depoliticized concept of a guild of pilots joined in collective secret inalienable knowledge.

A year after Ajeet's accident I spoke to Tapan from London. I asked how Ajeet was doing this month and whether the electronic charts were useful. Tapan replied that Ajeet was working the river again and had overcome his problems. Yet I was very surprised to hear that Tapan had opted only to carry out harbor work or to guide ships on the VTMS. This, he explained, was because he was finding it difficult to continue on the river with the stress of such difficult journeys and so many near misses. He explained that the electronic charts were helping, although they could not be used on the upper reaches near Kolkata. But he added enthusiastically that he had a plan to correct some of their limits. At times the electronic charts froze on the screen or didn't work at all, so he was creating his own version to serve as a backup to them. This he would issue directly to pilots for their own laptops so that they could use them when the officially issued charts failed. That, he suggested, would help all his "poor fellow mariners going out on the river." The reverberations of Ajeet's accidents appeared to have been contained. However, it was striking to me that the dangers of working conditions still continued, and less stressful lives for river pilots remained elusive. None of the key issues of prediction or policy in conditions of austerity had been addressed, let alone solved. Pilots remained at the center of the contradictions in rhythms of public deficit, international commerce, river tides and predictive technologies. Their labor of circulation continued to be risky and unstable, even though it was crucial to international flows of trade.

Conclusion: Austerity Capitalism and Contingent Circulation

What, then, do the responses and solutions to Ajeet's accident reveal about the ethical fixes that reproduce contemporary austerity capitalism? Generated from experiences of a timespace of labor, shaped by ethics and fears of radicalism, the electronic charts provided a temporary fix in austerity capitalism on the Hooghly. They have for a while contained the social and physical contradictions generated by austerity policy. Their symbolic value, along with their technological features, allows pilots to "adjust" to these contradictions. It is through their ethical fix that Kolkata can continue to receive the consumption goods of "globalization," international shippers can secure profits and the government can repay its debts. It is such piecemeal, popular mediations that occur in ethical registers which permit the reproduction of austerity capitalism. Capital circulation is not a large-scale process with a single logic working its way through history. Its contradictions are not fixed by large-scale mechanisms such as those of credit described by Marx, Harvey and Castree. Capital circulation is a contingent effect of the conduct of productivity that emerges from specific time-spaces of work. Unless our theoretical and ethnographic accounts take notice of this, we will not be able to explain either the experiences or forms of circulation in contemporary (or any form of) capitalism.

Throughout this chapter it has become clear that the contradictions of austerity capitalism are primarily experienced as problems *in time and timing*. Timespaces of labor are now full of incommensurable forms of social and nonhuman time that are increasingly in conflict. As a result all of us, like river pilots, are frequently faced with the challenge of trying to bring into relation through our labor divergent rhythms and temporal representations (Marx [1884] 1992; Althusser 1970; Negri 2003). Circulation will continue as long as we continue to see these difficulties as *only a problem of time*. If we stopped our labor and asked why these conflicts in time exist, what alternative solutions might become possible? Ajeet had to do this in the wake of his accident. Yet he experienced this not as a release or a new beginning, but as an unbearable failure and loss of agency. How might it be possible to externalize our experiences of conflicts in time and not lose our selves, which are formed from the labor of mediating these? How could Ajeet recognize that his accident was beyond his control and still be a man of skill with the potential for heroic agency? This is the dilemma that austerity capitalism offers us. If we start to reflect on this dilemma, we realize both the significance of, and the limits to, our own agency. It is perhaps through such reflection that a political analytics of austerity capitalism that looks beyond the problem of time can begin.

Fig. 7. Endurance at Venture Ltd

Chapter 6

Uncertain Futures and Eternal Returns: Timespaces of Production in an Informalized Shipyard

SINCE THE 1980S there has been a growth of informalized, unprotected labor along the Hooghly. With the complicity of unions, political parties and local state bureaucrats, firms have taken a specific form. They are based on a short-term, low-investment capitalism in which workers have no rights or benefits. This has occurred although West Bengal has more prolabor laws than any other state in India and a deep history of union activism (Chakravarty 2010). I came to fully understand the insecurities of this work from months spent in Venture Ltd, a private-sector shipyard. Its five yards are wedged between the Hooghly River and the narrow strip of *bustees* (slums) lining Waterfront Road. Sweeping fly-overs leading from the bridge abruptly give way to a narrow potholed track. Trucks loaded with iron plate and machinery for the yards career dodging small children playing with mud and sticks. Inside the yards fifteen hundred men work on projects outsourced from government ports, state-run shipyards and foreign firms. The work process for many vessels is pressed into constricted fingers of land. This makes movement potentially hazardous until the dangers are felt instinctively. But even then, cranes carrying huge plates of steel create unexpected obstacles in an unpredictable rhythm. The yards are uncovered, filled with rented machinery and affected by seasonal or daily shifts in weather. Their uncemented, muddy surface bleeds into the river and becomes part of it at high tide. Frequently men, wires and machinery become marooned in pools of water. Often workers joke about the ironic difference between the utopian slogan painted on a hired, new yellow crane used in the yards and their actual position. It reads: *Jai Jawan. Jai Bigyan. Jai Kisan.* This phrase is well known from a previous era of state socialism, meaning "Victory to the Soldier. Victory to Science. Victory to the Peasant." According to the men, this ideal is upheld only among the ranks of permanent employees in the Garden Reach Navy shipyard or the former state Shalimar works. There, better pay, conditions and infrastructure exist. Yet work in these settings can be acquired now only for temporary employees and is a rare resource, since it relies on seeking favor with union brokers. Workers remark on the absurdity of their precarious, devalued situation, since the navy and state yards outsource work to Venture. As a result, these elite yards announce in public relations spectacles their ability to exceed their targets for production.

Venture Ltd is a particularly significant site for examining the new informalized labor developing on the Hooghly, and across India and the world. The company is forged from a uniting of family, state and international capital and makes products for state and international clients. Run and owned by two brothers, it is a "family firm" that appears to be outside the formal, regulated and unionized capitalist networks of these clients (Yanagisako 2008). As we will see, it realizes in an extreme form the logics of austerity and outsourcing—a decrease of infrastructure, accountability and the costs of labor to the absolute minimum. Its form generates a timescape of labor filled with contradictions that are experienced as problems of *permanence* and *prediction in time.*

Although informalized urban labor has always been in the majority, the increase in precarious work along the Hooghly follows recent Indian and global patterns (Hirway and Shah 2011; Sanyal and Bhattacharyya 2009). Pioneering research has long tracked the reality of the majority of "footloose" temporary workers that make up the industrial workforce in India (Breman 1996; Parry 1999, 2013). These studies have focused on the reduction of privileges among state employees, the current lack of opportunities to join an aristocracy of labor, and the coping strategies of the working poor (Gooptu 2001, 2007; Picherit 2012). However, we have not fully explored how liberalization state policies and new forms of global capital investment are cocreating exclusions that have a distinct origin and form (De Neve 2009; Vijay 2009; Breman 2010). Nor have we traced the unstable forms of capital developing (Mezzadri 2010). As we will see in India, the financialization of sovereign debt has contributed to the creation of a short-term disordered capitalism. Its timespaces of production are filled with contradictions. For managers and workers laboring within these timespaces, there is an acute uncertainty about the future. Contradictions are experienced as a problem of *permanence in time* and of *predicting the future.* People maintain their hope that these unstable workplaces will sustain their own and their families' futures by placing trust (*bishash*) in the qualities of men and their masculine skill. This masculine skill is amplified and given permanence through association with the eternal, cyclical returns of natural and ritual rhythms. In addition, the durable products of skill (especially the vast ice class ships that are being built for foreign clients) form a *res publica* through which men build connections with and claims on each other. All of these forms of permanence are condensed for men in two events—the launching of ships and the celebrations of Vishwakarma puja.

In exploring these issues I draw on, but develop, arguments made by Arendt and Sennett. Arendt brings together questions of temporality, labor and ethical action in her typology of *animal laborans* and *homo faber*. For Arendt capitalism is marked by a meaningless short-term cycle of production and consumption driven by the biological life-process. Such labor (by *animal laborans*), she suggests, cannot generate an ethical or political life for humans because it is individualizing. All that is experienced is the relation to a machine that sets the tempo for human labor in service to markets driven by acts of consumption. Within her typology the artisan and artist (*homo faber*) have the possibility for a greater, if utilitarian, ethical life because they generate a durable product in the world with which they have a permanent relation and that manifests a quality of their selfhood. Sennett has written against this typology, arguing that the act of work within capitalism can be a source of ethical insight (2009). Importantly, the short-term workplaces I am examining here show the limits and potential of both of these accounts of temporality, labor and ethics. It is certainly true that these informalized workplaces are brutally driven by the volatile, short-term cycles of the marketplace described by Arendt. Yet this temporality stimulates rather than limits ethical assertions and creates longings for permanence. These ethics are shaped in part by the experience of labor on material forms as suggested by Sennett, but they also draw on concepts of nature, ritual and kinship to project large-scale productive processes. In addition, men build a sense of common humanity based on the durable products of labor. So, in short, time is certainly experienced as an acute problem in contemporary austerity capitalism, as Arendt would have expected. Yet this experience *provokes* ethical claims built from the experience of labor and its durable products or *res publica*. These are human responses to the contradictions of current forms of capitalism that contribute to instabilities and inequalities or may even lead to a rejection of these.

Contradictions and the Timespaces of Short-term Capitalism

Austerity Extraction: Rentier Regimes and Short-term Capitalism

Venture Ltd has grown directly from state strategies. It first developed from the Kolkata Port Trust's austerity policies of outsourcing repair and construction work.[1] Port shipbuilding was carried out until the 1990s in unionized dockyards with large infrastructures such as the state-owned Garden Reach Shipyard or Hooghly Dock and Port Engineers Ltd. From 1998, ship construction, repair and technical projects were outsourced to small, nonunionized, private yards along the Hooghly such as Venture. More recently, state and unionized shipyards have started to outsource to these yards to cut costs and speed up production times.

Venture Ltd has also developed out of the rentier land regimes of the Kolkata Port Trust.[2] In its attempts to draw funds toward the central government, since 1986 MOST has urged the port trust to create income from the wide tracts of land it owns along the Hooghly, and especially in Kolkata. Most of this land was directly used by the port until the mid-1980s. As the port closed and decreased certain operations, this land became vacant. It has gradually been rented out in very small parcels on short fifteen-year leases.[3] Most plots are sublet, often illegally, without the requisite permission from the port trust. Local politicians frequently end up in control of these. They extend their influence and make a living from brokering subletting of plots. The port's leasing system has contributed to the emergence of an informalized rentier economy and enterprises focused on short time scales, which do not invest capital in permanent infrastructures. In spite of many plans for redevelopment of the waterfront proposed by port trust officials and encouragement from MOST, this leasing structure has been left in place.[4] Bureaucrats at the port trust have become focused on attempting to extract as much revenue from short-term subleasing as possible.

These outsourcing and rentier policies provide the basis for a new sort of shipyard on the Hooghly. Before the late 1990s, shipbuilding was carried out in the Kolkata docks, Garden Reach, Hooghly Port and Dock Engineers or Shalimar shipyards. These workplaces had large, permanent infrastructures. They also had stable, skilled workforces with apprenticeship schemes. The majority of men were permanent, unionized workers. Temporary workers were brought in for less skilled work and ship-repairing. If these men acquired skills, they could then rise into the ranks of permanent workers through apprenticeships. In these yards production processes were sequenced by the time taken to construct a vessel, not by deadlines external to production such as contractual delivery dates. Such yards are still present on the Hooghly. Yet they have become closed to a younger generation of workers on the river and are citadels of privilege. There is no longer any permanent recruitment. There is some temporary work, but this can be accessed only if you already have a relative working in the yards or influence with a union broker. The work regime in these places is quite distinct from that in the new temporary yards. They are well-provisioned and have much safer working conditions. The production process is orchestrated according to the time it takes to construct a vessel, with much longer periods elapsing between commissioning and delivery. Since the 1960s ship construction technologies have been introduced to these places at the same time as all over the world. These were differences that both workers and managers at Venture Ltd often reflected on during my fieldwork. Managers claimed that their newer workplaces were more cost-effective and efficient with faster production times than the older unionized firms with fixed infrastructure and workforces. In contrast, workers bitterly complained about the conditions of their labor: impossible delivery times; work in the open; faulty, inadequate equipment; and constant physical danger. How then do these workplaces relate precisely to the strategies of the port and what kind of timespaces are they?

Flexible Impermanence

Venture Ltd, like the other new enterprises on the Hooghly, was dominated by a strategy of flexible impermanence. This was founded in the short-term leases for land offered by the port trust and informalized brokering by politicians and union officials. Such leases meant that companies including Venture Ltd could grow or shrink in size according to the cycles of client demand. In recent years Venture Ltd has been able to increase exponentially to meet the rush of contracts from state and international clients. The founding brother, Subroto Chatterjee, started as an apprentice naval architect in a government-owned yard in the 1970s. With his brother he bought the lease of the shipyard, then based only in one yard, in the mid-1980s. Up until 2005 they carried out all the construction in this single narrow strip of land. From 1998 Venture Ltd started to receive orders for repair and building of vessels from the port. In 2003 this work greatly expanded with other state agencies also starting to outsource. Venture Ltd began to get orders for blocks for navy ships and commissions from other port trusts. To meet this demand at the least cost, Subroto sublet another nearby strip of land. In 2005 he accepted the commission to build a large tourist vessel, so again sublet another strip of land from a port lessee. Then in early 2006 a friend—a naval architect in a private shipyard in Mumbai—asked Subroto to take the contract for two large vessels for a Scandinavian company brokered through a firm, Seagrow in Cyprus. He then leased two more strips of land, one directly from the port and another from a sublessee. Subroto hoped that these would be the first two in a line of seven vessels they would build. The port's rentier land structure by 2006 supported profit-generation through cheap outsourcing by state agencies, national business and global firms. Costs of production were much lower

in such a private shipyard than other sites of production because there was no requirement to recoup large up-front investments in land. This rapid expansion with
very little financial investment is grounded in the port's extractive short-termism.
Their rentier system is "cost effective" for all the outsourcing agencies involved in
Venture Ltd.

The expansion strategies of Venture Ltd also rely on the informalized brokering networks that have been stimulated by the port trust's rentier and outsourcing
policies. When the firm requires more land or workers they come to terms with
local politicians and union officials who control their supply. Subroto has formed
an alliance with a local union leader who claims links with the CPI(M). This man
acts as a broker in two ways. He is one of the main suppliers of contractual workers
to the yard. He has also made an arrangement with Subroto that the union would
not recruit members at Venture Ltd nor take up the cause of men in the yard. Many
unions and their officials have taken such a role on the waterfront, stimulated by
the outsourcing mechanisms of the Kolkata Port Trust. When Subroto needs new
parcels of land, this also has to be negotiated through political brokers. I learned
more about this when a slum on port land next to Venture Ltd burned down. The
newspapers reported this as an accident, but shipyard workers and people who
lived in the settlement speculated that someone associated with Venture had organized it. Of course this rumor may well be unfounded, yet in any case a middle
manager later told me that Venture was now attempting to lease this land. But the
local politician who negotiates access along this stretch of the waterfront had not
yet been willing to ease this transaction. It is the Kolkata port trust's rentier and
outsourcing regimes that support these strategies of flexible impermanence and
brokering power.

Unstable Workplaces and Uncertain Futures

This flexible impermanence extends into the employment structures and infrastructure of Venture Ltd. Like land, men and machines are also "rented" for short
periods of time. Contractual arrangements and work processes cut costs by devolving financial risks from outsourcing agencies and entrepreneurs to contractors and
workers. Overall, this combination of practices creates an unstable workplace with
intense uncertainty in the production process. This affected everyone involved, but
workers become the bearers of the greatest amount of physical and monetary insecurity.

Turning first to the employment structures of Venture Ltd, workers subsidized the costs of production by their contractual labor. Five contractors supplied the workforce. Some highly skilled workers (around forty) were paid monthly, but the rest were hired each day at variable rates. No written contracts existed between workers and their brokers. Nor did contractors offer credit to workers to bind them to them—preferring flexibility and lack of ties allowing instant responses to the labor requirements of the work process. Men were moved around between yards and laid off according to the daily demands of the construction process. Contractors also evaded the costs of restrictive employment regulations. Rather than using a single contractor, several provided men at once. This was a strategy to keep the number of employees per contractor below the figure that legally requires the offering of medical, accident and other benefits. The risks of production were devolved to contractors and their workers. Contractors are only retrospectively paid for the work carried out once a block has passed the final tests from the quality control inspectors. If the block fails, then the cost of making it good is carried by the brokers, who transfer some of this cost to workers through reduced wages. The temporary use of labor in small groups keeps the costs and risks of production down for both outsourcing agencies and the owners of Venture Ltd.

Machinery too was temporarily assembled in the yards and ships were built with the minimum amount of automated, capital-intensive equipment. Only one plate-cutting machine was present in the yard. There were only three cranes, which were often inadequate for lifting the weight of sheets of metal they raised. Obsolete technologies such as lofting instead of computer-aided design and the transport of steel sheets with ropes and hooks were used. The physical infrastructure of the yards were almost nonexistent. Instead of a dry dock, there was a pit of mud that had been excavated and enclosed by a mud dam. The surfaces of yards were uncovered and uncemented, turning to mud in the rain and burning in the sun. There were no rest areas for workers to eat or sleep in, so they collected under the ship or in store rooms at breaks. This temporary structure held great physical dangers for workers. Managers and workers related stories of almost being sliced in two by sheets of steel that had dropped during the process of lifting. The previous year two men had died while working in the yard. There were about ten minor accidents each day. The reasoning behind this strategy of low investment was succinctly conveyed to me by one of the managers of Venture Ltd:

It does not make sense to put money into introducing a machine or further levels of automation. We define ourselves as being efficient if we are doing the same thing as the mechanized yards but at a lower cost. It is better for us to keep the workers skill levels low and use of machinery low, so that we can continue to maintain low wages.

These strategies of impermanence make production highly unstable and unpredictable. The labor supply is uncertain, as men are regularly absent because of the ill-effects of work. It is also very difficult to persuade men to work overtime because they have to carefully calculate whether the cost of exhaustion on one day would be worth the possibility of sickness or tiredness (and therefore lack of wages) for the following days. The conditions lead to a slow attrition of valuable skilled workers. In particular, ambitious young unmarried welders in their twenties hearing of work would leave for two months or so with contractors to the Andaman Islands, Gujarat or Goa.

The temporary infrastructure and low mechanization also make production time unpredictable. Work has to stop in the uncovered yard whenever rain falls during the three months of northwest storms, and then monsoons from May to August. Lack of machinery means that the yard production speed was much more dependent on the sheer physical strength of its workforce. The single makeshift dry dock leads to the interruption of work because of the flooding of the dock at high tide. No one could say exactly when ships would be completed, with delivery dates constantly slipping further into the future. There is an intensified uncertainty at Venture Ltd produced by its short-term structures. Predicting a future of labor and production is extremely difficult for managers and contractors, let alone for workers.

This already unstable workplace is made even more problematic by test regimes linked to financial contracts. When Venture Ltd agrees to work with outsourcing agencies, their contracts tie payment schedules to successful completion of stages of construction and testing. But the test regimes linked to these contracts disrupt the production process. Weekly inspections by external auditors (foreign managers or Lloyds of India inspectors) orchestrate the pace of production across teams. The dates of larger structural tests specified in contracts are the targets for monthly production. These dates are not based on the work conditions in the yard, but on an ideal project completion schedule that is linked in to loan terms with foreign and local banks to outsourcing agents. If these dates are missed, then the loans used to provide capital for the project could be withdrawn or the terms altered. The pace of these inspections has no relationship to what it is feasible to produce in the difficult conditions of labor. Workers bitterly complained of these unrealistic deadlines. Severe and minor accidents clustered around testing dates. Further uncertainty is generated by these delivery and testing regimes tied into financial contracts.

The contradictions of this short-term capitalism are experienced as problems of permanence in time and of predicting the future. Managers, supervisors and workers pay close attention to the progress of work each day and the outcome of tests trying to predict from these how much work, and wages, would be available in the week and months to come. Rumors on these subjects cluster in conversations at the end of the day or around test events. But even this close monitoring is not enough, as workers, and sometimes supervisors and middle managers found themselves laid off at short notice. This chronic uncertainty leads all ranks to defer activities associated with long-term social reproduction. Young men said they could not get married because their wages were too insecure and insufficient. Older men said they could not educate or marry off their children, as their income was uncertain. The greatest fear of workers is that they might suffer an accident or become too weak and old for work. Sudden health crises or even simply the aging process threatens the long-term future of their families, as they have no savings. Ultimately, it is only the quality of *shahosh* or masculine courage, strength and skill that could make the short-term and long-term future at all secure or predictable. Men describe how this *shahosh* grows gradually inside you through the act of labor. It reduces your fear of dangerous conditions and increases your ability to make a living. This *shahosh* also forms the foundation for reciprocal relations of solidarity and admiration between men. As we will see, this trust (*bishash*) in the qualities of men gives hope that an individual and collective productive future could exist.

Affective Relations in the Shipyard: The Ties That Bind Men

The current scale of enterprise in Venture Ltd is sustained by relations of friendship based on admiration of *shahosh*. Managers had come to work at the firm through family or professional friendships formed originally through practices of *jogajog kora*. Most senior managers had worked previously in public-sector jobs on the Hooghly and had joined Venture Ltd after retiring from these. Middle- and lower-ranking ones were trained in the company itself. Once men had joined the company, pragmatic friendships had turned into stronger ties founded in admiration for Subroto's daring and technical expertise. The managers' excitement about the limitless possibilities ahead when led by such a man is palpable. On the other hand, any failure or setback is experienced as the betrayal of an emotional connection. Managers are also linked by their class and caste status—all managers had risen from similar lower-middle-class backgrounds and were from Brahmin or Kayastho castes.

Similar affective ties draw and keep shipyard workers in the company. Overall, the shipyard is the most emotional environment I have ever been in. Ties of affection and admiration between men, which workers and managers call the "love" (*bhalobhasha*) of men, are pervasive. Men are recruited through word of mouth along networks of friendship and kinship from neighborhoods along the Andul road. Most have worked together in other places and live near each other. Some friendships turn into even stronger ties as men arrange marriages between female relatives and fellow workers. These friendships are framed through kinship concepts of the brotherhood and relations characteristic of lineage groups (*bongsho*) and in-laws (*kutum*). These relations should be reciprocal and mutually sustaining conduits for flows of information and resources. Affection is regularly displayed between workers in small signs of mutual care. The majority of workers are from similar low-caste and Dalit groups and are predominantly Hindu (unlike the more varied structure of the workforce in the formal and state-sector shipyards), creating further ground for solidarity.

The dangerous work process makes reciprocal ties of friendship vitally important in day-to-day labor. Mutual support within groups working on a single block of a vessel is essential to maintaining safety and health. This was true for managers, but even more so for workers. For welders, labor is most individualized, since they are put to work specific seams and enclosed in a mask through which you can see only the blue spark of the welding flame. Grinders are similarly absorbed in avoiding bursts of sparks and metal dust and staying on the seam. But dependencies cross-cut these tasks, since in each team older, experienced men teach their young helpers. These older men, in turn, are entirely reliant on the younger men for their own safety. For example, helpers watch out for electric wires falling into pools of water; warn welders inside the cavities of the ship when other workers are coming too close; and caution grinders if plates are approaching on cranes overhead. Workers understand these mutual relations to be similar to the brotherhood forged through kinship relations. This became clear from shipyard workers' confusion as to why ships abroad were given women's names. They insisted that ships should only ever be given men's names. As Rajas Biswas, a thirty-five-year-old khalasi, put it one day:

But we associate the use of the women's name if the father is dead. Then the son will go to the mother's family. This is why here we give men's names to the ships. Otherwise it would seem that the father is dead or something. That we who made the ship are no longer alive anymore.

For workers it is a skilled collectivity of "brothers" united in "the love of men" equivalent to a kinship group that creates ships.

Managers and workers associated the sociality of work in Venture Ltd with a liberating egalitarianism. Men claimed that here they could forge their own futures through *shahosh* or daring and skill. This was contrasted with the old state paternalism of the port and state shipyards, where men said work tasks had originally been assigned to specific caste and community groups. Managers boasted that they were offering low-status groups access to new technical skills and promoting only on merit rather than on age and caste/community criteria. Workers insisted that everyone who labored together was *somman* (equal). When I first started fieldwork in the yard, I began with questions about skill. As soon as I showed my interest in this workers talked enthusiastically to me. The barrier created by my foreignness and gender was suddenly breached. It was even better if I tried out the work or asked men to pretend I was a helper. My questions and actions were a recognition that I (unlike the foreign inspectors who flew in from other places and could not speak to them in Bengali) thought that they had skill. But one question I asked led to puzzled, abrupt responses. This was, "What special qualities or essences did you need to learn their work?" Everyone insisted that the important thing was that anyone could learn it. Men asserted that their work was part of a universal system of technical skill that was open to all as long as you were willing to be brave, strong and do *hater kaj* (work of the hands). Labor in the yard was associated with equality and social mobility for these low-caste and Dalit workers, who were predominantly from scheduled and other backward castes. It was the antithesis of the logics of caste.

This sense of freedom through labor is enhanced by the decentralized command of the yard. Workers in their small teams debate with their overseers the value of different technical procedures, making them accept their solutions. Lohit Sahana, a fifty-year-old fitter, described this meritocratic equality in the following universal terms:

There is a compass box that we use with five compasses and with this all the things in the world can be constructed. People have BSc and are engineers and can work abroad; we don't have this but we have this box and this is exactly the same knowledge they use. You can go anywhere in the world and there is no difference in this knowledge.

Positions within the yard are said to be secured by the degree of daring and skill a man possesses. Qualitative rankings of skill are the same as the wage structure of the contractors. At the top are loftsmen who map out the patterns of segments of vessels. Then the markers who map the patterns onto the plates. Then followed the welders and gas-cutters who cut and join the plates together. Next the sanders, and finally the *khalasies,* or riggers, who lift plates and blocks by hand or on cranes. Foremen for groups are chosen by their ability to produce *shotik kaj* (fine, accurate work); to command the *bhalobhasha* of men; and to transmit reliable information to managers and contractors about the fragmented teams in the yards. Young men can rise comparatively fast in this structure. Caste discourses were entirely illegitimate in the yard. Workers laughed when I suggested that men ate in distinct groups according to caste rank. They explained that the separate groups were formed on the basis of teams of men who had come to know each other through the years because they worked regularly for the same contractors. The society of the yard was ideally a meritocracy of skill, tied together by mutual support and admiration for the qualities of men.

It is these same qualities of men that give managers and workers hope that a productive future could exist. For managers Subroto represents a larger than life figure who fully embodies the admired qualities of masculine technical skill. However, for workers it is their collective labor and its durable products that most display these qualities. Importantly, in both groups masculine skill is amplified by bringing it into relation with the eternal, cyclical rhythms of nature and ritual. It is through such representations of what we might call (after Arendt) *homo deus* that men sustain the hope that a productive future can be realized in the unstable, dangerous work conditions that surround them.

Shipyard Managers: Technical Charisma, Tides and the Fierce Beauty of Launches

At the muddy bank of the river in one of Venture Ltd's yards, I frequently used the wreck of a small hovercraft to climb from the shore onto barges that had come in for repair. I did not realize its significance until one morning the rumor spread that Subroto was trying again to build a hovercraft that would float 15 feet above the ground. This time, unlike the previous attempt (the remains of which I scrambled over), all the managers and supervisors were certain that he would be successful. They discussed how once Venture Ltd began to manufacture the hovercraft for clients such as the Indian Navy, all their fortunes would rise. Men insisted that I immediately take a look at the prototype Subroto was working on. When I reached the yard, all the middle managers were clustered on a raised pallet bent over the prototype cobbled together from a large industrial fan and plywood. They tenderly looked at the parts of the machine and discussed its technical details. Looking on all around were workers who had strolled in, hearing the news. Everyone had stopped work to take in the sight. The collective feeling of awe and expectation was palpable. Subroto was a larger than life, exemplary man who could change everyone's fortunes through his technical skill and daring.

This atmosphere of excitement also surrounded one other, more frequent event—Subroto "fairing the curves" in the planning loft. Subroto would supplant the meticulous authority of the loftsman, who had spent two weeks drawing the outline of a vessel or block on the smooth iron surface. The lines mapped onto the loft are three-dimensional sections of the hull drawn on a grid using strings and chalk. They are carefully placed according to mathematical formulas to match CAD plans. Many supervisors and managers told me I should watch Subroto's interventions that led to a "beautifying of the curves." At the loft Subroto rushed over to me to explain that on the computer you can't "feel the perfection" of the curve of the vessel. Subroto then set about changing the dimensions of the curves by 3 inches or more by freehand drawing. The marker in the planning loft, a senior experienced man, was left in his wake to correct all the other relational measurements. He did this in a dutiful but depressed fashion for another week. The middle managers and supervisors discussed at length with me the fact that only Subroto could draw the lines with a free hand like that. No one else, they said, had the skill and courage on such a scale to dare to do this. Such assertions were followed by excited speculation about how Subroto had managed to bring foreign work to the yard and what future prospects for the business there were. Subroto was admired for his opaque abilities to tap into hidden networks with his daring and skill.

Subroto's exemplary charisma was amplified by his knowledge of the Hooghly, in particular of the cyclical rhythms of its tides. Whenever managers spoke of the river it was strongly associated with the myth of Ma Ganga and the ritual uses of the purifying power of Ganga water. Commentary on the river's nature and the ability of Subroto to tap into natural rhythms contained a sense of the imminent divine in nature. In particular, managers referenced Ma Ganga's force, which was manifested during her descent to earth when Siva had to catch her in his locks in order to control her power. They had a shared passion for the more dramatic rhythms of the river and the river itself. They carefully photocopied pages from the tide table so I would remember to come at certain times to see these. They especially insisted that I should witness a bore tide. This is the periodic arrival of a wave upriver accompanied by a cooling wind that rushes along the Howrah bank in an abrupt display of the river's strength. One day I arrived in Subroto's office for an interview with him. His office overlooks the river, and he explained that he never closes his window because he has to have the wind coming in to remind him of the river. We talked for a while, and then Subroto suddenly jumped up, looked out of the window and then at his tide table. He said excitedly, "Have you ever seen a bore tide?" He then hurried me out of the office to the steps to the river. His whole body strained with excitement to see the wave coming. His enthusiasm was shared by his managers, who described Subroto as a man who was completely in tune with the force and rhythms of the Ganga.

These exemplary aspects of Subroto came together in what managers called the "fierce beauty" of ship launching. The first time I met Subroto he explained the technical feat of launching one of the vast ice class vessels sideways into the Hooghly. It had to be launched at the perfect still point between ebb and flood at night, during one of the deepest tides of the year. There were only ten minutes before the tide changed course. I asked why he had launched the vessel sideways. Subroto explained that "you can't pull the ship from the river, so instead you take the help of god [meant literally], which is called gravity." So I said knowledge of the river is vital for your work. Subroto said, "Yes I know it very well. I have sat 30 feet from it for the past thirty years." All the managers in turn played me their DVDs of this launch, which for them fully expressed the divine nature of the river in perfect combination with Subroto's skill. This was most clearly described to me by one manager, Udeep. He explained that the shipyard contained a fierce beauty and that was what I should write about. He added that he had seen this most vividly when the ice class vessel was launched. He went on to describe this event:

For one hour before not a pin dropped, so silent in the yard that was usually so full of hammering, welding, etc. The only noise was Subroto-da announcing instructions for the letting off of charges gradually step by step under the boat. All the VIPs were on a launch in the river. Everything was silent until the boat hit the water. Then there was a spontaneous shout from every single worker in the yard. Everyone came out of the office and everyone danced with everyone else all together. That is fierce beauty.

Udeep continued to explain that the most intense fierce beauty he had ever seen was in the Sundarbans at the place where land ends and it is only water. He continued: "There is a Bengali saying—this is where you go when the last blow of the broom comes down on you. This is the place where there is the last blow of land before the ocean. This is fierce beauty where death and beauty and the river are all mixed together."

Fierce beauty is a sublime aesthetic that combines awe at the vastness of nature and a terror of the fragile mortality of humans. The Ganga is emblematic of this, since for Hindus it is associated with funeral rites and ancestral rituals. It also holds the possibility of rebirth and purification. As Udeep explained, there is a solace in the mixture of terror, beauty and the river in which you acknowledge your vulnerable mortality and transcend it. According to managers Subroto had become the orchestrator of a technological sublime in the launching of ships (Nye 1992, 1994). He towered over these events with his agency uniting men in extraordinary achievements. He worked with the rhythms of a divine nature and technical skill combining them in vast acts of productivity in which men's vulnerability is for a moment transcended. Subroto's extraordinary powers gave managers the hope that the unstable, dangerous short-term capitalism of the yard would yield a prosperous future for them all. These powers were amplified into those of a *homo deus* through Subroto's association with the cyclical rhythms of the river that are understood to be manifestations of the imminent divine in nature.

Shipyard Workers: The Burning of the Stomach, Vishwakarma and Collective Powers

Shipyard workers were bitter about the chronically uncertain, short-term and dangerous environment of Venture Ltd. They complained about the lack of unions and the complicity of local union representatives and politicians with Subroto. They explained that the company used them until their bodies became injured or aged and then they would throw them away. They "insured" themselves against these by daily household pujas to Kali. During Kali puja they filled their neighborhoods with many small pandals to the goddess put up by two or three related or friendly households. Yet they asserted that pujas to Kali (especially the one held by Subroto after a man was decapitated in the yard) could not on their own resolve the instability of their work. For that they would need a real, genuine union or political advocates.

Workers ethically grounded their political analysis in claims that their situation was generated by an amoral individualistic appetite, which they called "the burning of the stomach." It was this corrosive force that they suggested had led to the lack of care for them or recognition for their work. It was demonstrated by Subroto's selfish acts of consumption, such as the purchase of expensive foreign cars for managers to use. They argued that they were gradually dying as a result of this individualism.

This ruthless hunger is destructive. It was described as the antithesis of the collective sociality expressed in domestic and public pujas in which food blessed by deities is shared. This sociality that recognizes reciprocity and connection makes the forces of life (*shakti*) expand, while the individualistic burning of the stomach extends uncertainty, decay and death. Importantly, workers described their skill, acts of labor and products of work as manifestations of this same productive life.

This became clear to me as men would make a repeated gesture in the yard. They would place their hand on the side of the ships they were constructing and affirm with emotion, *E shorir amra shorir*, "This body is our body." Some of them would expand on this claim. They would map physical functions on to parts of the ship. Others saw the ship as a man lying down. For example, Anup Haldar, a supervisor who had risen up the ranks in Venture Ltd, said, "The spine is the keel plate; the first section of the ship that is made at the beginning and supports the rest. The ship is like a man lying on their back with their head at the prow and feet aft. Then there are the ribs—that when you are building the ship look exactly like an x-ray of a human being." Each time someone spoke of this they would map the ship onto their body gesturing with their hands. The attraction of this image was very strong, particularly since the seams on the ship were x-rayed each night to check for leaks or weaknesses. It also had a compulsive pull because when yard overseers gave instructions to men they would draw the plan of the parts of the ship on the other man's body. Every time the center line of the ship was referred to, men would slice this line down from their foreheads along their own body. But this was stronger than an image for workers, since they insisted that the ship took the incarnation, *roop*, of a man, not that it was just like a man in shape. This word *roop* is associated with the ritual moment when priests make idols alive with community sacrifices at the beginning of puja cycles. The ship was experienced and described as a scaled-up body produced from the sacrifice of the collective energy of workers. It was inhabited by this energy too. When you work in the ship you can feel this because it shudders slightly as if it is alive and is filled with the sound of echoes of labor. Workers often remarked on these and smiled when I said the ship felt *shojib*.

Men also talked explicitly of how their *shakti* passed into the ship during their acts of labor. Vishwajeet Sikdar, a forty-year-old welder, and Bharavi, his seventeen-year-old helper, talked one day about how their work diminishes their *shakti* and how they have to eat bananas (*kola*) and milk (*dud*) both to take away the sting of the fumes in their lungs from welding and to revive their *shakti*. Vishwajeet added: "When you are old and worn out, all your *shakti* is gone, then the company will

not care. They will throw you away and you will just not be able to get work." The life that disappears from a person through the course of labor enters into the ship itself and makes it alive. In fact the ship is not an alienated object, but a durable *res publica* that allows workers to perceive their individual power amplified into a collective achievement through sacrifice.

Workers sought recognition for this sacrifice and their skill in the annual Vishwakarma puja in the yard. Vishwakarma puja is held every year on 17 September. For the working classes of Kolkata it marks the start of the puja season. It is widely understood as the time when machinery is worshipped and as the occasion for the heads of firms to feed their employees (in a gesture of reciprocal sustenance) a meal of meat and alcohol by their own hands. Lavish celebrations are sponsored by unions, where they operate. In Venture Ltd this puja takes a specific form that emphasizes workers' acts of skilled labor. Men's powers are amplified into those of a *homo deus* and are given permanence in the cyclical return of this ritual. This was visible to me when I spent the puja day in the yard.

Early in the morning, men were taking small children dressed in their best clothes inside the yards to see the ten idols paid for by contractors. In the absence of managers, workers had appropriated all the spaces of work. For example, the office peon, Taksheel, was in charge in the main office arranging the offerings to a huge Vishwakarma idol that had been set up there with a set of neatly rolled plans for the ship next to it. Workers crowded the office taking *prasad* and raising their hands to the *thakur*. Near the *thakur* was a small toy boat floating in a steel tank of water. A little boy brought by his father said, "What is that, Dad?" excitedly. The democracy of technical skill was being asserted through these appropriations of space, but alongside this the *shakti* and sacrifice of men was made manifest.

This became even clearer as a young welder, Sudhir Laskar, and his friend Aritra, a fitter, led me around the yard saying, "Let me show you all round inside the ship, all our work." We climbed up inside and he carefully led us into the second tank area, describing in detail all the technical requirements—Why the tanks were there, how the seams were made, and all the testing that was done. Another man came in to see what we were doing, a welder too, and they began to talk about the most difficult positions to weld in. They had to lie on their backs facing upward in the back section of the ship and the sparks flew into their faces. Sudhir kept displaying his technical knowledge of the ship—that it would have hydraulic pumps here and why it had water tanks so that it could pump in water when it was empty and not roll over. As we walked back through the dark passage into the first tank area of

the ship, I asked Sudhir why this was such a special day for them. He said, "Because we are Vishwakarmas we are men of *loha* (iron, steel), so for that reason we celebrate today." We walked past the huge cranes festooned with flowers, and one of the workers came up and gave us his *prasad* to eat—wanting us to share it with him. As we walked toward the planning loft where I had watched Subroto fairing the curves, I saw the area was full of workers. In the loft above the lines marked on the steel was another *thakur* of Vishwakarma. This was placed on the seat of knowledge and skill with the puja in progress. Workers had taken over the nearby managers' office too. We sat down in here because the rain was suddenly fierce. I asked Sudhir how his day had begun. He said he came at dawn to the yard and cleaned all his tools properly and did his own puja over them. This, he added, was the most important thing that he had to do right today. I asked, "What would happen if they did not worship Vishwakarma on this day and do the puja properly? Would it mean that their work would be spoiled or they would have accidents?" Sudhir said, "No, not like that. This is a puja that makes our minds calm and focused so that we can do good work; it does not protect us. We worship Vishwakarma because he is a very highly skillful man so he helps to make us skillful." Aritra said to me, "Once only when we were in Garden Reach they allowed us to bring all our families on Vishwakarma day. Before that none of our family cared or thought or felt emotion about our work. But afterward they too started to feel the emotions we feel for the work." I looked around and realized this was exactly why so many people had brought their young sons and daughters. The workers had taken over the yard, their place of labor and the ships, the product of their labor for one day. They worshipped themselves in the absence of their managers as skillful, powerful men with technical knowledge. Around them stood the permanent products of their work that as *res publica* manifested their collective sacrifice and skill. The durable quality of the steel that they worked on (they always called it *loha,* or iron) also became a quality of themselves as men of iron. For one day their vulnerability and the uncertainties of their work were overcome in an assertion of their permanent skill, ironlike strength and life-giving sacrifice. Their collectivity was made up of enduring *homo dei.*

The significance of the recognition associated with Vishwakarma puja was made even plainer because of events on that specific day. Subroto did not properly acknowledge his workers' productive powers. He had not given them packets of food with his own hand. To add to the insult he had sent small packets of vegetables and sweets not *mangsho* (meat). Talking with workers the next day I found that they were intensely angry. They complained that they felt *oshuk* (unwell, unhappy),

that Subroto was not giving them the strength of *mangsho* so they could work. Others complained that at the Shalimar yard because there is a tie up with the union they give you huge amounts of food and drink, but here they give nothing. The spiral of *oshuk* continued in the weeks to come as more and more workers complained to me that their contribution had not been fully recognized at Vishwakarma puja. They said that here was the final sign that the burning of the stomach was in control in the yard. Any men who could, especially skilled, unmarried young men, left to try their luck in other workplaces.

Not surprisingly, workers had a different interpretation of the launching of ships from that of managers. They did not see these events as the culmination of Subroto's technical charisma, but of their own collective productive powers as *homo dei*. Men explained that the recent launching of the ice class ship was the same as the immersion of the Vishwakarma image that ends the festival with the lifeless idol entering the *Ganga*. For example, Rahi Mondal, one of the team supervisors, said: "The immersion time of Vishwakarma is like the launching of the ship. When you launch a ship and immerse the idol you have the same emotions and feeling. You do the same things, singing and dancing and putting it into the *Ganga* at last." The arrangements for launches cross the forms of pujas and immersions: the ship is decorated with flowers; a coconut is smashed on its hull by the owner of the ship; loudspeakers blare Hindi film music; and there is dancing after the launch. All workers spoke of how incredible these events were because all the men danced together in joy (*annondo*). They said that at the launching of the ice class vessel in particular they had experienced the greatest joy (*annondo*) of their lives. As we watched a DVD of the ice class launching together (which I had received from Subroto), men pointed out the vast shadows cast by floodlights on the hull of the ship. These were the giant figures of workers made huge as they danced in celebration of their powers. In launches (as well as in Vishwakarma puja) the durable product of labor formed a *res publica* for workers in which their joint achievement of a technological sublime was visible.

Caught within the uncertain, short-term capitalism of Venture Ltd, shipyard workers asserted the value of their skill and labor. They understood their bodies, acts of work and products as manifestations of vast, durable and eternal life-forces. The cyclical return of Vishwakarma puja each year sustained their trust in these forces. However unstable their future and worn out their bodies, they were Vishwakarmas (*homo dei*), men of iron united within a democracy of technical skill. This scaled-up ethics of labor provided the ground for their demands for recognition.

From within it workers judged the politics and economics guided by the burning of the stomach and found it immoral. This ethics had its limits. It filled the workplace with Hindu associations, which left the non-Hindu workers in the yard apart, not sharing in public emotions. For example, when I asked Muslim workers about their experience of the launch of the ice class vessel, they looked puzzled and said it was nothing important because their work would continue both before and after the event in the same oppressive rhythms and difficult conditions. They did not attend Vishwakarma puja, nor did they share in the multiplying emotional crescendo of the puja season that it inaugurates. There were limits to the class solidarities generated out of the new short-term capitalism of Venture Ltd.

Conclusion

In Venture Ltd the contradictions of austerity capitalism are experienced as problems of time—in particular of permanence and of predicting the future. Once again as on the Hooghly among river pilots it is the dimension of time that thickens with dilemmas and impossibilities. Many theories of capitalism predict that the use of abstract time-measures as the basis for wages and a drive to intensification of surplus value extracted during the working day would lead to conflicts at the level of experienced time (Negri 2003; Postone 1993). Others focus on how present forms of capitalism aim for greater speed in realization of value (Castells 2000; Harvey 1989; Hope 2006). Anthropologists have noted that we seem to live in an age of uncertain futures that they link to the mobility of capital or the time-horizons of neoliberal economic policy (Comaroff, Comaroff and Weller 2001; Guyer 2007). Here I have offered a different approach to contemporary conflicts in and of time. I have analyzed why time in particular is experienced as a problem, diagnosing the constellation of government policies, market activities and political relations that make it problematic. Then, at a separate level of analysis, I have traced the technologies, representations, social disciplines of time and rhythms in time that have to be mediated in the act of labor in order for accumulation to occur. Finally I have followed the emergence of ethical understandings of individual and collective agency in time from these experiences of labor. Many of the anthropological and sociological accounts of capitalist time focus on only one or another of these elements. In addition, without this separation of analytical levels we are in danger of collapsing together representations, ethical debates, technologies and experiences of time (Bear 2014). We would be left with a partial or misleading account of both conflicts in time and of the social relations that they emerge from.

Arendt first raised these questions of temporality, labor and ethical action for us. Yet we need to push beyond her answers. She was writing in a world divided politically along the lines of the Cold War and that in the immediate postwar period appeared to be moving toward the dominance of socialist and capitalist mass production and large-scale capital investment. Our austerity capitalism is profoundly different from that and more similar to a longer history of capitalism (Yanagisako 2012; Tsing 2005). As I have shown in these two chapters its rhythms are short term, producing precarity and acts of labor that are difficult to realize. Such conditions stimulate and diversify ethical engagement. In this case they are associated not with an *animal laborans* or even a *homo faber*, but a *homo deus*. This *homo deus* overcomes uncertainty by associating their powers with the permanence and eternal return of the life forces of nature and the divine. I would expect this figure to be much more widely present within all forms of capitalism than has been so far acknowledged. The postwar period was an exception to the usual precarity and disorder of capitalism. And even Marx, as Arendt herself pointed out, grounded his vision of the essential productivity of the act of labor in a secularized version of the Protestant transcendent divine.

This figure of *homo deus* grounds claims that the act of labor is productive, creating a greater abundance of life in the face of death. What is potentially excluded from this ethics is an acknowledgment of the waste and destruction that labor can cause. But shipyard workers simultaneously assert the expansive power of labor *and* that it involves a sacrifice. They also measure productive action according to the social relationships it generates of individual selfishness or mutuality. As we will see in the next, concluding section, this makes their ethics of labor different from any other form on the Hooghly. It is possible to generate a new measure of value from their ethics—a social calculus that has profound political implications.

Section V

Beyond Austerity

Fig. 8. Viswakarma puja on the planning loft at Venture Ltd

Conclusion 1

Toward a New Social Calculus

IN ANTHROPOLOGY AND SOCIOLOGY, reference to a calculus brings to mind a very particular approach to the economy. This is associated with the analysis of economization or the "divergent analyses scholarly and lay that define, explain and enact economic forms of life" (Caliskan and Callon 2010, 2). Such work has focused on the formal, heuristic theories of the economy, institutional and technical arrangements and valuation processes (Li Puma and Lee 2004; Miyazaki 2013; Riles 2011). It has emphasized the diversity of calculi through which the world becomes economic. Yet my ethnography has navigated a quite different path, and now I will deploy it to argue for a theoretical and political counterpoint to such approaches. This is encapsulated in the concept of a social calculus.

What do I mean by a social calculus? To answer this question let us reflect on what my ethnography has revealed about processes of economization. My account began with a transformation in the form of state debt, which was redefined by technocrats as a solely economic problem and was tied into financial market mechanisms. So far, it would seem that my approach follows a focus on calculative reason and its ordering of relations between humans, technologies and the world. Yet the observation of this new framing was only a starting point for my investigation of the divergent social calculi, conflictual social relations and unstable infrastructures that were let loose by these new calculations. My ethnography followed these far beyond the markets in sovereign debt, into the crises, ethical dilemmas, contradictions in time and precarious forms of accumulation that a commitment to them generates. What makes my approach different, therefore, is that I reveal the hidden socialities of economic life generated in relation to formal calculi. Rather than focusing solely on heuristic acts of valuation and exchange, I trace their relationship to acts of labor and productivity. In this I make a move parallel to Marx's tracking the implications of the schemas of capitalist exchange for social relations. While there is room for attention to inequality and accumulation in approaches that focus on economization, much of the research oriented toward this examines a bracketed universe of calculi apart from the disordered diverse capitalism they are part of (Bear et al. 2015).

How then should we understand this diverse capitalism? What exactly are the relations between calculi and the diverse social? How can a focus on labor help us to answer these questions? Importantly, attention to acts of work (those of bureaucrats and financial experts seeking to govern the economy as well as to those of people laboring to produce within it) reveals the centrality of the conduct of productivity to capitalism. As Ho, Yanagisako and Zaloom have argued, economic practices are enacted as part of the pursuit of becoming a particular kind of person, family or community (Ho 2009; Yanagisako 2002; Zaloom 2004). It is therefore explicitly ethical projects that frame economic action as part of acts of labor. As wages or profits are sought through the mediating action of labor in specific timespaces, capitalist measures of value become associated with acts of judgment and self-fulfillment. The forms of these ethics are shaped in part by the experience of laboring to mediate between conflictual rhythms in time, technical devices and recalcitrant nonhuman things. These ethics often project large-scale productive powers in the world, drawing on the forms of ritual and kinship. In this book, as a counterpoint to most recent accounts of the economy, I have particularly focused on the ethics or "senses of workmanship" that are generated in labor. These both emerge unpredictably from, and underpin, the legitimacy of the contradictory social and class relations of capitalism. When viewed from the analytical perspective of labor (rather than of exchange), the economic is always an ethical arena in which subjectivity, community and the public good are at stake.

The calculi described in accounts of economization act as technical translation devices between divergent ethical projects and their associated social relations. They enable people to convert different forms of value through a grid of comparability in an apparently neutral fashion. They also sustain the separation of these forms of value from each other. They are a line of demarcation, transformation and hidden struggle supported by the authority of international political institutions and states (Mitchell 2007; Carrier and Miller 1998). In this book we have encountered many of these, including economic projections, figures of public deficit, debt contracts, fiscal targets, wages and outsourcing agreements. The most significant one has been the mechanism of state debt, which, as I have shown, fundamentally affects the forms taken by livelihoods, politics, market and state institutions. It also gives life to wide-reaching political, ethical and fiscal obligations that are not explicitly written into its formal agreements. As I have shown throughout the book, we cannot read off the conduct of productivity, its ethics or social relations from the explicit content of economizing devices such as state debt. Instead we must analyze these for what they are—grids of conversion between divergent forms of value and their associated social relations. It is true that their technocratic, calculative forms have increased in significance in recent decades through the rising influence of economic technocrats within international and national organizations (Anders 2008, 2010). However, it is not accurate to suggest that capitalism is now sustained by a calculative, marketizing ethic or the acceptance of this as a ground for social relations. As always, capitalism generates, and consists of, a diversity of ethical forms and social relations. Without these no profits could be made from acts of conversion between various kinds of exploitation and accumulation (Tsing 2009, 2015).

Once we put economizing devices in their place, it also becomes evident that it is not sufficient to focus on practices of valuation. Instead, equally crucial are prospective practices of speculation. These, as I have shown (especially in Chapter 4), are particularly central to current market and state relations. Speculation is different from valuation in its temporal orientation. It seeks to discern hidden, opaque, expansive and incalculable future possibilities beyond the surface of things. It proceeds through social entanglements most epitomized by the relations of *jogajog kora*, in which it is the formation of creative relationships that is sought. Speculation is the unacknowledged twin of the transparent processes of valuation. It is expunged from formal calculative devices and from the discipline of economics or even economic sociology, which reduces it to a question of information flow or trust within markets (Bear 2015). We need to recognize its significance in our analytical approaches. Otherwise we will miss new features of the present that include speculative state planning and its volatile, unequal outcomes. We are also at risk of underestimating the degree to which the conduct of productivity proceeds not through information exchange or trust, but through the performance of charismatic personas, secrecy, complicity and fear.

Finally attention to a social calculus casts new light on the significance of material infrastructures. Materiality, networks and nonhuman agency have figured large in analyses of "agencement" or how technical and logistical infrastructures affect the competencies, skills and emotions of humans as they act economically. Throughout my account of the infrastructures of global trade on the Hooghly, I have traced a different insight. It is important to study infrastructures because they are technical *res publica,* or public things, that extend political community in time and space. They provide a figurative *topos* of a public in relation to which individual political and ethical judgments are made (Marshall 2010). Some forms of infrastructure can contribute to the emergence of a generation of care for the world. Others do not provide such a ground, but undermine the possibility for politics because they limit the "space of appearance" of humans to humans (Arendt 1958, 1968, 1982). So the study of infrastructures matters because they are a ground for political and ethical encounters between citizens. Once again I am placing the human social at the center of my account. To do this I have adapted Arendt's discussion of political action and *res publica,* moving beyond her typologies of labor, work and action. For Arendt, infrastructure, or the durable products of labor that provide the "home for mortal men," would have belonged to the realm of homo faber and work (1958). In her schema infrastructure, which is a product that is not consumed, could provide solace to people caught up in the world of labor, or *animal laborans,* as a form of durable solidity in the endless cycle of labor and consumption. But she would have expected infrastructure to be associated with the politics and ethics of *homo faber*. This politics she describes as utilitarian, based on an ethic of use value and the public space of the market. This is for her an inadequate politics because it focuses on utility and uses this to measure the value of the human. But I would like to rescue *homo faber* from this typology. I would also like to explore to what extent we can think of their products—including infrastructure—as *res publica*. Can we think of infrastructure as containing the potential to extend political community, make the human visible and as generative of senses of care for the world?

If we bring Simondon's work into dialogue with that of Arendt, it would seem that we might be able to think of infrastructure in this way. For Simondon the technician and the technical are not inevitably associated with a single utilitarian ethics. In fact, he argues that economistic values and technical values are not necessarily in alignment with each other. Human uniqueness is not obliterated by technological forms, but instead is supported by particular technological milieu (Combes 2013). Even more important, Simondon argues that technical objects contain a transposed human element with which humans can engage (1958). From this a politics and ethics different from that of economistic utilitarianism can emerge. Humans can relate to the human in technology. Through this recognition they can generate a relation to other humans and the machine form itself. I think that if we combine this approach with that of Arendt's *res publica,* we have a very productive way of understanding infrastructures. Infrastructures are not experienced as only nonhuman, nor are they necessarily permeated with a utilitarian ethic. They are a technical *res publica* that contains a human element. As such they can become the ground for the imagination of relations to other humans and to technological objects. They provide a figurative *topoi* for ethical judgment.

A key point throughout my book has been that the current financialized forms of infrastructures, such as those of global trade on the Hooghly, are particularly fragmenting in their effects. They generate disaggregated publics and classes starkly divided between state and market, and the public and informalized "sectors." Within these distinctions are made between productive and unproductive humans, with a consistent devaluation of private-sector contractual, precarious workers. What commonwealths exist are limited in their extent, focused on the well-being of segmented class groups. State employees focus on the historical resonances of infrastructures and interpret their own skill as a manifestation of a tradition of river labor. The political scale they relate their work and the infrastructures of the Hooghly to is that of the nation. The ordering principle in this ethics is the benevolent state, while disorder is created by the private sector. Private entrepreneurs enunciate and practice a public good of flexibility, making themselves and their firms as fluid as the revolutions in capital. For them work is related to the scale of the family. The ordering principle is that of transcendent capital, while disordering principles originate in the state. In these ethics the mutual interdependence of state and private-sector institutions on the river is rendered invisible. Most significantly, these commonwealths bracket ethics from politics, focusing on caring relations with the river or attention to the needs of the nation. Yet there is, as we will see, one ethic that refuses these segregations. This is an ethic of labor and life among informalized shipyard workers and their families. This radically points to the significance of a totalizing social calculus that is applied to all forms of economic activity. By now turning to an account of this ethic I will reveal it as the foundation for my theoretical and political critique throughout this book.

Shipyard workers and their families are members of an established working class in Howrah that stretches back at least three generations. These men and women deploy a social calculus based on a scaling up of the household and its kin relations, to judge urban, capitalist relations. Labor for them should be for the generation and amplification of life and sociality (something expected from peasant, but not capitalist, contexts; see Gudeman 2001, 2008; Harris 2007). They understand all participants in the river economy, whether private or state sector, as equally subject to the judgments of this ethic. This ethic is totalizing and cosmopolitical in its analysis, uniting domains that all other participants in the river economy hold apart. As explained in the previous chapter, the inequalities of capitalist relations are understood as an expression of "the burning of the stomach," or individualistic, selfish appetites that cause disordered social relations. Labor, on the other hand, was associated with the expression of a life-force (*shakti*). This was renewed in the rituals of Vishwakarma puja that made men into enduring *homo dei*. This life-force encompasses not just the workplace but also the household. Even more significantly, it is associated with the reproductive, fertile power and long-term kinship ties of the household that are scaled up through rituals to the goddess Ma Monosha. This ethic is expressed in accounts and ritual practices that link the cosmos, the household, work and the city.

The majority of men who work at Venture Ltd live with their extended families in working-class neighborhoods along the Andul road. Women work nearby, stitching in small garment units, doing piecework at home or providing domestic labor. Social connections are built around uncles and brothers in the paternal line who live close together, clustered in the narrow lanes. Their one-room mud houses are constructed gradually on land on which they have squatted. There is a large amount of intermarriage between families in these neighborhoods. This is achieved through arranged marriages negotiated as part of male friendships at work or love marriages that develop from friendships formed during local festivals.

Each single household is described as a segment of a total family that is formed by a group of brothers arranged in precedence by birth order. They share a lineage (*bongsho*) linked by "blood" (*rokto*) from which sisters move out and into which wives are adopted. The ideal household would be that of all the brothers and their wives grouped in a single home of connected one-room buildings. The movement of sisters out of these homes through marriage is a necessary evil that reduces the wealth and productive power of the family. It is necessary because the life force of women is only realized through their reproductive role and work as wives. As a proverb among these families expresses, "A woman is born in one house and works in another." Marriage is necessary too because it strengthens the productivity of the household in another way: it creates ever-widening networks of *kutum,* or in-laws. The formation of *kutum* is an expansive practice that draws extensive social networks into the orbit of households. Your *kutum* are not only relatives through marriage but also those people with whom you have strong friendships in neighborhoods and workplaces. Friends are also part of the *kutum.* These expansive networks are mobilized for the metasociality of festivals and for practical help. *Kutum* are made through the sharing in puja celebrations, through working together and, most important, are expressed by eating in one's home.

The civic world of the city is understood through these household kinship terms and practices. Neighborhoods are described as formed by ties of *kutum*, actual and potential allies in marriage and friendship. Calling friends *kutum* (wife-takers) places them in a hierarchical relationship with you that can never be ended. It is a social debt that demands long-term connection and leads to a constant flow of food, information and affection between households. The outermost limits of these ties is the boundary of ancestral origin (*gotro*), or what is commonly described as caste status. Within the universe of the city the broadest circle of connection is "type of person" (*jati*). This aspect of identity is imagined as constructed upward from the essential household ties of *bongsho*, *kutum* and *gotro*. It is marked by a variety of kinds of distinction from region, religion and nation, but not caste, which should not limit sociality. The city is described as a collection of *jatis* arranged like the five fingers on one hand. They are all different, but they all have both good and bad people within them. Humanity is achieved through a progressive construction upward from the household and its particular forms of identity, which are minimal guarantees of being human. Ties at all levels should ideally be marked by affection (*bhalobasha*) and trust (*bishash*). These affective ties are quite distinct from the temporary ties of monetary relations because they take time and effort to forge.

The sharing of food is central to creating these ties of affection and *bishash* that join society together. Its agency provides the wellness and fertility of individuals and households, and its offering and consumption are a sign of acceptance of a relationship. Collective eating and sociality, especially during rituals, provides the source and expression of life-sustaining relationships. It also dramatically displays the productive fertility of households and neighborhoods in the numbers of people eating together and the quantities of food that are offered. These displays reach their highest and most accentuated form in the ritual of Ranna puja, which is twinned with Vishwakarma puja. The paired rituals link together all forms of productive power in a spectacular display of the work, fertility and sociability that is necessary for their continuing realization. These practices deploy a deeper history of Monosha puja within a new urban form. This festival is associated with village rituals of agricultural fertility. Monosha puja is now the basis for Ranna puja, or cooking puja, which conjoins the world of the household and the world of urban labor. Shipyard workers and their families describe Ranna and Vishwakarma puja as first in the annual cycle of celebrations, which create "joy" (*annondo*) and will make the family and its work "stay well" (*bhalo thake*). "Staying well" is an inclusive phrase that involves prosperity, *sukh* (individual good health and happiness), fertility and prevention of accidents. *Annondo* is an equalizing, shared emotion associated only with pujas that is amplified as more people take part in rituals together. The twinned practice of Ranna and Vishwakarma pujas exactly materializes the desired circulations of productive power or *shakti*.

Ranna, or "cooking," puja is the collective project of households. Families join financial resources and women cook together with no "selfishness" (*hingso*) for the celebration. Preparations for both Ranna puja and Vishwakarma puja start on 16 September. Wives and mothers in law clean the household together with the usual domestic tools such as *shil nora* (grinding stone). They use a wide range of sacred resources to purify the house. These include, Ganges water (*ganga jol*), and basil water associated with Siva (*tulsi jol*). Simultaneously, men clean all their tools and machinery at their workplaces with Ganges water. Women take the opportunity to make this act of cleaning a dramatic display of their daily routines—complaining how hard and difficult these are. Each assertion makes visible their contribution of work to the fertility of the household alongside that of their husband and his brothers. Extra labor is also required for the festival because multiple, complicated dishes are cooked to be offered to the goddess Ma Monosha. These are placed on the floor in a "beautiful" display, given to Ma Monosha and then eaten by people in the household and the closest *kutum*, people who belong to the mother's uncle's house (*mamabari*). On the morning of the 17th women carry out a domestic puja to the goddess Monosha at the same time men worship Vishwakarma in the yards. On this day extended networks of *kutum* come to eat with you. Houses overflow with people who are the materialization of the household's productive powers. People eat together in an acceptance of idealized relationships of mutual sustenance. When men celebrate their own status as *homo deus* in Vishwakarma puja, this is part of a larger practice of recognizing the productive powers of life. This life flows from households, into neighborhoods and civic relations as well as the workplace. Its existence elicits a series of long-term social obligations based on kinship that should cross-cut all of these spaces. It is expressed and realized in long-term relations of trust and affection that are quite different from the short-term monetary ties associated with "the burning of the stomach." Ideally, work should be an act that takes place as part of reciprocal circulations of life. It is encompassed within a social calculus—how much social productivity it materializes and supports.

The mythology of Ranna and Vishwakarma puja further scales up the life-forces of these rituals to the cosmopolitical. They connect the affection and trust that creates life among humans to the reciprocity between humans and the divine. Shipyard families state that Ranna puja and Vishwakarma puja are held on the same day because of the role of the man-god in the myth of Behula and Lokhindar. They then relate this story of the confrontation between a wealthy ship merchant, Chandsadagar, and Mother Monosha, the snake-goddess. Monosha is banished from heaven by Siva. He orders her to return only if she can acquire a large number of worshipers. She appears to Chandsadagar and requests him to worship her, but he rejects her. She then becomes vengeful, vowing to end all of his prosperity and fertility. She kills all of his sons while they are voyaging on his vessels. A few years later another son, Lokhindar, is born who, when he reaches adulthood, decides to wed Behula. Behula tries to protect Lokhindar from Monosha on their wedding night. She asks Vishwakarma to build an iron room for them to safely sleep in. Monosha forces Vishwakarma to make a small hole in the corner of the room. On the wedding night Monosha's favorite snake enters through this and kills Lokhindar. Behula carries his body downriver to the kingdom of the gods on a boat of banana leaves built by Vishwakarma. Once there she vows to worship Monosha herself and to persuade Chandsadagar to carry out grand pujas for her. Lokhindar is restored to life. How then, do people relate this story of the importance of trust (*bishash*) or mutual recognition between goddesses and humans for the continuance of life to the household and shipyard?

For both men and women, Chandsadagar is a great ship company owner like Subroto Chatterjee who founded Venture Ltd. When women recount the myth they focus on the struggle for recognition of Monosha as a female goddess, and a woman, whose *bishash* was denied. Women make her the center of the drama, echoing the emphasis on women's productivity and fertility that is recognized in Ranna puja. When men tell this myth they narrow in on the role of Vishwakarma in the story. They forgot that he had been intimidated by Monosha. Instead they assert that he had made the room "water-tight" to protect a fellow man, Lokhinder, but due to technical constraints—he had to get out of the room at the end of the work—a hole had been left. Yet they also emphasize *bishash* as the core theme of the myth. It was in conversations around this myth that the multiple contexts for *bishash* were explicitly linked. As Rajas Biswas explained:

See, Laura has been to my house about ten times! There is special trust. That is what is important; without *bishash* nothing can be. I have an unwritten contract with my contractor.

My only contract with him relies on *bishash*. She has *bishash* in my family so she comes to my house. *Bishash* is everything to a man and to the gods and goddesses too.

For women it is *bishash* as trust in the fertile power of female goddesses that is significant, linked to the recognition of the productive powers of women. For men it is the expansive social meanings of *bishash* that create obligations between men that are most salient. Overall, the myth of Monosha and its associated pujas affirm an ethic in which flows of life (which generate fertility and productivity) can only be maintained if long-term ties of obligation are honored. An absence of *bishash* will generate a world like that inhabited by the vengeful Monosha in which the forces of death and decay triumph.

In this ethic based on the obligations of the *oikos* acts of work, both female and male should be part of reciprocal flows of life between people who recognize their obligations to each other. Labor should exist only in the context of long-term social debts and mutual recognition of these debts. Labor belongs to life and life is for creating more reciprocal flows of life. Economic activity here is placed inside a totalizing social calculus and judged by it. Although Arendt argued that such scaling up of the household was characteristic of the apolitical life of capitalism, with its emphasis on production and reproduction, this ethic is radical. It insists on the value of both female and male reproductive and wage labor as creative acts that express a cosmic life-force. It is a demand for recognition that capitalist relations should sustain precarious workers and create mutualistic ties of sustenance and obligation. It at times obscures exclusions from, and inequalities within, households and monetary debt dependencies between male friends. Its moral community also has a Hindu valence. Nevertheless it asserts an ethic of expansive community that places the rights of both male and female labor and mutuality at its center. It is this ethic that provides the foundation for my utopian arguments in my last, prospective chapter. Shipyard families provide us with a social calculus for measuring the economy that, as I will show, has radical political implications.

Conclusion 2

Sovereign Debt, Equality and Redistribution

Financial Crisis and New Opportunities

When the financial crisis hit in 2007–8, and as the "great recession" continued, my research into austerity policy on the Hooghly River suddenly took on new significance. Public-sector institutions across the world, and especially in Europe and America, entered into fiscal crisis. My findings could no longer be confined to a particular region. It was clear that the austerity policies applied from the 1980s in emerging and low-income countries in South Asia, Latin America and Africa were reaching new arenas. These shifts came close to me during this period. The UK civil service unit in which my husband worked was axed to make savings in public expenditure by the Conservative–Liberal Democrat government. My own university followed the policy mood, instructing all departments to cut their budgets by 3 percent shortly after the UK election of May 2010. The US fiscal crisis pressed in too. This book might never have been published. A series it was aimed for that was subsidized by the US federal government lost its funding because of congressional negotiations over the growing deficit in the fall of 2010. I do not mention these events because my experience was equivalent to that of the working poor on the Hooghly or elsewhere. I do so because these replays and echoes have important analytical and political potential.

The analytical opportunity created is the chance to forge a new approach to sovereign debt. Activists, legal scholars and economists have so far focused on sovereign debt crises in emerging and low-income countries. Their vitally important work followed the lead of the influential Jubilee movement for the cancellation of Third World debt of the 1990s. It focused on development inequality; exchanges between First and Third World economies and international financial institutions (IFIs) such as the IMF, World Bank and the regional development banks. But the recent extension of austerity policies means that we now need to take further steps. We have to develop a model of the relations and mechanisms of sovereign debt that encompasses the global situation. This needs to look beyond crisis to reveal the normal, everyday operations of public financing. It also must tackle the increasing importance of financial markets to sovereign debt policy. The first part of this conclusion offers such a model.

Through our experiences of the financial recession we also have an opportunity to rethink sovereign debt policy and its politics. Austerity measures across the world have made starkly clear the growing conflict between the social investment, redistributive and extractive techniques of state institutions. This contradiction pushes us to imagine innovations in government financing that will reinforce the redistributive aspects of government. In particular we are challenged to look beyond an economic definition of the public good toward other ethical and political possibilities. In the second part of this conclusion I assess new policy proposals for sovereign debt and public-sector financing. I weigh these according to a social calculus. In other words, according to how they affect social relations. I suggest that all government financing policy should be judged through such a frame. I will also propose some alternative approaches. My suggestions come from my analysis of the inequalities produced by the current relations and mechanisms of sovereign debt. I will end by commenting on how the financial crisis has created the potential for new solidarities. The volatility and inequality produced by relations of sovereign debt are finally, after thirty years, equally visible to people across the world. We can now generate collective projects that can lead to public demand to alter these relations.

An Anthropologist among Economists and Legalists

It is with tentative steps that I move into the territory of economists and legal scholars. In my arguments I draw greatly on their pioneering discussions of sovereign debt. Yet, what I add is an anthropological perspective. What is this anthropological perspective? Economic arguments focus on sovereign debt as a transaction between agents in a marketplace (Jochnick and Preston 2006; Herman, Ocampo and Spiegel 2010). For neo-Keynesians this interaction is affected by social externalities manifest in information asymmetries and these, in turn, generate further social impact (Stiglitz 2002, 2006, 2010a, 2010b). Microeconomists and public choice theorists influenced by Hayek show the "distortions" the state and politics introduce to sovereign debt decisions (Wagner 2013). Behavioral economists examine how decision-making associated with sovereign debt contracts is affected by social, emotional and cognitive factors (Kletzer and Wright 2000; Flandreau and Flores

2008). Legal arguments focus too on the nature of the contract between parties to sovereign debt. They seek ways to make these agreements more just in their effects within and between generations (Barry and Tomitova 2007; Gosseries 2007). An anthropological perspective starts from a different premise from all of these approaches. It begins with social relations, their ethics, politics and inequality. It does not accept that sovereign debt can be understood as a market exchange. Instead, it critically assesses the concept of the market. It explores how people use technologies, formal models and ethical assertions in order to construct such a realm of activity (Mitchell 2002; Zaloom 2006, 2009;Yanagisako 2002, 2013). It is this anthropological perspective that has been applied throughout this book. I have not tracked market interactions associated with sovereign debt. I have analyzed the diverse bureaucratic and popular ethics that combine to generate productive forms on the Hooghly. These emerge as a response to new sovereign debt policies that are *also* always ethical technologies. For an anthropologist, sovereign debt is a social relationship that is misrecognized as "only" a market exchange. To analyze it we would bring into view all the complex relationships it relies on and generates. Logically, therefore, it is only by tracking the effects of sovereign debt as a social relation that we can develop more equitable forms of it. I will offer such an analysis of contemporary relations of sovereign debt. This forms the foundation for my discussion of new opportunities for policy and political engagement.

An Ideal Type of Sovereign Debt

Much of the analysis of the recent financial crisis focuses on the practices that led to a freeze in the global banking system in 2007–8 (Krugman 2013; Reinhart and Rogoff 2009; Stiglitz 2010a; Tett 2010). The key elements in these events were new shadow banking and financing practices in the US corporate sector; the decline of banks' liquidity ratios; the growth of complex derivatives and securities based on volatile property markets; and credit bubbles caused by the extension of the Euro to peripheral states (Blyth 2013). These financial practices were supported by new kinds of risk analysis through calculation that developed from the 1980s. The limit of these techniques was that they could not include in their frameworks knowledge of the vast architecture that emerged from derivatives and securities (Lee and Li Puma and Lee 2004). The liquidity freeze in the international banking system certainly had complex proximate origins. However, we need to look beyond these immediate events in order to explain why government bailouts to the financial sector and austerity emerged as the "only possible" response. The events did not contain their own policy solution. Nor can the existence of economic theories of austerity alone (such as those of Alisina and Silvia Ardenya) explain the turn to them in the wake of the crisis. Instead we need to explore how the technical practices of state and market institutions pushed governments toward these measures. In particular, we need to trace the new relations and mechanisms of sovereign debt that have emerged since the 1980s. It is beyond the scope of this conclusion to fully outline this history. Instead, presented here is an ideal type. This is drawn from my historical ethnography of sovereign debt in India; policy documents from the OECD, IMF, World Bank and UNDP; and the writings of economists.

Before I move onto this ideal type, we should pause to consider the nature of sovereign debt. We need to do this in order to understand why *how* it is transacted matters so much for citizenship rights and equality. As economists have repeatedly puzzled over, sovereign debt is unlike any other form of credit relation. It is made up of obligations to repay that are uncollateralized by other assets. Instead, these obligations are taken on between debtors and creditors according to the perception of the reputation and power of the government. They are the responsibility of the total population of the country, which is bound in a political relationship with their sovereign. Sovereign debt contracts are a wager that a government has enough power to extract revenue from its citizens. They are guaranteed by social relations that are not within the market exchange. Hence many economists puzzle over whether democratic or authoritarian governments are more likely to repay their debts (Alichi 2008). They also wonder how, and if, corporate bankruptcy can ever be a model for sovereign default (Raffer 2007; Stiglitz 2010b). So, in sovereign debt, we have a market transaction that does not only obey the rules of market and monetary value. In its contracts political and ethical relationships are turned into a financial relationship. Sovereign debt contracts are the unstable mediators between two systems of value—political-ethical and monetary. They are also, therefore, a key arena for negotiation between market and state institutions. The current forms of sovereign debt are one historical development of this relation between the state and the market. These reduce the ability of governments to set their own policies. Instead, there is a strong tendency to change the public sector into a fiscally disciplined adjunct to the rules and rhythms of financial markets. This formation compromises the social investment and redistributive aspects of rule and leads to an intense extraction of value from public institutions. It has developed across low-income, transitional and emerging countries imposed by the lending practices and financial reforms of the international financial institutions such as the World Bank and IMF. Its features such as central bank independence and the use of repos were also put in place through the 1980s–90s in Europe through both legal imposition by EU treaties and the European Central Bank, along with enthusiastic adoption by some state governments. In the United States it existed in embryo in the Federal Reserve Act of 1913 but was not fully realized until the 1980s. As I have shown in the case of India and the Kolkata Port Trust, it has led to a progressive disestablishment of public-sector jobs, infrastructure and resources. What then are the social relations of sovereign debt that amplify market rules and rhythms? What are the ethics and mechanisms of value that orient these relations? What are the consequences for fiscal policy, politics and inequality when current forms of sovereign debt work "normally"?

The core social relation of sovereign debt is that between governments and central banks. Since the 1980s there has been a push from economic policy makers and IFIs to create central bank independence. From the foundation of the Bank of England, all of these (apart from the German Bundesbank and to some extent the Federal Reserve) had been entirely subject to the political will of sovereign governments. From the 1960s, public choice theory (led by George Stigler, James Buchanan, Richard Wagner, Finn Kydland and Edward Prescott) critiqued the failures of democratic governments to support the cyclical patterns of the economy (Blyth 2013). This argued that politicians could not be trusted to make the right fiscal decisions, as their policies were driven by short-term attempts to win electorates. Through the 1980s technocrats in central banks were given authority to set interest rates, manage government debt and control inflation. This model was pushed strongly by the IFIs as they set about "reforming" through loans, structural adjustment and HIPC initiatives in emerging and low-income economies. It also was applied across the UK and Europe as the European Union and the European Central Bank set new standards for government practices. Key elements of fiscal policy were no longer under the direct and sole control of politicians and civil servants.

Alongside this devolving of fiscal authority, new technical mechanisms exist that have altered the relationship between the government, central banks and financial markets. The old method of meeting public financing through automatic monetizing (the issuing of debt to the government and of money to the market/public—"printing money") has been rejected as a failed inflationary practice driven by political interests. Markets in public debt bonds have also been restructured to ensure that government borrowing is disciplined by the market (Arvani and Heinin 2008; Currie, Dethier and Togo 2003; IMF and World Bank 2003). Central banks have sought to develop thriving international and domestic primary and secondary markets in public debt bonds. Fiscal policy in relation to these financial markets is now handled as a single consolidated problem by specific technocratic bureau either within central banks, treasuries or by separate debt management offices. The ideal is that these offices should deal with sovereign debt as a technical issue of bond issuance and management. Their goals are to balance out monetary indicators of economic health and supply the government with the lowest possible cost funding. These offices formulate government debt management strategy within a corporate assets and liabilities management framework. Tax revenues, public resources and expenditures are now treated as budgetary risks similar to corporate risks that have to be offset by portfolio management by financial-sector experts. Within these institutions sovereign debt is detached from the political concerns of the state. It is governed and measured by the value systems of financial markets. It is also used to manage the supply of money in the "economy" rather than simply to provide funding for political projects. A survey of the central banks and debt managers in eleven countries in 1997 (Mexico, Italy, Spain, UK, Pakistan, Sweden, France, Japan, Canada, Ireland and the United States) captures the qualities of this practice well. They agreed that their aims were to:

adopt market based methods for the primary issuance of government debt; improve the liquidity of institutional investments in the secondary market; develop markets in derivatives in government debt; publicize to transmit signals to the market efficiently; develop an investor consultancy and relations program to serve the needs of investors and be transparent to them; develop regular reporting so "market makers," investors, credit ratings agencies have up to date information on the debt management programme ... [and to] convert private household savings into investments in bonds and derivatives.[1]

In the new forms of the "independent" central bank and debt management office, the needs of the market are made crucial to the management of sovereign debt. The rules and rhythms of the market are discerned and enforced. They become the orienting values for sovereign debt policy.

This subordination of fiscal policy to the rules and rhythms of markets continues in the technical uses of debt bonds and their derivatives. The central bank and/or debt management office assign privileged status to primary dealers (usually large global or national banks and investment firms). These "market-makers" are permitted to buy bonds and "repos." A repo is the sale of a government debt bond along with an agreement to buy it back at a later specified date at a price greater than the first sale price. The difference in price acts as interest on the loan. Repos were first used by the Federal Reserve in 1918, but since the 1980s they have become the primary mechanism used by central banks to manage monetary policy and by debt offices to manage government funds. They are also the architecture on which complex financial derivatives have developed (Choudhry 2006). They are now deployed to deflate or inflate the economy; cover over gaps in income; correct currency imbalances caused by trade or to provide cover for capitalizing guarantees. Primary dealers sell on derivatives from these bonds to other investors including further repos, futures and credit default swaps. These investors vary greatly from domestic pension funds or investment firms to international banks and global firms. Further contracts, such as securities based on sovereign debt, appear and expand once the secondary market is established.

Repos are central to the new relations of sovereign debt. They are the technical mechanism that mediates between the funding needs of the government, central bank decisions and financial market rhythms and productive action in the wider society. Although gilts and treasury bills (vehicles through which to buy government debt) have long existed, these were not the same in their effects as repos. These were contracts designed to deal with the provision of government funds that were only tied to the rhythms and needs of state institutions. Repos, on the other hand, are also a monetary management mechanism. They are traded on financial markets in order to support the rhythms of "the economy." They become the basis for an unpredictable derivatives and securities architecture. This means that their value and use will fluctuate according to the rhythms of market exchanges. This is a reversal of the original relationship between state and the market that existed in the foundation of central banks. In this older relationship, the sovereign guaranteed market exchanges. The ruler stood behind these with his/her autocratic power in exchange for bonds turned into money. But with the use of repos, the political and ethical power of the sovereign is hollowed out. Sovereign debt becomes subordinated to the value-giving practices and exchanges of the financial markets and the fluctuations of the economy. Primary dealers help governments to structure their bond offerings, market them and underwrite their issue (Herman 2007). Secondary dealers also are called upon for their financial expertise in government debt. The interests of the government, the central bank and the largest international banks are tightly tied together through these bond and repo mechanisms. There has been a change in the technical instruments of sovereign debt that reduces the ability of governments to assert a long-term political and ethical value for their fiscal policy.

These new relationships and mechanisms also make the fiscal policy of the government subject to the volatile behavior of investors. Economists have rightly argued that international and national creditors have practiced predatory lending to emerging and low-income countries since the 1980s. Private creditors, knowing that they will be bailed out by their own governments, continue to buy risky, high-return bonds and derivatives in sovereign debt (Stiglitz 2010b). This has been a profitable strategy for private creditors. In spite of write-downs and restructuring of emerging and low-income countries' debt, creditors have consistently made long-term yields in excess of other corporate bonds (Spiegel 2010). Commercial banks have been incentivized to lend more to riskier sovereign clients by the high yields on their bonds (Herman 2007). This has been further supported by the use of short-term quarterly reports to shareholders, which has oriented investors to quick profits. Their purchase of risky bonds and dumping of them back into the markets produce spikes and troughs in sovereign debt bond yields. Government bonds are usually just one part of an investment portfolio of securities, so they are bought and sold according to the trading rhythms in other equities, derivatives and securities. In recent years the rush of investors toward and away from them has come to echo the fortunes of other sovereign debtors and the peaks and troughs of the equities markets. This introduces unpredictable volatility in the costs of borrowing for governments. It also produces an intense attention to the sentiment of the markets. Increasingly, governments, central banks and debt management offices have been pushed toward a new kind of government fiscal measure. These are actions that support the sentiments of the markets in sovereign debt.

At the center of this management of the sentiment of the markets are the grades allocated by private ratings agencies, Standard and Poors, Moody and Fitch. These unaccountable organizations amplify volatile patterns of investment (Stiglitz 2010a). In the 1980s, for the first time, they began to rate the credit-worthiness of sovereign bond issuers rather than of individual bond issues. They began to adjudicate on the reputation of countries and their future prospects. In 1986, Moody and Standard and Poor's began to rate countries issuing securities not in US dollars so that subnational public-sector companies and municipalities could receive ratings and loans (Gaillard 2011). But it was the effects of the Brady plan in the 1990s that hugely raised the number of countries receiving sovereign ratings. The US treasury secretary, Nicolas Brady, led the move to reduce the sovereign debt of countries in crisis through swapping bank debts for bonds funded by the IFIs. This led to the rebirth in speculation in the international sovereign bond market and growth of derivatives (Salamanca 2010). There was another increase in the early 2000s, when Fitch, the US State Department and UNDP in two separate agreements contracted to rate fifteen sub-Saharan countries. It has been widely argued that ratings agencies are far from independent, as they are funded by fees from government debt offices and buy-side investment and international banks (Herman 2007, 2010). But what, of course, is even more important is that their measures of value reinforce the estimation of sovereign debt only according to financial market principles.

Importantly the growth of speculative secondary markets in sovereign debt has produced great waves of investment boom and bust in various emerging country debt-bonds. This has adversely affected these countries because the Baker and Brady sovereign debt workouts created overconfidence in lending to these arenas in the 1980s–90s. During the same period IMF/World Bank restructuring measures forced the opening up of capital markets to such investment as a condition of lending. This trend was further fueled by the reduced capital weights in the Basel I Agreement, which meant that international banks rushed to lend in the short term to emerging countries, which led to the Asian financial crises of the 1990s (Raffer 2007). Now countries across the globe are subject to booms and busts of investment in sovereign debt bonds and the various financial instruments attached to them. The relative positioning of countries in the tributary networks of sovereign debt rests on their levels of public deficit and investor confidence in their future prosperity (Stiglitz 2010b). The availability of investor funds depends on an international competitive marketplace and in particular on US and Chinese fiscal policy. US Treasury decisions often shape the international movements of capital. This is because US bonds and derivatives are perceived by investors as the most potentially valuable debt. They are desired because they pay in dollars, which at present is the global reserve and trade currency. As US Treasury bond yields rise and fall, investors move funds in and out of US markets. China's fiscal policy is also very important because it holds the largest amount of US Treasury notes (debt bonds with a length of two to ten years). Chinese government decisions on whether to trade or hold these affects values and therefore capital movements. All of these factors have made it more difficult to enact monetary policy, as foreign currency floods in and out of domestic financial markets in an unpredictable fashion (Panizza 2010).

Governments entered into the new sovereign debt arrangements because they seemed to promise potentially limitless access to funds for public financing and good economic management tools. But, instead, fiscal policy is increasingly constrained by financial market values and rhythms. Governments are now no longer even able to ensure a measure of control over fiscal policy by issuing domestic currency debt rather than external foreign currency debt. After the Asian financial crises of the 1990s, governments, especially in emerging economies and low-income countries, turned to domestic debt financing, as they argued it would be less subject to flight. This was a more expensive option because domestic debt tends to have shorter maturity times and is subject to much more rollover risk with higher rates of interest. The IMF, for example, reported in 2006 that domestic debt accounted for 21 percent of the total debt in the sixty-five low-income countries, but that it absorbed 42 percent of the total interest bill (ibid.). Therefore it drives up the price of borrowing for governments even though it was turned to as a means to underpin a steady, regular supply of funds to the government and for progressive economic "growth." But domestic debt has turned out not to be a source of stability. International investors have entered the domestic markets of developing countries, and domestic investors are now holding bonds issued in the international market. All a central bank, debt management office or government can monitor is the amount of debt that is issued under its state regulations. They do not know where the profits of that debt are going or whether they are entering the country's money supply. Nor do they know who holds this debt. Again, although government debt markets were constructed to make debt management and monetary policy more controllable, they have not done so. Governments can no longer manage their debt predictably as the cost of borrowing rises and falls according to currently unknowable factors.

The IFIs (the World Bank, IMF and regional development banks) contribute to the continuation of market driven fiscal policy focused on public debt reduction. Along with the private-sector London Club and official-sector Paris Club, they negotiate routines of repayment. They also make public debt the key constraint on the fiscal policy of governments. Their existence as institutions for lending and negotiation of sovereign debt sustains creditor-debtor relationships (Raffer 2007). Sovereign debts were the high-risk junk bonds of the eighteenth and nineteenth century (ibid.). Defaults were common (Flandreau and Flores 2008; Tomz 2007). In the twentieth century up to the early post–World War II period, sovereign debts were often written down, forgiven or made subject to Bisque clauses (moratoriums on repayment if it would adversely affect the borrower's economy) (Cosio-Pascal 2010). Without the IFIs, this would be the situation still. These institutions have consistently acted in the sovereign debt crises from 1980s to the present to establish, and then expand, lending by official and market institutions (Raffer 2007). Their actions provided the underpinnings for the growth of international and national sovereign debt markets. In particular, the Baker (1985–88) and Brady (1988–98) plans brought together international banks, IFIs and governments to create new sovereign debt bond primary and secondary markets (Salamanca 2010). The HIPC initiatives of the 1990s and partial forgiveness of debt in the 2000s reduced the debts of individual countries, but maintained the status quo of relations of sovereign debt. Without the actions of the IFIs, repayments to official lenders, the profits of international commercial banks and the speculative markets in sovereign debt would have collapsed under the weight of unsustainable financial demands on low-income countries (Raffer 2007). Outside situations of sovereign debt crisis, the IFIs impose measurement practices that orient financial policy toward public deficit reduction and the market management of public debt (Herman 2007). The IFIs discipline governments to focus on fiscal policy that will enable the repayment of, and trading in, sovereign debt bonds to continue.

The last relation significant for understanding sovereign debt is that between financial markets and millions of middle- and lower-middle-class investors and credit holders. The macroeconomic project of the IFIs and governments from the mid-1980s was focused on mobilizing private household savings to produce investment and "growth." The development of government bond markets was intended to act to draw this private capital into the banking system. Private individuals have benefited through returns from investment vehicles and funds that have speculated in these new markets. They have also received credit from banks funded in part via government bonds. This credit has subsidized the consumption-led growth with decline in the relative value of wages that has occurred globally since the 1980s. These payments are redistribution from the public sector to private individuals. These middle-class citizens benefit from the fiscal discipline, sales of assets and use of lower-paid contractual labor in the public sector across the world.

In current forms of sovereign debt the government gains funding from private resources and the banking system but loses control over fiscal policy and often has to pay higher borrowing costs. Fiscal policy is now a performance of responsibility, constraint and discipline. It also aims to reduce the costs of the public sector through lay-offs, out-sourcing, privatization and greater extraction from public resources. Such actions seek to communicate to the "investment community" transparent messages that will lead to lower costs of borrowing for the government (Holmes 2009, 2013). The rhythms and values of financial markets constrain and extract value from state institutions in new, pervasive ways.

Financial Crisis and Austerity Revisited

How does this ideal type help us to understand the financial crisis and austerity policy? Since 2007–8, vast amounts of public debt have been taken on in the United States, UK and EU in order to recapitalize international and national commercial banks. Governments have then introduced radical austerity policies in the public sector to maintain their sovereign debt ratings in the markets, hoping to counteract their steep levels of public borrowing. Politicians and civil servants are confined to the role of cutting expenditure with an anxious eye on their sovereign debt status in the markets. Central banks govern the economy using quantitative easing in order to shore up commercial banks. Quantitative easing is a complete reversal of the older mechanisms of sovereign debt that existed to fund political action. This is the buying back by the central bank of sovereign debt bonds from private-sector financial institutions to make their balance sheets more viable. Sovereign debt is now bought back by central banks and thereby increased *in order to make the financial markets work,* not to support the long-term political and ethical policy of state institutions. This is a total capture of state fiscal policy by financial markets that completely realizes the market-oriented tendencies in current sovereign debt relations.

The reports on global sovereign debt in the wake of the financial crisis issued by the World Bank, IMF and UN fully capture this situation (Blommenstein et al. 2010; Blommenstein, Harwood and Holland 2012). In 2010 and 2011, government debt managers, central bankers and private-sector bankers from twenty-three advanced and emerging market economies met in Washington to discuss the postcrisis outlook. The penetration of government policy by market values and rhythms is fully visible in the responses of debt managers to the global financial crisis of 2007–9. As the liquidity in the international banking system collapsed, the ability of governments to issue bonds in the primary market declined as well. This threatened their borrowing programs through which they manage both revenue flows to the public sector and monetary policy. Debt managers described how in some countries government bond auctions and secondary derivative trading had to be suspended, as there was no demand. At the same time, debt managers attempted to borrow more short-term debt to counteract the sudden short-falls in the public finances that were caused by quantitative easing or the recapitalization of nationalized insolvent banks. The crisis was a moment in which governments fully experienced their dependency on the volatile rhythms of the financial sector.

Instead of looking for alternatives, governments began to focus more intensely on anticipating investor demand above any other goal, including the costs to their citizens. First governments are advised in the report not to end their liquidity measures and asset purchase programs too early, but to sustain them to calm investor fears (Blommestein et al. 2010). Then they are instructed to follow the example of emerging market countries in the 1990s to maintain investor confidence. Their fiscal measures must be oriented to sound deficit-reducing policies. They are explicitly advised to follow the model of India in the 1990s. They must *overshoot* the required debt reduction, even if this means a slower recovery in growth. Only this would achieve the aim of restoring market confidence. Public expenditure reductions and structural reforms in the public sector need to be effectively communicated to the markets at every possible opportunity. This has become even more important for the "mature economies," since investors now are only focused on whether a country is investment or noninvestment grade in its credit ratings. Credit quality has become the central element determining the flow of currency across borders, and they now compete directly with emerging market countries. Government fiscal policy needs to be austere, otherwise states will lose the race for capital. Policies also must not become too restrictive on the financial sector. They should allow banks to operate without too severe liquidity and capital requirements, as these would constrain the banks' ability to extend credit.

The report also lays bare the inability of governments to manage the behavior of the investors that they rely on for their borrowing. It describes how investor sentiment is driven by rumor and fear, not macroeconomic fundamentals. Large numbers of uninformed and irrational investors are said to have moved into the sovereign debt market. They skew the yields on bonds when they dump investments they no longer want. These rumors were sparked by the very mechanisms of the market itself. This is because conventional credit ratings do not reflect the expected risk of default by a sovereign. Instead they track the patterns of market supply and demand for sovereign bonds and their derivatives and securities. Supply and demand has become even more volatile because investors not well versed in government bonds are entering the market seeking a safe haven for investments. As they are inexperienced, they have been taking on inappropriate investments. This creates the risk of destabilizing the market when they realize their mistake and need to adjust their portfolios. Here policies of austerity emerge as the only answer to the volatility and unpredictability of the market mechanisms of sovereign debt. There has been a total retreat from long-term political and ethical goals for fiscal governance.

Extractive States and Amplified Inequality: India and Singapore

What then, are the consequences of these relations and mechanisms of sovereign debt for citizens? State institutions are barely able to maintain the policy space to enact policies of redistribution, welfare and public investment. They are also extractive in new ways. They do not only tax their citizens. They also draw monetary resources upward from public-sector institutions in a tributary structure. They redirect these resources to fund financial market transactions and to signal responsibility to their creditors. These practices bring into conflict the social investment, redistributive and extractive practices of state institutions.

This conflict plays out very differently depending on the historical form of the state, bureaucracy and polity. But even in countries with a welfare bureaucracy and democratic politics social investment, redistribution and extraction are placed permanently in tension. To understand this tension it is helpful to examine the different trajectories of India and Singapore. These are interesting cases to compare because both countries began to develop deeper primary and secondary markets in sovereign debt bonds in the same decade from the 1990s to 2000s. Yet they are entirely distinct in their histories of state welfare, political form and pre-existing levels of public debt. How then have these differences played out in relation to their incorporation into the new relations and mechanisms of sovereign debt?

As this book has shown in India, the introduction of primary and secondary markets in sovereign debt was part of a broader reorientation of the public sector toward the repayment of government debt. This would be achieved through the privatization of public-sector units; the development of public-private partnerships; and the growing use of contractual labor. Greater revenues would also be drawn out of public-sector labor and the intensified use of public resources. In the 1980s and early 1990s these policies were motivated by attempts to repay IFIs and appear "responsible" in relation to their structural adjustment policies. With the creation of sovereign debt markets, the government continued these strategies to support new monetary mechanisms; reduce the cost of government borrowing; and ensure profits for primary dealers. If central government debts were reduced through greater extraction from tutelary agencies such as the Kolkata Port Trust, then such markets would be more viable. The tenor of this policy is visible in the links made by Usha Thorat (then executive director of the Reserve Bank of India) writing in 2002. She argued that the fiscal responsibility bill and the cutting of deficits by public-sector agencies would lead to a more vibrant market in government bonds (Thorat 2002). If this occurred, the goal of developing "efficient markets" that worked for "information processing to facilitate efficient asset pricing and resource allocation" would be achieved.[2] But the problem with this tactic is the effect it has on public institutions. These enter a crisis mode of austerity policy. Increasingly they use exploited informalized private-sector labor. They lack the funds for infrastructure investments. Their planning occurs through chaotic speculative relations.

In addition, such austerity policies increase existing inequalities between institutions and regions. State resources are not redistributed between these. Instead, the state presses harder on public institutions and the regions that are already in deficit, because of low tax revenues or lower rates of trade, than it does on more prosperous sites. Therefore the state no longer redistributes or corrects the market but amplifies its patterns of unequal distribution. Also, further lower-cost private-sector investment can be attracted by already prosperous institutions and regions. In India this pattern is clearly visible in the differences between the ports in Kolkata and Mumbai. In Mumbai the already thriving facilities were able to attract further investment and public-private partnerships to develop the Jawarhalal Nehru docks (Secretariat for Infrastructure 2007). While in Kolkata the Port Trust has been burdened with demands to repay central government debts and, therefore, has to extract more from dwindling public resources and declining infrastructures.

Similarly, at the level of states and municipalities (which now also seek funding through market mechanisms of public debt bonds), prosperous institutions have the potential to attract private capital, while others are chronically starved of funds. The 1996 Rakesh Mohan Infrastructure Committee and the 1997 Ninth Plan approach paper suggested the formation of public-private partnerships and the issuance of commercial bonds to provide urban infrastructures (Mohan 2003). This was the same logic as sovereign debt financing mechanisms except writ small. This measure would lead to cuts in central and state government spending on urban infrastructure, thereby reducing deficits and would deepen the liquidity of primary and secondary financial markets with private corporate and household funds. The government tried to stimulate the growth of this market through the introduction of tax exemptions on yields from municipal bonds, provision of a pooled finance development fund and viability gap funding for public private partnerships. In addition, the Jawarhalal Nehru Renewal Mission supported mechanisms for issuing credit ratings for municipalities and aimed to help municipalities achieve good ratings. But these measures have had a slow start. In 1998 the first municipal bonds were issued to Ahmedabad, but since then there have been very few bond issues. The few municipalities with AAA rating have this rating because they have been favored with government funds and are prosperous already (Mehta and Mehta 2010). So they have not needed to seek further funding from bond issues, even though they potentially could. Other municipalities with low ratings because of existing high levels of deficit cannot attract either PPPs or funding. State social investment and redistribution of revenues as a counterpoint to the market has been undermined at the center, state and municipal level. Instead, the rhythms and inequalities produced by market institutions have been amplified. Democracy does make a difference here, however. We can understand the raft of welfare initiatives in India since 2005 (the national rural employment guarantee scheme; food security act and land compensation act) as attempts to reinstate redistributive aspects of rule. But these welfare measures do nothing to alter the historical change in the character of the public-sector bureaucracy. Its tributary structure and orientation toward fiscal policies that sustain the national and international market in sovereign debt bonds continue. These give the Indian state an extractive character and generate practices that amplify the volatile rhythms and inequalities of market practices.

How then has the nondemocratic, restricted welfare and deficitless city-state of Singapore fared? Importantly, the government has had a budget surplus since the 1980s. This is in a large part because it has never undertaken welfare responsibilities. There is no unemployment benefit or health care provision for its citizens (although they do have the right to public housing and retraining). This freedom from debt and democratic, welfare constraints gives Singapore a privileged position. It does not have to fear the volatile rhythms and sentiments of the market nor discipline its public sector with austerity policies. The fiscal policy of the government has used this policy room to further increase its wealth through financial speculation. It acts like an investment bank seeking credit to fund expansionist international financial activity. In addition various public-sector units have used the government's strong sovereign rating to support their own bond issues. The public sector below the level of the government has also become similar in its practices to an investment bank, directly acquiring government debt bonds and derivatives in order to gain credit.

In 2000 the Singaporean government began to issue very large amounts of domestic sovereign debt bonds in Singaporean dollars (Ngiam and Loh 2002). This was in order to develop as an international financial center and, even more important, to access international funding without receiving foreign currency loans. This strategy was adopted so as to avoid experiencing the instability that had occurred in the Asian Financial Crisis in 1997 (this was sparked by changes in exchange rates that made foreign currency loan repayments unsustainable). Within the country state agencies such as statutory boards and government corporations access foreign funding through the domestic bond market. For example, in 2000 the Jurong Town Corporation launched a twelve-year issue of 200 million Singapore dollars. SingTel followed in 2001 with a 1 billion five-year issue (ibid.). State agencies also act like investment banks with the government-run pension fund, the central provident fund, being the single largest holder of long-term government bonds. Reportedly, the proceeds from this purchase have been used by the government of Singapore sovereign wealth fund for further investment in foreign assets. As a deficit-free, nonwelfare state, Singapore was able to fully incorporate financial market mechanisms without imposing austerity policy. Its public-sector institutions flush with capital can mobilize this to further amplify their wealth in the financial marketplace. As a result, it has become a leading player in the international financial markets. It has also been able to provide public infrastructure for its citizens. The Singaporean government's strategy is now a policy exemplar. For example, its bureaucrats have become key advisors in "best practice" on infrastructure provisioning and financing for the World Bank (World Bank 2011). However, the Singaporean government has only been able to achieve such spectacular results because of its exceptional character. Singapore most fully realizes the utopian version of the financial market practices that now drive state fiscal policy. In the case of the city-state, in contrast to India, these practices amplify existing state wealth. However its status as an exemplar is fundamentally misleading. The rest of the world cannot become Singapore. Unlike the majority of governments in the world it does not have to intensively extract from its own public sector and it is a nonwelfare state.

The Indian and Singaporean examples show that the *normal operation* of sovereign debt relations amplifies inequalities both within and between countries and regions. What policy and political interventions might alter this? How can we counterbalance the financial market rhythms and values that now dominate in fiscal policy? What new forms of government funding can we imagine that would contribute to the growth of redistribution? What kinds of social movements could push for this potential change?

A Social Calculus for Sovereign Debt

Whatever the solutions are that are proposed they need to be evaluated according to a social calculus. By a social calculus I mean a measure that traces the effects of forms of government financing on redistribution and social relations. This is not the same as social audit or triple bottom line accounting of the impact of organizations (Spreckley 1981; New Economics Institute 2013). Nor is it similar to the economists' concept of public goods. Following Samuelson, they work with a definition of public goods as goods with "non-rival and/or non-exclusive benefits and costs" (Kaul et al. 2006, xii). Both of these approaches use the model of the market as the foundation for the understanding of the ethical and the political. Citizens are stakeholders in the society, environment and institution. Or they are consumers of "goods" provided by institutions that cannot be private property. Instead, the challenge for us is to use ethical and political frames to measure the value of market actions. Or, in other words, to carry out a qualitative analysis of the social relations that forms of government financing generate and the extent to which these support processes of redistribution. Quantitative analysis has a part to play, but only in a subsidiary position to an evaluation of the ethical and political qualities of the relationships involved. These social relations should not only be measured through the human development indices now common in international organizations. They should be evaluated according to the degree of redistribution they produce and the extent to which they enable the political rights of citizenship.

Recent proposals for changes in government financing do not bear up well under such a social calculus. Many of these focus on resolving sovereign debt crises more equitably. They do not propose alternative relations and mechanisms of sovereign debt. For example economists, the IMF and UN policy-makers have debated the value of an international sovereign debt bankruptcy court. Many have suggested that only a legal body using procedures similar to those of the US Chapter 9 Municipal Bankruptcy law would be able to resolve current inequalities. In spite of its apparent radicalism, this is a preservationist approach that is designed to create processes of "orderly workout." It would keep current forms of financial market speculation and government fiscal policy in place.

Pressure groups associated with development approaches suggest that greater citizen participation in the form of NGO and activist groups would correct inequalities. "Citizens conditionality" has been proposed in sovereign debt crisis countries. In this model, a country making a bankruptcy settlement or debt cancellation with one of the IFIs would be required to deposit an amount equal to its monthly debt payments into a trust account. This would be used for poverty alleviation. It would be run by concerned citizens and monitored by international organizations (Barry and Tomitova 2007). But this measure would not correct the distortions to government fiscal policy produced by the "normal" operation of sovereign debt. It also maintains the existing authority of IFIs. Neither of these proposals would correct the erosion of long-term political and ethical policy space that has occurred. Nor would they lead to an increase in government practices of redistribution.

Quite the opposite of these preservationist approaches, are activist suggestions that individual governments or coalitions of debtor countries should use their political power to repudiate debt payments or carry out mass coordinated defaults (Ambrose 2005). These would lead to a resetting of the system on the model of the biblical Jubilee. However, this deconstruction on its own would not be enough. We also need to propose some more equalizing methods of sovereign debt financing that could be used after such an event. Otherwise we are at risk of simply returning to the mechanisms of secondary markets, repos and the dominance of market rhythms and values. Activist proposals are important in provoking public debate on equity and redistribution. However, they have rarely offered solutions that would meet the criteria of a social calculus.

Alongside these reflections on sovereign debt crises more pragmatic policy initiatives are underway across the world. These aim to overcome the contradictions that emerge from current forms of government financing. It is the provision of public infrastructures that becomes compromised. It is not surprising, therefore, that the IFIs have identified an "infrastructure financing gap" in the global south. This difference between the required level of funding and that actually received was calculated in 2008 in the Asia Pacific region to be $180 billion per year (Kingombe 2011). The effects of the redistribution of public-sector resources and labor value to the private sector have now become patently clear in crumbling infrastructures. The solution offered by the IFIs is to promote greater public-private participation in infrastructure development through international subsidies and national government credit guarantees. But this measure also fails a social calculus. It secures the further extraction of value from the public sector toward the private organizations that predominate in infrastructure provision in the global south. These are the investment banks (Nomura Securities, Barclays, Standard chartered bank, Goldman Sachs) and the sovereign wealth funds (Singapore, Abu Dhabi and the China Investment Corporation) that are already dominant. For example, the World Bank Report on Infrastructure in 2012 argued that it should "leverage" its existing capital by using it to bring in more private-sector financing into infrastructure (World Bank 2011). It would do this by offering World Bank guarantees and funding to projects. Its commercial arm, the IFC, would set up a global equity fund into which private agents could invest that would be used to finance infrastructure in emerging markets. The World Bank would offer access to countries to these facilities if they also drew in private capital through government guarantees at the national level. They would be advised on how to achieve this by the government of Singapore, with which in 2009 the World Bank set up an infrastructure finance center of excellence. South Asia (and India in particular) is targeted as a key site for these initiatives. The World Bank would help toward India's 12th Plan goals to scale up its investment in roads, ports, power, logistics and supply chains by providing expertise and access to partial funding. It would thereby help to produce a deepening of its capital markets. The World Bank plan fails the test of a social calculus. Its methods cannot produce greater equality between regions and countries. This is because it does nothing to alter the dominance of market values and relations in fiscal policy. Regions and countries with better government sovereign credit ratings that are already prosperous will continue to attract the most private investment. The proposal seeks a "deepening" of these market practices that leads to inequality. Further reducing the possibility for social equality, this policy also uses World Bank capital and national government guarantees to sustain profits and cut the "risks" for international private companies.

The implications of such IFI support for PPP becomes clear if we look in more detail at the recent history of the Indian case. In 2006 the India Infrastructure Finance Company was set up to provide long-term loans for infrastructure projects. The funding for this was raised from domestically issued sovereign debt bonds and funding from the IFIs (World Bank and Asian Development Bank). By 2012, Rs40,373 crore for 229 projects had been lent (including 340 crore to private enterprises in the Port sector) (High Level Committee for Financing Infrastructure 2013). In 2010 the India Infrastructure Finance Company Ltd (IIFCL) took on a new subsidizing role in relation to the Indian banks. It started to take on transferred loans from initial lenders for up to 50 percent of the outstanding balance. This was in order to refinance projects that were over-running or over-budget. In June 2012 the IIFCL began to subsidize the borrowing of private developers within the financial markets. It issued partial guarantees to developers for up to 50 percent of their bond issue so that their bonds could receive a high credit rating, thereby cutting their costs of borrowing. This guarantor role has recently expanded further with World Bank help and has become the main role for the IIFC. In 2013, seeking to deepen markets and foreign investment for infrastructure bonds, the IIFC now provides "credit enhancement" for bonds issued by infrastructure companies for up to 20 percent of the project cost. This amounts to public risk and public subsidy to ensure private profits, a pattern seen widely in PPPs (Mazzucato 2013). This would not matter so much if the already existing infrastructures of the public sector were not being pushed so hard. They must continue to repay their deficits to ensure central state budgets are healthy, the financial markets remain prosperous and to finance such subsidies to private firms. This model of public-sector financing only adds to the pressures on places such as the Kolkata Port Trust. It will do nothing to alter the unequal practices of speculative planning, informalized labor relations and extraction of value from public resources described in this book. Such measures fail when measured on a social calculus. They are most likely to sustain inequality and "deepen" financial market activity and private benefit.

In Europe, the UK and the United States in the wake of the financial crisis there are similar moves to devolve infrastructure, and even welfare, provisioning to capital markets and private investors. A common policy solution, the use of "community bonds," is proposed. In 2010 in the United States the Small Business Jobs act included the creation of a community development financial institutions guarantee program. The Treasury will provide guarantees up to $500 million in 2013 alone to "Community Development Financial Institutions" that provide money for supporting commercial activities that will create revitalization of poor areas, including provision of social housing, financial services to the poor and job creation (CDFI 2013). This sum of money would subsidize their borrowing from the regular financial sector and seeks to make this capital patient and socially productive. The European Central Bank has also recently introduced subsidies and guarantees for infrastructure development bonds (European Central Bank 2013). In 2013 in the UK, Cameron announced the launch of a social stock exchange, tax breaks for investors in social enterprises and a £250 million community asset promise. The think tank Res Publica, supported by the Chancellor of the Exchequer, Osborne, has proposed a new model of infrastructure community bonds (Res Publica and the Canary Wharf Group 2012). In these the role of government institutions in providing welfare and infrastructure is entirely eroded. For example, the infrastructure bonds "outside the constraints of public administration" would be issued by special purpose investment vehicles. Yields on these bonds would be paid from a combination of public budgets, private sector contributions, future tax revenues, land value capture, citizens' philanthropic contributions and "efficiency savings" in government. These moves also do not meet the criteria of a social calculus. Here market investors take on the provisioning role of the state in the special purpose vehicle and use state money to guarantee regular profits to other private investors. In each of these measures from the United States to Europe the act of state provisioning and redistribution becomes a source of private profit. This is unlikely to produce greater social and political equality over the long run. There are even more public actions that can be profited from. There will be no space left to assert a political and ethical value outside of market relations and evaluations.

A Utopia: Founding a New Public Conversation

How then might we imagine a utopian form of government financing? Only techniques that amplify the long-term ethical and political aspects of rule and deepen the relationships between citizens and governments can achieve this. The aims of social investment, redistribution and equality must be at the core of these. My suggestions that follow are not "practical" in the usual sense of policy measures. They are intended to create the space for an entirely different public conversation about sovereign debt and government financing. I am sure that many more and better ideas will emerge from future discussions. Each of my suggestions is intended to rebalance the relationship between the financial markets, state institutions and citizens.

First, the technocratic authority of debt offices and central banks should be made accountable. This could be achieved through the democratic election rather than appointment of central boards of these organizations. Campaigns would offer an opportunity for economic policies to be challenged by a social calculus in the public debate surrounding them. Once in authority, central bank boards would have to explain and justify their measures to the public. They would be constrained by the effects of the social inequalities they might produce.

Secondly, the other important players in international debt relations, the IFIs, must be completely remade. It is important (as many activists have argued) that all country debts are simultaneously forgiven. This would, in effect, lead to the disestablishment of the World Bank and IMF. Once this had occurred in order to counteract the mobile, amorality of capital we need a substitute for the IFIs—an activist international taxation organization. This would track and redistribute to the poorest countries, regions and citizens the offshore profits of corporations and investment institutions (Piketty 2014). Strengthened by the existence of this organization, national governments would argue again for taxation as a valid form of redistribution. Alongside this new tax regime, as credit relations resumed between sovereigns and lenders, an international organization of debtors and one of creditors would be formed with equal rights in a new international bankruptcy court. As each of these policies were introduced we would have to ask, what kinds of social relations do they produce and are these redistributive and equalizing?

Thirdly, to create greater space for an ethical and political fiscal policy it is important to end the secondary market in sovereign debt bond derivatives. The same ban should apply to the derivatives and securities trading in municipal and infrastructure bonds. All of these "political" bonds should also only be made over extended time frames of at least thirty years. This would ensure that they would attract the permanent support of long-term investors, especially organizations such as pension funds that also exist ultimately for social benefits. Community bonds in the true sense of the term would be introduced as a source of public financing. These would be direct credit transactions between institutions, citizens and state bodies that would bypass the intermediary of the market. Instead, organizations that exist primarily not for a profit motive such as trusts, charities, universities and religious institutions would lend directly to their own treasury, taking out tax-credit bonds. They would be repaid by a reduction in the taxes that they had to pay. Money could be pooled in citizen's cooperative vehicles (on the model of tontines, perhaps, in which once all the participants expire the bond disappears, thus preventing the inheritance of debt). The money gathered would be issued to the government in return for "yield" in income tax reductions. The principle behind these utopian measures is not the dissolving of state institutions as in other proposals for community bonds. Instead, these practices would buttress the redistributive role of the state, providing room for it to operate not according to market rhythms and values. It would also produce an amplification of institutions that do not exist for profit alone in society. An international practice of these community bonds could be developed within the new international taxation organization. Here yields on bonds would be paid from the taxed assets of international corporations rather than from the treasuries of emerging and low-income countries. If ratings agencies were still to exist, they would be required to measure the value of sovereign debt bonds on the international stage according to new criteria. Reflecting the long-term interests of investors, they would predict the degree to which countries can maintain the welfare of their citizens over time.

The most important "check" within this framework would be citizen move-ments. Citizen-led movements can bring a new public debate on sovereign debt into being. These would not turn an ethical and political argument into a human development or economic framework. Instead, they would do the reverse. They would turn economic facts back into ethical and political questions of the nature of the state and of the rights of the global public. They would focus on how in practi-cal terms citizens can claim back a right to their *res publica*, or public good, in the true meaning of that term. They would seek to end the extractive mechanisms that have drawn economic value from public goods and eroded their contributions to a collective political existence (Arendt 1958). Such a movement would replace an economic definition of public good with a political and ethical one. It would be founded on an act of asserting, We are the public, return to us our collective pos-sessions that have been taken from us. It might include an extension of the public debt audit strategies carried out in places such as Argentina. These audits would go beyond the question of the role of IFIs and public officials to tackle the ques-tion of private financial profits from sovereign debt and government financing. The numerical fact of public debt would, through these audits, be turned back into a social and political question. Overall, the foundations of this movement would be in an assertion of the inherent value of the public spaces, practices and infrastruc-tures that create collective political dialogue in society (ibid.). Activism would draw from frustration about the absence or decline of rural and urban infrastructure. It would take as its sites attempts to save specific public objects and spaces that have been eroded over time. At its core would be an exploration of the question of what state institutions are for. How and to what extent they can support redistribution and end exploitative labor relations? In forging this politics we can draw from the experiences of the people I worked with on the Hooghly River. Their lives show the limits and potential of remaking the economic into an ethical, and ultimately political, question.

Reference Matter

Notes

Introduction

1. I am very grateful indeed to Brenda Chalfin for her use of this phrase *res publica* in the workshop that Nayanika Mathur and I convened, "The New Public Good: The Affects and Techniques of Flexible Bureaucracies," at the Centre for Research in the Arts and Social Sciences, Cambridge University, in March 2012, which inspired my further research on the use of Arendt in relation to infrastructures. For her interpretation, see "Public Things, Excremental Politics and the Infrastructure of Bare Life in Ghana's City of Tema."

Section I

1. For any events or organisations pre-2001 the name Calcutta is used, while Kolkata is used for any events or organisations after this date when the city was renamed.

Chapter 1

1. Calcutta Port Trust Board Meetings, 9th meeting, 2 June 1958, vol. 92: 534.
2. Ibid., 1st meeting, 1 Jan. 1962, vol. 98: 381.
3. Ibid., 5th meeting, 28 Mar. 1968, vol. 102: 315.
4. Ibid., (budget) 12th meeting, 31 Oct. 1966, vol. 100.
5. Ibid., 7th meeting, 18 May 1973, vol. 106.
6. Ibid., 14th meeting, 20 Nov. 1976, vol.Nov.–Dec.: 683.
7. Ibid., 3rd meeting, 26 Feb. 1980, vol. Jan.–Mar.: 7.
8. Ibid., 1st meeting, 27 Jan. 1994, vol. 1: 6.
9. Ibid., 1st meeting, 25 Mar. 1986, vol. Jan.–Mar.: 29.
10. Ibid., 5th meeting, 12 Nov. 1989, vol. Oct.–Dec. 1989.
11. Ibid., 1st meeting, 29 Jan. 1991, vol. Jan.–Mar.: 38.
12. Ibid., 4th meeting, 10 Mar. 2000.
13. Ibid., 8th meeting, 25 Aug. 1992.
14. Special Meeting on Labor Situation, 6 Mar. 1981, vol. Jan.–Mar. 1981.
15. Ibid., 61.
16. Ibid., 183.
17. Ibid., 188.
18. Calcutta Port Trust Board Meetings, 10th meeting, 31 Aug. 1984, vol. Aug.–Dec.
19. Ibid., 2nd meeting, Jan. 1986, vol. Jan.–Mar.
20. Ibid., 12th meeting, 25 Oct. 1985, vol. Aug.–Dec.

21. Ibid., 8th meeting, 31 July 1991, vol. May–July.

22. Ibid., 10th meeting, 29 Aug. 1990, vol. Aug.–Oct.

23. Ibid., 10th meeting, 28 Sept. 1995, vol. Sept.–Nov.

24. Ibid., 4th meeting, 31 Mar. 2000.

25. Ibid., 1st meeting, 21 Jan. 2000, vol. Jan.: 45.

26. Ibid.

27. Ibid., 7th meeting, 22 June 1984, vol. May–Aug.: 162.

28. Ibid., 11th meeting, Monday 28 Oct 1991, vol. Oct.–Dec.

29. Ibid., 11th meeting, 20 Nov. 1992, vol. Nov.

30. Ibid., 2nd meeting, Item no. 427, 10 Jan. 1994, vol. Jan.–Feb.

31. Ibid., 10th meeting, Item no. 19, 27 Aug. 1997, vol. Aug.–Sept.

32. Ibid., 13th Meeting, Appendix II, 13 Nov. 1998, vol. Nov.–Dec.: 54.

33. Ibid., 7th June meeting, Item no. 5, vol. June–Aug. 2002.:40.

34. Ibid., 4th meeting, 26 Mar. 1975, vol. Jan.–June: 65.

35. Ibid., 13th meeting, 28 Nov. 2000, vol. Nov.–Dec.

36. Ibid., 4th meeting, 23 Mar. 1982, vol. Jan.–Mar.

37. Ibid., 2nd meeting, Part iv, Item 1, 20 Jan. 1989, vol. Jan.–June.

38. Ibid., 2nd meeting, 20 Jan. 1989.

39. Ibid., 4th meeting, 7 Oct. 1996, vol. Oct.

40. Ibid., 3rd meeting, 26 Feb. 1980, vol. Jan.–Feb.

41. Ibid., 10th meeting, 30 Aug. 1993, vol. June–Aug.

42. Ibid., 13th meeting, 8 Dec. 1989, vol. Nov.–Dec.

43. Ibid., 14th meeting, 31 Dec. 1990, vol. Nov.–Dec.: 292.

44. Ibid., 5th meeting, 31 May 1994, vol. Apr.–May: 6.

45. Ibid., 5th meeting, 22 May 1995, vol. May–June: 66.

46. Ibid., 8th meeting, 27 Aug. 1996, vol. July–Aug.

47. Ibid., 8th meeting, 25 Aug. 1992, vol. July–Aug.

48. Ibid.,10th meeting, 28 Sept. 1995, vol. Sept.–Nov.

49. Ibid., 8th Meeting, 24 June 1998, vol. June–July.

50. Ibid., 11th meeting, 17 Oct. 2001, vol. Oct. –Dec.

51. Ibid., 10th meeting, Item 4, 20 Sept. 2000, vol. Sept.–Oct.

52. Ibid., 9th meeting, 29 Sept. 2003, vol. Sept.–Oct.

53. Kolkata Port Trust Board Meetings, 3rd meeting, 24 Feb. 2004, vol. Jan.–Mar.

54. Ibid., 10th meeting, 16 Dec. 2005, vol. Oct.–Dec.

55. See the awarding of a contract for this to a UK-based company. "Kolkata to Have Its Own London Eye," *The Hindu*, 23 May 2014.

56. See "Kolkata Port, Railways Plan Sagar Island Project," available at *thehindubusinessline.com*, 10 Feb. 2011.

57. See "Kolkata Port Scraps Sagar Island Project," *Business Standard*, 27 Mar. 2012.

58. See "Phase 1 of Sagar Island Seaport to Begin in 2017," *Business Standard*, Monday 19 Sept. 2013.

59. "Na Mo-Na Mo Meets No-No," *The Telegraph*, 22 Mar. 2014.

Chapter 2

1. See Chapter 1, under *"Austerity Labor: Devaluing the Working Classes and Imperma-nent Livelihoods."*

2. See J. Chatterjee (2007) on B. C. Ray's attempts to regenerate West Bengal after the loss of its old economic links.

3. The Inland Water Training Institute was set up by B. C. Ray, the first chief minister of Bengal. Calcutta Port Trust Board Meetings, 24 July 1951, vol. 84.

4. Ibid., 18 Sept. 1950, vol. 84, and 20 Sept. 1951, vol. 85.

5. Ibid., 8 July 1958, vol. 92.

6. Ibid., 20 July 1959, vol. 94.

7. Ibid., 24 Aug. 1959, vol. 93, and 11 Jan. 1965, vol. Jan.–Feb. 1965.

8. On the imagery of Bengali husbands as Siva in Uma and other popular songs, see R. McDermott 2001.

Chapter 3

1. See Chapter 1, "Austerity Technologies."

2. For important accounts of such representations of "family capital," see Chari 2004 and Yanagisako 2002.

3. Calcutta Port Trust Board Meetings, 11th meeting, 29 Aug. 1988, vol. July–Sept.: 465.

4. Ibid.

5. Captain D. K. Dutta to Chairman, 20 June 1981, Appendix to meeting, Friday 31 Aug. 1984, vol. July–Sept.: 8910.

6. Science City is described on its official website as the largest science museum and convention center in the subcontinent, and it is located in a symbolically important way on the newer outskirts of Kolkata. It is administered by the National Council of Science Museums. The "Maritime Centre," to which the members of the marine department con-tributed, sits alongside the Earth Exploration Hall, the Dynamotion Hall, Space Odyssey and Evolution Park Theme Tour.

Section 3

1. See Chapter 1, "Austerity Property."

2. Simmel 1908, 464.

3. Ibid., 465.

4. Here my argument differs from that of Simmel. Simmel assumed that the public-ity of accounting, archiving and democracy meant that complicit friendship had become unimportant to state capitalism. He argued that the secret had retreated to the sphere of personal relationships. But this teleological model tells only part of the story because it leaves out the practice of speculation. In fact, the promise of transparency generates a proliferating emphasis on relationships founded on the sharing or withholding of secrets.

5. The older anthropological literature shows that friendship has always been sig-nificant to state-society relationships, so how are we to understand its new uses? Are these simply a continuation of older practices of seeking influence? Other ethnogra-

phies would suggest not. These demonstrate that with the retreat of large-scale, state-led projects, policies now aim to harness personal relationships in new ways. Elyachar (2010, 2012a), for example, has traced how NGO-microfinanced programs in Egypt incorporate networks of *wasta*. Egyptians of all classes have long relied on these connections with intermediaries in order to make their livelihoods, but microfinance formalizes and financializes these relations. As the chapter that follows shows, a quite similar process is at work on the Hooghly in relation to *jogajog kora*. Popular urban connections are becoming more closely tied to the revenue streams and planning of the state. Except these relations are not simply harnessed, as Elyachar suggests, but are amplified.

Chapter 4

1. See Chapter 1, "Austerity Property."

Section 4

1. See Chapter 1, "Unpredictable Circulations."

Chapter 5

1. See Chapter 1, "Austerity Nature" and "Austerity Technologies."

2. J. Law and A. Mol 2002, 13.

3. This makes Hutchins's analysis of navigation problematic: he focuses on a context for navigation that is purified of its usual contradictions—that is, the making of profit and manipulation of technical objects and data in relation to a recalcitrant world. It is only because he chooses such a context that his discussion of navigation can remain one about cognitive practices and devices. His context helps to produce his theory that ultimately technologies, including that of navigation, are simply part of a project of cognition, a human will to know certain things and achieve certain crystallizations of practical knowledge about the world.

4. First-grade pilots have more than twenty years of service, grade two more than four to five years of service, grade three less than four years of service.

Chapter 6

1. See Chapter 1, "Austerity Technologies."

2. See Chapter 1, "Austerity Property."

3. Board Meetings of the Port, 5th meeting, 9 Apr. 1930.

4. Board Meetings of the Port, 20 Jan. 1989, Item 9, appendix II.

Conclusion 2

1. Carracedo and Dattels 1997, 105.

2. Thorat 2002, 55.

References

Primary Sources

1950–2000. *Board Meetings of the Calcutta Port Trust.* Calcutta: Port Trust Press.

2001–2006. *Board Meetings of the Kolkata Port Trust.* Kolkata: Port Trust Press.

"Kolkata Port Scraps Sagar Island Project." *Business Standard*, 27 Mar. 2012.

"Phase 1 of Sagar Island Seaport to Begin in 2017." *Business Standard*, Monday 19 Sept. 2013.

CDFI. 2013. Available at www.cdfifund.gov/what_we_do/programs_id.asp?programID=14.

Ernst and Young. 2012. *India Infrastructure Summit.* New Delhi: Ernst and Young.

European Central Bank. 2013. *The Europe 2020 Project Bond Initiative.* Available at www.eib. org/products/project-bonds.

Government of India. 2010. *Report on Indian Infrastructure Debt Fund.* New Delhi: Government of India.

High Level Committee for Financing Infrastructure. 2013. *Interim Report.* New Delhi: Planning Commission, Government of India.

International Monetary Fund and World Bank. 2003. *Guidelines for Public Debt Management.* Washington: IMF Publications

"Kolkata to Have Its Own London Eye." *The Hindu*, 23 May 2014.

"Kolkata Port, Railways Plan Sagar Island Project." *Thehindubusinessline.com*, 10 Feb. 2011.

Ministry of Finance. 2004. *Tenth Status Report on India's External Debt.* New Delhi: Government of India.

Ministry of Finance. 2008. *Report of the Internal Working Group on Debt Management.* New Delhi: Government of India.

Ministry of Surface Transport. 2000. *Status Paper on Private Sector Participation in the Port Sector.* New Delhi: Government of India.

Ministry of Shipping. 2011. *Report of Working Group on the Port Sector for the Twelfth Five Year Plan.* New Delhi: Government of India.

"Na Mo-Na Mo Meets No-No," *The Telegraph*, 22 Mar. 2014.

Reserve Bank of India. 2007. "Government Securities." *Report on Currency and Finance 2005–6.* New Delhi: Government of India.

Res Publica and the Canary Wharf Group. 2012. *Financing for Growth: A New Model to Unlock Infrastructure Investment.* London: Res Publica.

Secretariat for Infrastructure. 2007. *Report of the Task Force: Financing Plan for Ports.* New Delhi: Planning Commission, Government of India.

————. 2010a. *Compendium of PPP Projects in Infrastructure*. New Delhi: Planning Commission, Government of India.

————. 2010b. *Private Participation in Infrastructure*. New Delhi: Planning Commission, Government of India.

————. 2011. *Investment in Infrastructure during the Eleventh Five Year Plan*. New Delhi: Planning Commission, Government of India.

World Bank. 2011. *Transformation through Infrastructure: Infrastructure Strategy Update*.

Secondary Sources

Abelin, Mireille. 2012. "'Entrenched in the BMW': Argentinian Elites and the Terror of Fiscal Obligation." *Public Culture* 24(2): 329–356.

Abram, Simone, and Gisa Weszkalnys. 2011. "Anthropologies of Planning: Temporality, Imagination and Ethnography." *Focaal* 61: 3–18.

Adam, Barbara. 1998. *Timescapes of Modernity: The Environment and Invisible Hazards*. London: Routledge.

Adam, Barbara, and Chris Groves. 2007. *Future Matters: Action, Knowledge, Ethics*, Leiden: Brill.

Acharya, Shankar, and Rakesh Mohan, eds. 2010. *India's Economy: Performances and Challenges, Essays in Honour of Montek Singh Ahluwalia*. New Delhi: Oxford University Press.

Agarwala, Rina. 2013. *Informal Labor, Formal Politics, and Dignified Discontent in India*. Cambridge: Cambridge University Press.

Aglietta, Michel, and Andre Orleans, eds. 1998. *La Monnaie Souveraine*. Paris: Odile Jacob.

Agrawal, Arun. 2005. *Environmentality: Technologies of Government and the Making of Subjects*. Durham, NC: Duke University Press.

Alexander, Catherine, and Josh Reno. 2012. *Economies of Recycling: The Global Transformation of Materials, Values and Social Relations*. London: Zed.

Ali, Daud, and Anand Pandian, eds. 2010. *Ethical Life in South Asia*. Bloomington: Indiana University Press.

Alichi, Ali. 2008. *A Model of Sovereign Debt in Democracies*. WP/108/152 IMF Working Papers.

Alley, Kirsty. 2002. *On the Banks of the Ganga: When Wastewater Meets a Sacred River*. Ann Arbor: University of Michigan Press.

Althusser, Louis, and Etienne Balibar. 1970. *Reading Capital*. London: New Left Books.

Aluwahlia, Montek Singh. 1994. "India's Quiet Economic Revolution." *The Columbia Journal of World Business* 29(1): 6–12.

Ambrose, Soren. 2005. "Social Movements and the Politics of Debt Cancellation." *Chicago Journal of International Law* 6(1): 267–285.

Amrith, Sunil. 2013. *Crossing the Bay of Bengal: The Furies of Nature and the Fortunes of Migrants*. Cambridge, MA: Harvard University Press.

Anand, Nikil. 2011. "Pressure: The PoliTechnics of Water Supply in Mumbai." *Cultural Anthropology* 26(4): 542–563.

Anders, Gerhard. 2008. "The Normativity of Numbers: World Bank and IMF Conditionality." *Political and Legal Anthropology Review* 31(2): 187–202.

———. 2010. *In the Shadow of Good Governance: An Ethnography of Civil Service Reform in Africa.* Leiden: Brill.

Anjaria, Jonathan Shapiro. 2006. "Street Hawkers and Public Space in Mumbai." *Economic and Political Weekly* 41(21): 2140–46.

Anjaria, Jonathan Shapiro, and Colin McFarlane, eds. 2011. *Urban Navigations: Politics, Space and the City in South Asia.* London: Routledge.

Appadurai, Arjun. 2002. "Deep Democracy: Urban Governmentality and the Horizon of Politics." *Public Culture* 14(1): 21–47.

———. 2011. "The Ghost in the Financial Machine." *Public Culture* 23(3): 517–539.

———. 2013. *The Future as Cultural Fact: Essays on the Global Condition.* London: Verso.

Arendt, H. 1958. *The Human Condition.* Chicago: Chicago University Press.

———. 1968. *Between Past and Future.* New York: Penguin Books.

———. 1982. *Lectures on Kant's Political Philosophy.* Ed. Robert Beiner. Chicago: Chicago University Press.

Arnold, David, and Eric Dewald, eds. 2012. "Everyday Technology in South and South-East Asia." *Modern Asian Studies* 46(1): 1–17.

Arvani, Zsofia, and Geffrey Heinen. 2008. *A Framework for Developing Security Markets for Government Securities.* International Monetary Fund Working Paper. Washington: IMF Publications

Balachandran, G. 2006. "Circulation through Seafaring: Indian Seamen 1890–1945." In C. Markovits et al., *Society and Circulation.*

———. 2007. "South Asian Seafarers and Their Worlds c.1870–1930s." In J. H. Bentley, R. Bridenthal and K. Wigen, eds., S*eascapes: Maritime Histories, Littoral Cultures, and Transoceanic Exchanges.* Honolulu: University of Hawai'i Press.

Barros-Grela, Eduardo, and Jose Liste-Noya, eds. 2011. *American Secrets: The Politics and Poetics of Secrecy in the Literature and Culture of the U.S.* Madison, NJ: FDU Press.

Barry, Andrew. 2002. "The Anti-Political Economy." *Economy and Society* 31(2): 268–284.

Barry, Christian, and Anna Tomitova. 2007. "Fairness in Sovereign Debt." *Ethics and International Affairs* 21(1): 41–79.

Baviskar, Amita. 1998. *In the Belly of the River: Tribal Conflicts over Development in the Narmada Valley.* New Delhi: Oxford University Press.

———, ed. 2007. *Waterscapes: The Cultural Politics of a Natural Resource.* New Delhi: Permanent Black.

Baviskar, Amita, and Nandini Sundar. 2008. "Democracy versus Economic Transformation?" *Economic and Political Weekly* 43(46): 87–89.

Bear, Laura. 2007. *Lines of the Nation: Indian Railway Workers, Bureaucracy and the Intimate Historical Self.* New York: Columbia University Press.

———. 2013 . "The Antinomies of Audit: Opacity, Instability and Charisma in the Economic Governance of a Hooghly Shipyard." *Economy and Society* 42(3): 375–397.

———. 2014a. "Capital and Time: Uncertainty and Qualitative Measures of Inequality," Piketty Symposium." *British Journal of Sociology*, 65(4): 639–49..

———. 2014b. "Doubt, Conflict and Mediation: An Anthropology of Modern Time." *Journal of the Royal Anthropological Institute* 20(S1): 3–30.

———. 2015. "Capitalist Divination: Popularist Speculators and Technologies of Imagination on the Hooghly River." *Comparative Studies in South Asia, Africa and the Middle East*, 35(2).

Bear, Laura, Karen Ho, Anna Tsing and Sylvia Yanagisako. 2015. "GENS: a Feminist Manifesto for the Study of Capitalism." *Theorising the Contemporary, Current Anthropology website.*

Bear, Laura, and Ritu Birla and Stine Puri. 2015. "Speculation: India, Uncertainty and New Economic Imaginaries." *Comparative Studies in South Asia, Africa and the Middle East, Comparative Studies in South Asia, Africa and the Middle East*, 35(2).

Bear, Laura, and Nayanika Mathur. 2015. "Remaking the Public Good: a New Anthropology of Bureaucracy." *Cambridge Journal of Anthropology*, 33(1).

Bellamy Foster, John. 2000. *Marx's Ecology: Materialism and Nature.* New York: Monthly Review Press.

Benei, Veronique. 2008. *Schooling Passions: Nation, History and Language in Contemporary Western India.* Stanford: Stanford University Press.

Bennett, Jane. 2001. *The Enchantment of Modern Life: Attachments, Crossings and Ethics,* Princeton: Princeton University Press.

Best, Jacqueline. 2012. "Bureaucratic Ambiguity." *Economy and Society* 41(1): 84–106.

Bestor, Theodore. 2001. "Supply-side Sushi: Commodity, Market and the Global City." *American Anthropologist* 103(1): 76–95.

———. 2004. *Tsukiji.* Berkeley: University of California Press.

Bhattacharya, Tithi. 2007. "Tracking the Goddess: Religion, Community, and Identity in the Durga Puja Ceremonies of Nineteenth-Century Calcutta." *Journal of Asian Studies* 66(4): 919–962.

Birla, Ritu. 2009. *Law, Culture and Market Governance in Late Colonial India.* Durham, NC: Duke University Press.

———. 2010. "Vernacular Capitalists and the Modern Subject in India: Law, Cultural Politics and Market Ethics." In Anand Pandian and Daud Ali, eds., *Ethical Life in South Asia.* Indianapolis: University of Indiana Press.

Bloch, Maurice. 1977. "The Past in the Present and the Present in the Past." *Man* 12(2): 278–292.

Blom Hansen, Thomas. 2012. *Melancholia of Freedom: Social Life in an Indian Township in South Africa.* Princeton: Princeton University Press.

Blom Hansen, Thomas, and Oskar Verkaaik, eds. 2009. "Introduction: Urban Charisma or Everyday Mythologies in the City." *Critique of Anthropology* 29(5): 5–26.

Blommestein Hans, Vincenzo Guzzo, Alison Holland and Yibin Mu. 2010. "Debt Markets: Policy Challenges in the Post-Crisis Landscape." *OECD Journal: Financial Market Trends* 1: 143–169.

Blommestein, Hans, Alison Harwood and Allison Holland. 2012. "The Future of Debt Markets." *OECD Journal: Financial Market Trends* 2: 263–281.

Blommestein, Hans, and Philip Turner. 2012. "Interactions between Sovereign Debt Management and Monetary Policy under Fiscal Dominance and Financial Instability." *OECD Working Papers on Sovereign Borrowing and Public Debt Management* 3.

Blyth, Mark. 2013. *Austerity: The History of a Dangerous Idea.* Oxford: Oxford University Press.

Bogaert, M. 1970. *Trade Unionism in Indian Ports: A Case Study at Calcutta and Bombay.* New Delhi: New India Press.

Bolt, Maxim. 2010. "Camaraderie and Its Discontents: Class Consciousness, Ethnicity and Divergent Masculinities among Zimbabwean Migrant Farm Workers." *Journal of Southern African Studies* 36(2): 377–93

———. 2012. "Waged Entrepreneurs, Policed Informality: Work, the Regulation of Space and the Economy of the Zimbabwean-South African Border." *Africa: Journal of the International African Institute* 82(1):111–30

———. 2013. "Producing Permanence: Employment, Domesticity and the Flexible Future on a South African Border Farm." *Economy and Society* 42(4): 197–225.

Bond, Daniel, Daniel Platz and Magnus Magnusson. 2012. *Financing Small-scale Infrastructure Investments in Developing Countries. United Nations: Department of Economic and Social Affairs* Working Paper 114, http://www.un.org/en/development/desa/papers.

Bourdieu, Pierre. 1990. *The Logic of Practice.* Stanford: Stanford University Press.

Breman, Jan. 1996. *Footloose Labour: Working in India's Informal Economy.* Cambridge: Cambridge University Press.

———. 2004. *The Making and Unmaking of an Industrial Working Class: Sliding down the Labour Hierarchy in Ahmedabad, India.* New Delhi: Oxford University Press India.

———. 2010. "India's Social Question in a State of Denial." *Economic and Political Weekly* 45(23): 42–46.

Browne, Katherine E., and B. Lynne Milgram. 2009. *Economics and Morality: Anthropological Approaches.* Plymouth, UK & Lanham, MD: AltaMira Press.

Bryan, Dick, Randy Martin, Johanna Montgomerie and Karel Williams. 2012. "An Important Failure: Knowledge Limits and the Financial Crisis." *Economy and Society* 41(3): 299–315.

Caliskan, Koray. 2010. *Market Threads: How Cotton Farmers and Traders Create a Global Commodity.* Princeton: Princeton University Press.

Caliskan, Koray, and Michel Callon. 2009. "Economization Part I: Shifting Attention from the Economy Towards Processes of Economization." *Economy and Society* 38(3): 369–398.

——————. 2010. "Economization Part II: a Reseach Programme for the Study of Markets." *Economy and Society* 39(1): 1–32.

Callon, Michel, Milo Yuval and Fabian Muniesa. 2007. *Market Devices.* London: Blackwell.

Campbell, John K. 1964. *Honour, Family and Patronage: A Study of Institutions and Moral Values in a Greek Mountain Community.* Oxford: Clarendon.

————. 1968. "Two Case Studies of Marketing and Patronage in Greece." In J. G. Peristiany, ed., *Contributions to Mediterranean Sociology*. The Hague: Mouton.

Canuto, Otaviano, and Lili Liu. 2013. *Until Debt Do Us Part: Subnational Debt, Insolvency and Markets*. Washington, DC: World Bank.

Carracedo, Montserrat Ferre, and Peter Dattels. 1997. "Survey of Public Debt Management Frameworks in Selected Countries." In V. Sundararajan, Peter Dattels and Hans Blommestein, eds., *Coordinating Public Debt and Monetary Management*, 96–162. Washington, DC: International Monetary Fund.

Carrier, James, and Danny Miller. 1998. *Virtualism: A New Political Economy*. Oxford: Berg.

Carswell, Greta, and Geert De Neve. 2013a. "Labouring for Global Markets: Conceptualising Labour Agency in Global Production Networks." *Geoforum* 44(1): 62–70.

————. 2013b. "From Field to factory: Tracing Transformations in Bonded Labour in the Tiruppur Region, South India." *Economy and Society* 42(3): 430–454.

Castells, Manuel. 2000. *The Rise of the Network Society*. Oxford: Wiley.

Castree, Noel. 2009. "The Spatio-Temporality of Capitalism." *Time and Society* 18(1): 26–61.

Cederloff, Gunnel, and K. Sivaramakrishnan. 2006. *Ecological Nationalisms: Nature, Livelihoods and Identities in South Asia*. Seattle: University of Washington.

Chakrabarti, Prafulla. 1999. *Marginal Men: The Refugees and the Left Political Syndrome in West Bengal*. Kolkata: Naya Udyog Publishers.

Chakrabarty, Dipesh. 1989. *Rethinking Working Class History: Bengal 1890–1940*. New Delhi: Oxford University Press.

Chakravarty, Deepita. 2010. "Trade Unions and Business Firms: Unorganised Manufacturing in West Bengal." *Economic and Political Weekly* 45(6): 45–52.

Chalfin, Brenda. 2010. *Neoliberal Frontiers: An Ethnography of Sovereignty in West Africa*. Chicago: Chicago University Press.

————. 2014. "Public Things, Excremental Politics and the Infrastructure of Bare Life in Ghana's City of Tema." *American Ethnologist* 41(1): 92–109.

Chari, Sharad. 2004. *Fraternal Capital: Peasant-Workers, Self-Made Men and Globalization in Provincial India*. Stanford: Stanford University Press.

Chatterjee, Partha. 2004. *The Politics of the Governed*. New York: Columbia University Press.

————. 2008. "Democracy and Economic Transformation in India." *Economic and Political Weekly* 43(16): 53–62.

Chatterji, Joya. 2007. *The Spoils of Partition: Bengal and India, 1947–1967*. Cambridge: Cambridge University Press.

Chong, Kimberly. 2012. "The Work of Financialization: An Ethnography of a Global Management Consultancy in Post-Mao China." Ph.D. thesis, LSE.

Chopra, R., Caroline Osella and Filippo Osella. 2004. *South Asian Masculinities: Context of Change, Sites of Continuity*. New Delhi: Women Unlimited an Associate of Kali for Women.

Choudhry, Moorad. 2006. *An Introduction to Repo Markets*. Chichester: John Wiley and Sons.

Coleman, Simon. 2010. "Afterword." In Amit Desai and Evan Killick, eds., *The Ways of Friendship: Anthropological Perspectives.* Oxford: Berghahn.

Collier, Stephen. 2009. "Topologies of Power: Foucault's Analysis of Political Government beyond 'Governmentality.'" 26(6): 78–108.

———. 2011. *Post-Soviet Social: Neo-liberalism, Social Modernity, Biopolitics.* Princeton: Princeton University Press.

Comaroff, Jean, John Comaroff and Robert Weller. 2001. *Millennial Capitalism and the Culture of Neo-liberalism,* Durham, NC: Duke University Press.

Combes, Muriel. 2013. *Gilbert Simondon and the Philosophy of the Transindividual.* Cambridge: MIT Press.

Cooper, Matthew. 1994. "Spatial Discourses and Social Boundaries: Re-imagining the Toronto Waterfront." *City and Society* 7(1): 93–117.

Corbridge, Stuart, and John Harriss. 2000. *Reinventing India: Liberalization, Hindu Nationalism and Popular Democracy.* Cambridge: Polity Press.

Corbridge, Stuart, and Manoj Srivastava. 2013. "Mapping the Social Order by Fund Flows: The Political Geography of Employment Assurance Schemes in India." *Economy and Society* 32(2): 455–479.

Corbridge, Stuart, Glyn Williams, Manoj Srivastava and Rene Veron. 2005. *Seeing the State: Governance and Governmentality in India.* Cambridge: Cambridge University Press.

Cosio-Pascal, Enrique. 2010. "Paris Club: Intergovernmental Relations in Debt Restructuring." In Barry Herman, Jose Ocampo and Shari Spiegel, eds., *Overcoming Developing Country Debt Crises.* 231–276. Oxford: Oxford University Press.

Cowell, Richard, and Hugh Thomas. 2002. "Managing Nature and Narratives of Dispossession: Reclaiming Territory in Cardiff Bay." *Urban Studies* 39(7): 1241–1260.

Cross, Jamie. 2010. "Neo-Liberalism as Unexceptional: Economic Zones and the Everyday Precariousness of Working Life in South India." *Critique of Anthropology* 30(4): 355–373.

———. 2011. "Detachment as Corporate Ethic: Materializing CSR in the Diamond Supply Chain." *Focaal* 60: 34–46.

Currie, Elizabeth, Jean-Jacques Dethier and Eriko Togo. 2003. *Institutional Arrangements for Public Debt Management.* The World Bank, Working Paper 3021.

Das, Udaibir, Michael Papaioannou and Magdalena Polan. 2008. "Strategic Considerations for First-time Sovereign Bond Issuers." WP/08/261 IMF Working Papers.

Dash, Kishore. 1999. "India's International Monetary Fund Loans: Finessing Win-set Negotiations within Domestic and International Politics." *Asian Survey* 13(6): 884–907.

Davies, Sam, Colin Davis, David de Vries, Lex Heerma van Voss, Lidwij Hsselink and Klaus Weinhauer. 2000. *Dock Workers: International Explorations in Comparative Labour History, 1790–1970.* Aldershot: Ashgate.

De Genova, Nicholas. 2010. "The Management of 'Quality': Class Decomposition and Racial Formation in a Chicago Factory." *Dialectical Anthropology* 49: 249–272.

De Haan, Arjan. 1994. *Unsettled Settlers: Migrant Workers and Industrial Capitalism in Calcutta.* Hilversum: Verloren.

———. 2002. "Migration and Livelihoods in Historical Perspective: A Case Study of Bihar, India." *Journal of Development Studies* 38(5): 115–142.

De Neve, Geert. 2005. *The Everyday Politics of Labour: Working Lives in India's Informal Economy*. Delhi: Social Science Press/Oxford: Berghahn.

———. 2008. "We Are All *Sondukarar* (Relatives)!: Kinship and Its Morality in an Urban Industry of Tamil Nadu, South India." *Modern Asian Studies* 42(1): 211–246.

———. 2009. "Power, Inequality and Corporate Social Responsibility: The Politics of Ethical Compliance in the South Indian Garment Industry." *Economic and Political Weekly* 44(22): 63–71.

———. 2013. "Fordism, Flexible Specialization and CSR: How Indian Garment Workers Critique Neo-liberal Regimes." *Ethnography* (forthcoming).

Dean, Jodi. 2001. *Publicity's Secret: How Technoculture Capitalizes on Democracy*. Ithaca, NY: Cornell University Press.

Derrida, Jacques. 1992. *Given Time 1: Counterfeit Money*. Chicago: Chicago University Press.

Dev, S. M., and J. Mooij. 2002. "Social Sector Expenditure in the 1990s: Analysis of Central and State Budgets." *Economic and Political Weekly* (2 Mar.): 853–866.

Dilley, Roy. 2010. "Reflections on Knowledge Practices and the Problem of Ignorance." *Journal of the Royal Anthropological Institute* 16(S1): 176–192.

Donnolly, Elizabeth A. 2007. "Making the Case for Jubilee: The Catholic Church and the Poor-country Debt Movement." *Ethics and International Affairs* 21(1): 107–133.

Doron, Assa. 2008. *Passages of Resistance: Caste, Occupation and Politics on the Ganges*. Surrey: Ashgate.

Dreze, Jean, and Amartya Sen. 2013. *An Uncertain Glory: India and Its Contradictions*. London: Allen Lane.

Du Gay, Paul. 2008. "Max Weber and the Moral Economy of Office." *Journal of Cultural Economy* 1(2): 129–144.

Dubbeld, Bernard. 2003. "Breaking the Buffalo: The Transformation of Stevedoring Work in Durban between 1970–1990." *International Review of Social History* 48: 97–122.

Dunn, Elizabeth. 2004. *Privatising Poland: Baby Food, Big Business and the Remaking of Labor*. Ithaca, NY: Cornell University Press.

Edensor, Tim. 2005. *Industrial Ruins: Space, Aesthetics and Materiality*. London: Berg.

Elyachar, Julia. 2010. "Phatic Labor, Infrastructure and the Question of Empowerment in Cairo." *American Ethnologist* 37(3): 452–464.

———. 2012a. "Before and after Neo-liberalism: Tacit Knowledge, Secrets of the Trade and the Public Sector in Egypt." *Current Anthropology* 27(1): 76–96.

———. 2012b. "Next Practices: Knowledge, Infrastructure and Public Goods at the Bottom of the Pyramid." *Public Culture* 24(1): 109–209.

Engelen, Ewald, Ismail Ertürk, Julie Froud, Sukhdev Johal, Adam Leaver, Michael Moran and Karel Williams. 2012. "Misrule of Experts? The Financial Crisis as Elite Debacle." *Economy and Society* 41(3): 360–382.

Escobar. Arturo. 1999. "After Nature: Steps to an Anti-Essentialist Political Ecology." *Current Anthropology* 40(1): 1–30.

Feldhaus, Anne. 1995. *Water and Womanhood: Religious Meanings of Rivers in Maharasthra.* Oxford: Oxford University Press.

———. 2003. *Connected Places: Region, Pilgrimage and Geographic Imagination in India.* New York: Palgrave Macmillan.

Fernandes, Leela. 1997. *Producing Workers: The Politics of Gender, Class and Culture in the Calcutta Jute Mills.* Philadelphia: University of Pennsylvania Press.

———. 1998. "Culture, Structure and Working Class Politics." *Economic and Political Weekly* 33(52): 53–60.

Ferguson, James. 1999. *Expectations of Modernity: Myths and Meanings of Urban Life on the Zambian Copperbelt.* Berkeley: University of California Press.

———. 2009. "The Uses of Neo-liberalism." *Antipode* 41(S1): 166–184.

Finn, Margot. 2003. *The Character of Credit: Personal Debt in English Culture, 1740–1914.* Cambridge: Cambridge University Press.

Fisher, Michael H. 2006. "Working across the Seas: Indian Maritime Labourers in India, Britain, and in between, 1600–1857." *International Review of Social History* 51(S14): 21–45.

Flandreau, Marc, and Juan Flores. 2008. "Of Bonds and Brands: Foundations of Sovereign Debt Markets 1820–1830." *Journal of Economic History* 69(3): 646–684.

Freeman, Carla. 2000. *High Tech and High Heels in the Global Economy: Women, Work and Pink Collar Identities in the Caribbean.* Durham, NC: Duke University Press.

———. 2007. "The Reputation of Neo-liberalism." *Critique of Anthropology* 34(2): 252–267.

Gaillard, Norbert. 2011. *A Century of Sovereign Ratings.* New York: Springer.

Gandy, Matthew. 2002. *Concrete and Clay: Reworking Nature in New York City.* Cambridge: MIT Press.

———. 2004. "Rethinking Urban Metabolism: Water, Space and the Modern City." *City: Analysis of Urban Trends, Culture, Theory, Policy, Action* 8(3): 371–387.

———. 2008. "Landscapes of Disaster: Water, Modernity and Urban Fragmentation in Mumbai." *Environment and Planning A* 40: 108–140.

Gelpern, Ann, and Mitu Gulati. 2010. "How CACs Became Boilerplate: Governments in 'Market-Based' Change." In Barry Herman, Jose Ocampo and Shari Spiegel, eds., *Overcoming Developing Country Debt Crises*, 347–388. Oxford: Oxford University Press.

Ghertner, Asher. 2010. "Calculating without Numbers: Aesthetic Governmentality in Delhi's Slums." *Economy and Society* 39(2): 185–217.

Ghosh, Anjan. 2000. "Spaces of Recognition: Puja and Power in Contemporary Calcutta." *Journal of Southern African Studies* 26(2): 289–299.

Ghosh, Arunabha. 2006. "Pathways through Financial Crisis: India." *Global Governance* 12: 413–29.

Ghosh, Papiya. 2008. *Community and Nation: Essays on Identity and Politics in Eastern India.* New York: Oxford University Press.

Gidwani, Vinay, and Rajyashree Reddy. 2011. "The Afterlives of 'Waste': Notes from India for a Minor History of Capitalist Surplus." *Antipode* 43(5): 1625–1658.

Gilliland, Jason. 2004. "Muddy Shore to Modern Port: Redimensioning the Montreal Water-front Time-Space." *Canadian Geographer* 48(4): 448–472.

Goodchild, Philip. 2009. *The Theology of Money*. Durham, NC: Duke University Press.

Gooptu, Nandini. 2001. *The Politics of the Urban Poor in Early-Twentieth Century India*. Cambridge University Press.

———. 2007. "Economic Liberalisation, Work and Democracy: Industrial Decline and the Urban Poor in Kolkata." *Economic and Political Weekly* 42(21): 1922–1933.

———. 2013a. *Enterprise Culture in Neoliberal India*. London: Routledge.

———. 2013b. "Servile Sentinels of the City: Private Security Guards, Organized Informal-ity, and Labour in Interactive Services in Globalized India." *International Review of So-cial History* 58(1): 9–38.

Gosseries, Alex. 2007. "Should They Honor the Promises of Their Parents' Lenders?" *Ethics and International Affairs* 21(1): 99–125.

Graeber, David. 2012. *Debt: The First 5000 Years*. London: Melville House.

Graham, Stephen, and Simon Marvin. 2001. *Splintering Urbanism: Networked Infrastruc-tures, Technological Mobilities and the Urban Condition*. London: Routledge.

Graham, Stephen, and Nigel Thrift. 2007. "Out of Order: Understanding Repair and Main-tenance." *Theory, Culture and Society* 24(3): 1–25.

Gudeman, Steven. 2001. *The Anthropology of Economy: Community, Market and Culture*. Oxford: Blackwell.

———. 2008. *Economy's Tension: The Dialectics of Community and Market*. Oxford: Berghahn.

Gupta, Akhil. 2012. *Red Tape: Bureaucracy, Structural Violence and Poverty in India*. Dur-ham, NC: Duke University Press.

———, and Kalyanakrishnan Sivaramakrishnan. 2011. *The State in India after Liberali-sation: Interdisciplinary Perspectives*. London: Routledge.

Gupta, S. P. 1994. "Debt Crisis and Economic Reforms." *Economic and Political Weekly* 29(23): 1411–1418.

Guyer, Jane, and La Ray Denzer. 2005. "The Craving for Intelligibility: Speech and Silence on the Economy under Structural Adjustment and Military Rule in Nigeria." In Steven Gudeman, ed., *Economic Persuasions*, 97–117. Oxford: Berghan.

———. 2007. "Prophecy and the Near Future: Thoughts on Macroeconomic, Evangeli-cal and Punctuated Time." *American Ethnologist* 34(3): 409–421.

Haberman, David. 2006. *River of Love in an Age of Pollution: The Yamuna River of Northern India*. Berkeley: University of California Press.

Han, Clara. 2012. *Life in Debt: Times of Care and Violence in Neo-liberal Chile*. Berkeley: Uni-versity of California Press.

Hancock, Mary, and Smriti Srinivas, eds. 2008. "Symposium on Religion and the Forma-tion of Modern Urban Space in Asia and Africa." *International Journal of Urban and Regional Research* 32(3), Special Issue.

Harris, Olivia. 2007. "What Makes People Work?" In Rita Astuti, Johnny Parry and Charles Stafford, eds., *Questions of Anthropology*. Oxford: Berg.

Harriss, John. 2011. "How Far Have India's Economic Reforms Been 'Guided by Compassion and Justice?' Social Policy in the Neoliberal Era." In Sanjay Ruparelia, Sanjay Reddy, John Harriss and Stuart Corbridge, eds., *Understanding India's New Political Economy: A Great Transformation?* 127–140. London: Routledge.

Harriss-White, Barbara. 2003. *India Working: Essays on Society and Economy.* Cambridge: Cambridge University Press.

Harvey, David. 1989. *The Condition of Post-Modernity.* Oxford: Blackwell.

———. 2000. *Spaces of Hope.* Edinburgh: Edinburgh University Press.

———. 2005. *A Brief History of Neoliberalism.* Oxford: Oxford University Press.

———. 2007 [1982]. *The Limits to Capital.* London: Verso.

Hell, Julia, and Andreas Schonle. 2010. *Ruins of Modernity.* Durham, NC: Duke University Press.

Henderson, Jeffrey. 1999. "Uneven Crises: Institutional Foundations of East Asian Financial Turmoil." *Economy and Society* 28(3): 327–368.

Herman, Barry. 2007. "The Players in the Game of Sovereign Debt." *Ethics and International Affairs* 21(1): 5–32.

———. 2010. "Why the Code of Conduct for Resolving Sovereign Debt Crises Falls Short." In Barry Herman, Jose Ocampo and Shari Spiegel, eds., *Overcoming Developing Country Debt Crises,* 389–427. Oxford: Oxford University Press.

Herman, Barry, Jose Antonio Ocampo and Shari Spiegel. 2010. *Overcoming Developing Country Debt Crises.* Oxford: Oxford University Press.

Herz, Noreena. 2004. *The Debt Threat: How Debt Is Destroying the Developing World.* New York: Harper Business.

Herzfeld, Michael. 1985. *The Poetics of Manhood: Contest and Ideology in a Cretan Mountain Village.* Princeton: Princeton University Press.

———. 1993 [1992]. *The Social Production of Indifference: The Symbolic Roots of Western Bureaucracy.* Chicago: University of Chicago Press.

———. 2004. *The Body Impolitic: Artisans and Artifice in the Global Hierarchy of Value.* Chicago: University of Chicago Press.

———. 2005 [1997]. *Cultural Intimacy: Social Poetics in the Nation-State.* New York: Routledge.

Hibou, Beatrice. 2004. *Privatizing the State.* London: C. Hurst and Co.

High, Holly, ed. 2012. "The Debt Issue." *Social Anthropology* 20(4), Special Issue.

Hirway, Indira, and Neha Shah. 2011. "Labour and Employment under Globalisation: The Case of Gujarat." *Economic and Political Weekly* 46(22): 57–65.

Ho, Karen. 2009. *Liquidated: An Ethnography of Wall Street.* Durham, NC: Duke University Press.

Hoag, Colin. 2010. "The Magic of the Populace: An Ethnography of Illegibility in the South African Immigration Bureaucracy," *POLAR* 33: 6–25.

Hoffmann, Michael. 2012. "Patronage, Exploitation and the Invisible Hand of Mao Tse Tung in an Urban Municipality in Western Nepal." Ph.D. thesis, LSE.

Holmes, Douglas R. 2000. *Integral Europe: Fast-Capitalism, Multiculturalism, Neo-Fascism.* Princeton: Princeton University Press.

———. 2009. "Economy of Words." *Cultural Anthropology* 24(3): 381–419.

———. 2013. *Economy of Words: Communicative Imperatives in Central Banks.* Chicago: Chicago University Press.

Hope, Wayne. 2006. "Global Capitalism and the Critique of Real Time." *Time and Society* 15(2/3): 275–302.

Hull, Matthew. 2003. "The File: Agency, Authority, and Autography in an Islamabad Bureaucracy." *Language and Communication* 23: 287–314.

———. 2012. *Government of Paper: The Materiality of Bureaucracy in Urban Pakistan.* Berkeley: University of California Press.

Humphries, Caroline. 2003. "Rethinking Infrastructure: Siberian Cities and the Great Freeze of January 2001." In J. Schneider and I. Susser, eds., *Wounded Cities: Destruction and Reconstruction in a Globalised World*, 91–107. London: Berg.

Hutchins, Edwin. 1995. *Cognition in the Wild.* Cambridge: MIT Press.

Ingham, Geoffrey. 2004. *The Nature of Money.* Cambridge: Polity Press.

Ingold, Tim. 1993. "The Temporality of the Landscape." *World Archaeology* 25(2): 24–174.

Jalais, Annu. 2009. *The Forest of Tigers: People, Politics and the Environment in the Sundarbans.* New Delhi: Routledge.

James, Erica Caple. 2012. "Witchcraft, Bureaucraft and the Social Life of US Aid in Haiti." *Cultural Anthropology* 27(1): 50–75.

Jassal, Smita. 2001. "Caste and the Colonial State: Mallahs in the Census." *Contributions to Indian Sociology* 35(3): 319–354.

Jochnick, Chris, and Fraser A. Preston. 2006. *Sovereign Debt at the Crossroads: Challenges and Proposals for Resolving the Third World Debt Crises.* Oxford: Oxford University Press.

Kalb, Don. 2009. "Conversations with a Polish Populist: Tracing Hidden Histories of Globalization, Class and Dispossession in Postsocialism (and Beyond)." *American Ethnologist* 36(2): 207–223.

Kalb, Don, and Gábor Halmai, eds. 2011. *Headlines of Nation: Subtexts of Class: Working Class Populism and the Return of the Repressed in Neoliberal Europe.* EASA Book Series. London: Berg.

Kaliskan, Corey, and Michel Callon. 2009. "Economization Part I: Shifting Attention from the Economy to Processes of Economization." *Economy and Society* 38(3): 369–398.

———. 2010. "Economization Part II: A Research Programme for the Study of Markets." 39(1): 1–32.

Kaul, Inge, Pedro Conceicao, Katell Le Goulven and Ronald U. Mendoza, eds. 2003. *Providing Global Public Goods: Managing Globalisation.* UNDP. Oxford: Oxford University Press.

———. 2006. *The New Public Finance: Responding to Global Challenges.* UNDP Oxford: Oxford University Press.

Kaur, Raminder. 2003. *Performative Politics and the Cultures of Hinduism*. New Delhi: Permanent Black.

Keane, Webb. 2007. *Christian Moderns: Freedom and Fetish in the Mission Encounter.* Berkeley: University of California Press.

Kideckel, David. 2008. *Getting By in Postsocialist Romania: Labor, the Body and Working-Class Culture*. Bloomington: Indiana University Press.

Kingfisher, Catherine, and Jeff Maskovsky. 2008. "The Limits of Neo-liberalism." *Critique of Anthropology* 28(2): 115–126.

Kingombe, Christian. 2011. *Mapping the New Infrastructure Financing Landscape*. Overseas Development Institute Background Notes. London: ODI.

Kipnis, Andrew. 2008. "Audit Cultures, Neo-liberal Governmentality, Socialist Legacy or Technologies of Governing?" *American Ethnologist* 35(2): 275–289.

Kletzer, Kenneth, and Brian Wright. 2000. "Sovereign Debt as Intertemporal Barter." *American Economic Review* 90(3): 621–639.

Krugman, Paul. 2013. *End This Depression Now!* New York: W. W. Norton and Company.

Laidlaw, James. 2013. *The Subject of Virtue: An Anthropology of Ethics and Freedom*. Cambridge: Cambridge University Press.

Lakoff, Andrew. 2007. "Preparing for the Next Emergency." *Public Culture* 19(2): 247–271.

Lambek, Michael, ed. 2010. *Ordinary Ethics: Anthropology, Language, and Action*. New York: Fordham University Press.

Larkin, Brian. 2008. *Signal and Noise: Media, Infrastructure and Urban Culture in Nigeria*. Durham, NC: Duke University Press.

Latour, Bruno. 1996. *Aramis, or, The Love of Technology*. Cambridge: Harvard University Press.

———. 2004. *Politics of Nature*. Cambridge: Harvard University Press.

Law, John. 2002. *Aircraft Stories: Decentering the Object in Technoscience*. Durham, NC: Duke University Press.

Law, John, and Ann-Marie Mol, eds. 2001. "Local Entanglements or Utopian Moves: An Inquiry into Train Accidents." Available at www.lancs.ac.uk/fass/sociology/papers/law-mol-local-entanglements-utopias-and train-accidents.pdf.

———. 2002. *Complexities: Social Studies of Knowledge Practices*. Durham, NC: Duke University Press.

Levinson, Mark. 2006. *The Box*. Princeton: Princeton University Press.

Li Puma, Edward, and Ben Lee. 2004. *Financial Derivatives and the Globalisation of Risk*. Durham, NC: Duke University Press.

Loizos, Peter, and E. Papataxiarchas. 1991. *Contested Identities: Gender and Kinship in Modern Greece*. Princeton: Princeton University Press.

Lyotard, Jean Francois. 1993. *Libidinal Economy*. Bloomington: Indiana University Press.

Mackenzie, A. 2001. "The Technicity of Time: From 1.00 Oscillations/Sex to 9192631770 Hz." *Time and Society* 10(2–3): 235–257.

Mains, Daniel. 2012. "Blackouts and Progress: Privatisation, Infrastructure and a Developmentalist State in Ethiopia." *Cultural Anthropology* 27(1): 3–27.

Mann, Bruce. 2003. *Republic of Debtors: Bankruptcy in the Age of Modern America.* Cambridge: Harvard University Press.

Marchand, Trevor. 2010. *Making Knowledge: Explorations of the Indissoluble Relation between Mind, Body and Environment.* London: Wiley-Blackwell.

Markovits, C., J. Pouchepadass and S. Subhramaniyam, eds. 2006. *Society and Circulation: Mobile People and Itinerant Cultures in South Asia 1750–1950.* London: Anthem.

Marshall, David L. 2010. "The Polis and Its Analogues in the Thought of Hannah Arendt." *Modern Intellectual History* 7(1): 123–149.

Martin, Matthew. 2010. "Ethiopian Debt Policy: The Long Road from Paris Club to the MDGs." In Barry Herman, Jose Ocampo and Shari Spiegel, eds., *Overcoming Developing Country Debt Crises.* Oxford: Oxford University Press.

Marx, Daniel, Jose Echague and Guido Sandleris. 2006. "Sovereign Debt and the Debt Crisis in Emerging Countries: The Experience of the 1990s." In Chris Jochnick and Fraser A. Preston, eds., *Sovereign Debt at the Crossroads: Challenges and Proposals for Resolving the Third World Debt Crisis.* Oxford: Oxford University Press.

Marx, Karl. 1991a [1884]. *The Process of Circulation of Capital, Capital: Volume 2.* London: Penguin.

———. 1991b [1884]. *The Process of Capitalist Production as a Whole, Capital: Volume 3.* London: Penguin.

Mathur, Chandana. 1998. "Transformation as Usual? The Meanings of a Changing Labour Process for Indiana Aluminium Workers." *Critique of Anthropology* 18(3): 263–277.

Mathur, Nayanika. 2012. "Transparent-making Documents and the Crisis of Implementation: A Rural Employment Law and Development Bureaucracy in India." *Political and Legal Anthropology Review* 35(2): 167–184.

Maurer, Bill. 2002. "Repressed Futures: Financial Derivatives' Theological Unconscious." *Economy and Society* 31(1): 15–36.

Mauss, Marcel. 1990 [1950]. *The Gift: The Form and Reason for Exchange in Archaic Societies.* London: Routledge.

Mazarella, William. 2006. "Internet X-ray: E-governance, Transparency and the Politics of Immediation in India." *Public Culture* 18(3): 473–506.

Mazzucato, Mariana. 2013. *The Entrepreneurial State: Debunking Public v. Private Myths.* London: Anthem Press.

Mbembe, Achille. 2003. "Necropolitics." *Public Culture* 15(1): 11–40.

Mbembe, Achille, and Janet Roitman. 1995. "Figures of the Subject in a Time of Crisis." *Public Culture* 7: 323–352.

McCall Howard, Penny. 2012. "Workplace Cosmopolitanization and "the Power and Pain of Class Relations at Sea." *Focaal* 62: 55–69.

McDaniel, June. 2004. *Offering Flowers, Feeding Skulls: Popular Goddess Worship in West Bengal.* Oxford: Oxford University Press.

McDermott, Rachel. 2001. *Mother of My Heart, Daughter of My Dreams: Kali and Uma in the Devotional Poetry of Bengal.* Oxford: Oxford University Press.

———. 2011. *Revelry, Rivalry and Longing for the Goddesses of Bengal: The Fortunes of Hindu Festivals*. New York: Columbia University Press.

McDowell, Linda. 2003. *Redundant Masculinities? Employment Change and White Working Class Youth*. Malden, MA: Blackwell.

McGoey, Linsey. 2007. "On the Will to Ignorance in Bureaucracy," *Economy and Society* 36(2): 212–235.

McHeyman, Josiah. 2004. "Ports of Entry as Nodes in the World System." *Identities: Global Studies in Culture and Power* 11: 303–327.

McIntyre, Michael, and Heidi J. Nast. 2011. "Bio(necropolitics): Marx, Surplus Populations, and the Spatial Dialectics of Reproduction and 'Race.'" *Antipode* 43(5): 1465–1488.

Mehta, Dinesh, and Meera Mehta. 2010. "A Glass Half Full? Urban Development from 1990s to 2010." *Economic and Political Weekly* 45(28): 20–23.

Mehta, Lyla. 2005. *The Politics and Poetics of Water: Naturalising Scarcity in Western India*. New Delhi: Oxford University Press.

Mezzadri, Alessandra. 2010. "Globalisation, Informalisation and the State in the Indian Garment Industry." *International Review of Sociology* 20(3): 491–511.

Michalowski, Sabine. 2008. "Sovereign Debt and Legal Rights—Legal Reflections on a Difficult Relationship." *Human Rights Law Review* 8(1): 35–68.

Miller, Danny. 2002. "Turning Callon the Right Way Up." *Economy and Society* 31(2): 218–233.

Mitchell, Timothy. 2002. *Rule of Experts: Egypt, Technopolitics, Modernity*. Berkeley: University of California Press.

———. 2007. "The Properties of Markets," in Donald Mackenzie, Fabian Munieza and Lucia Siu, eds., *Do Economists Make Markets?: On the Performativity of Economics*, 244–256. Princeton: Princeton University Press.

Miyazaki, Hirokazu. 2003. "The Temporalities of the Market." *American Ethnologist* 105(2): 255–265.

———. 2013. *Arbitraging Capitalism: Dreams of Capitalism at the End of Finance*. Berkeley: University of California Press.

Mohan, Rakesh. 2000. "Fiscal Correction for Economic Growth." *Economic and Political Weekly* 35(24): 2027–2036.

———. 2003. *Infrastructure Development in India: Emerging Challenges*. World Bank Annual Conference on Development Economics, 21–23 May.

———. 2008. "Growth Record of the Indian Economy 1950–2008." *Economic and Political Weekly* 43(19): 61–71.

Mollona, Mao. 2005. "Gifts of Labour: Steel Production and Technological Imagination in an Area of Urban Deprivation, Sheffield, U.K." *Critique of Anthropology* 25(2): 177–198.

Mosse, David. 2003. *The Rule of Water: Statecraft, Ecology and Collective Action in South Asia*. New Delhi: Oxford University Press.

Mukherjee, Nilmani. 1968. *The Port of Calcutta: A Short History*. Calcutta: Port Commissioners.

Mukherjee, Radhakamal. 1937. *The Changing Face of Bengal: A Study in Riverine Economy*. Calcutta University Readership Lectures, Kolkata University.

Munoz, Jose-Maria. 2011. "Talking Law in Times of Reform: Paradoxes of Legal Entitlement in Northern Cameroon." *Law and Society Review* 45(4): 893–922.

Murray-Li, Tanya. 2007a. "Practices of Assemblage and Community Forest Management." *Economy and Society* 36(2): 263–293.

———. 2007b. *The Will to Improve: Governmentality, Development and the Practice of Politics.* Durham, NC: Duke University Press.

Nash, June. 1979. *We Eat the Mines and the Mines Eat Us: Dependency and Exploitation in Bolivian Tin Mines.* New York: Columbia University Press.

Nassy Brown, Jacqueline. 2000. "Enslaving History: Narratives on Local Whiteness in a Black Atlantic Port." *American Ethnologist* 27(2): 340–370.

Negri, Antonio. 2003. *Time for Revolution.* London: Continuum Books.

New Economics Institute. 2013. See http://neweconomy.net/about_us.

Ngiam, Kee-Jin, and Lixia Loh. 2002. "Developing Debt Markets in Singapore: Rationale, Challenges and Prospects." *Asia-Pacific Development Journal* 9(1): 23–43.

Northover, Henry. 2010. "Human Development Advocacy for Debt Relief, Aid, and Governance." In Barry Herman, Jose Ocampo and Shari Spiegel, eds., *Overcoming Developing Country Debt Crises,* 298–316. Oxford: Oxford University Press.

Nye, David. 1992. *Electrifying America: The Social Meanings of a New Technology, 1880–1940.* Cambridge, MA: MIT Press.

———1994. *American Technological Sublime,* Cambridge, MA: MIT Press.

Ong, Aiwa. 2007. *Neoliberalism as Exception: Mutations in Citizenship and Sovereignty.* Durham, NC: Duke University Press.

Osella, Caroline, and Filippo Osella. 2006. *Men and Masculinities in South India.* New York: Anthem Press.

Osella, Filippo, and Caroline Osella. 2009. "Muslim Entrepreneurs in Public Life between India and the Gulf: Making Good and Doing Good." *Journal of the Royal Anthropological Institute* 15(S1): 202–221.

Ostor, Akos. 1980. *The Play of the Gods: Locality, Ideology, Structure and Time in the Festivals of a Bengali Town.* Chicago: University of Chicago Press.

Palley, Thomas I. 2003. "Sovereign Debt Restructuring Proposals: A Comparative Look." *Ethics and International Affairs* 17(2): 26–33.

Pandian, Anand. 2009. *Crooked Stalks: Cultivating Virtue in South India.* Durham, NC: Duke University Press.

Panizza, Ugo. 2010. "Is Domestic Debt the Answer to Debt Crises?" In Barry Herman, Jose Ocampo and Shari Spiegel, eds., *Overcoming Developing Country Debt Crises,* 91–110. Oxford: Oxford University Press.

Panjwani, Mariam Dossal. 2000. "Godis, Tolis and Mathadis: Dock Workers of Bombay." In Sam Davies et al., eds., *Dock Workers; Volume 1.* Aldershot: Ashgate Press.

Parry, Jonathan. 1994. *Death in Banaras.* Cambridge: Cambridge University Press.

———. 1999. "Two Cheers for Reservations: Satnamis and the Steel Plant." In J. Parry and R. Guha, eds., *Institutions and Inequalities: Essays in Honour of Andre Beteille.* New Delhi: Oxford University Press India.

———. 2007. "The Sacrifices of Modernity in a Soviet Built Steel Town in Central India." In J. Pina-Cabral and F. Pine, eds., *On the Margins of Religion*. Oxford: Berghahn.

———. 2008. "Cosmopolitan Values in a Central Indian Steel Town." In Pnina Werbner, ed., *Anthropology and the New Cosmopolitanism: Rooted, Feminist and Vernacular Perspectives*. European Association of Social Anthropologists Monographs. Oxford: Berg.

———. 2013. *Company and Contract Labour in a Central Indian Steel Plant. Economy and Society* 42(3): 348–374.

Patico, Jennifer. 2009. "Spinning the Market: The Moral Alchemy of Everyday Talk in Postsocialist Russia." *Critique of Anthropology* 29(2): 205–224.

Peck, Jamie, Nik Theodore and Neil Brenner. 2009. "Postneoliberalism and Its Malcontents." *Antipode* 41(S1): 94–116.

Peebles, Gustav. 2008. "Inverting the Panopticon: Money and the Nationalization of the Future." *Public Culture* 20(2): 233–265.

———. 2010. "The Anthropology of Credit and Debt." *Annual Review of Anthropology* 39: 225–240.

Perrow, Charles. 1984. *Normal Accidents: Living with High Risk Technologies*. New York: Basic Books.

Pettifor, Ann. 2003. "Resolving International Debt Crises Fairly." *Ethics and International Affairs* 17(2): 2–9.

Picherit, David. 2012. "Migrant Labourers' Struggles between Village and Urban Migration Sites: Labour Standards, Rural Development and Politics in South India." *Global Labour Journal* 3(1): 143–162.

Pickering, Andrew. 1995. *The Mangle of Practice: Time, Agency and Science*. Chicago: University of Chicago Press.

———. 2008. "New Ontologies." In A. Pickering and K. Guzik, eds., *The Mangle in Practice: Science, Society, and Becoming*. Durham, NC: Duke University Press.

Piketty, Thomas. 2014. *Capital in the 21st Century*. Harvard: Harvard University Press.

Pitt-Rivers, Julian. 1961. *The People of the Sierra*. Chicago: Chicago University Press.

Piot, Charles. 2010. *Nostalgia for the Future: West Africa After the Cold War*. Chicago: Chicago University Press.

Poovey, Mary. 2008. *Genres of the Credit Economy: Mediating Value in Eighteenth and Nineteenth Century England*. Chicago: Chicago University Press.

———. 2012. "Introduction: Issue on Financial Crisis." *Journal of Cultural Economy* 5(2): 139–146.

Porzecanski, Arturo. 2006. "Dealing with Sovereign Debt: Trends and Implications." In Chris Jochnick and Fraser A. Preston, eds., *Sovereign Debt at the Crossroads: Challenges and Proposals for Resolving the Third World Debt Crisis*. Oxford: Oxford University Press.

———. 2007. "The Constructive Role of Private Creditors." *Ethics and International Affairs* 21(1): 307–319.

Postone, Moishe. 1993. *Time, Labour and Social Domination*. Cambridge: Cambridge University Press.

Power, Michael. 1997. *The Audit Society: Rituals of Verification.* Oxford: Oxford University Press.

Prentice, Rebecca. 2009. "'Thiefing a Chance': Moral Meanings of Theft in a Trinidadian Garment Factory." In Katherine E. Browne and B. Lynne Milgram, *Economics and Morality: Anthropological Approaches,* 123–141. Society for Economic Anthropology Monographs, 26. Plymouth, UK & Lanham, MD: AltaMira Press.

———. 2012. "Kidnapping Go Build Back We Economy: Discourses of Crime at Work in Neoliberal Trinidad."*Journal of the Royal Anthropological Institute* 18(1): 45–64.

Rademacher, Anne. 2011. *Reigning the River: Urban Ecologies and Political Transformations in Urban Kathmandu.* Durham, NC: Duke University Press.

Raffer, Kunibert. 2007. "Risks of Lending and Liability of Lenders." *Ethics and International Affairs* 21(1): 85–106.

Reddy, Sanjay. 2007. "International Debt: The Constructive Implications of Some Moral Mathematics." *Ethics and International Affairs* 21(1): 81–98.

Reinhart, Carmen M., and Kenneth S. Rogoff. 2009. *This Time Is Different: Eight Centuries of Financial Folly.* Princeton: Princeton University Press.

Reith, Gerda. 2004. "Uncertain Times: The Notion of 'Risk' and the Development of Modernity." *Time and Society* 13 (2/3): 383–402.

Reno, Josh. 2009. "Your Trash Is Someone's Treasure: The Politics of Value at a Michigan Landfill." *Journal of Material Culture* 14(1): 29–46.

Richard, Annaliese, and Daromir Rudnyckyj. 2009. "Economies of Affect." *Journal of the Royal Anthropological Institute* 15(1): 57–77.

Riles, Annalise. 2004. "Real Time: Unwinding Technocratic and Anthropological Knowledge." *American Ethnologist* 31(30): 393–405.

———. 2006. "Real Time." In Michael Fisher and Greg Downey, eds., *Frontiers of Capital: Ethnographic Reflections on the New Economy,* 86–107. Durham, NC: Duke University Press.

———. 2011. *Collateral Knowledge: Legal Reasoning in the Global Financial Markets.* Chicago: University of Chicago Press.

Robbins, Brian. 2007. "The Smell of Infrastructure: Notes Towards an Archive." *Boundary* 234(1): 25–33.

Roitman, Janet. 2003. "Unsanctioned Wealth: Or, the Productivity of Debt in Northern Cameroon." *Public Culture* 15(2): 211–237.

———. 2005. *Fiscal Disobedience: An Anthropology of Economic Regulation in Central Africa.* Princeton: Princeton University Press.

———. 2011. "The Anti-Crisis." In *Political Concepts: A Critical Lexicon.* Available at politicalconcepts.org.

———. 2013. *Anti-Crisis.* Durham, NC: Duke University Press.

Roodman, David. 2006. "Creditor Initiatives in the 1980s and 1990s." In Chris Jochnick and Fraser A. Preston, eds., *Sovereign Debt at the Crossroads: Challenges and Proposals for Resolving the Third World Debt Crisis.* Oxford: Oxford University Press.

Rose, Nikolas. 1999. *Governing the Soul: The Shaping of the Private Self.* London: Free Association Books.

Rose, Sonya. 1992. *Limited Livelihoods: Gender and Class in Nineteenth Century England.* London: Routledge.

Rosenberg, David, and Sandra Harding. 2005. *Histories of the Future.* Durham, NC: Duke University Press.

Roy, Ananya. 2002. *City Requiem, Calcutta: Gender and the Politics of Poverty.* Minneapolis: University of Minnesota Press.

Roy, Ananya, and N. AlSayyad. 2003. *Urban Informality: Transnational Perspectives from the Middle East, Latin America, and South Asia.* Lanham, MD: Lexington Books.

Roy, Ananya, and Aiwa Ong, eds. 2011. *Worlding Cities: Asian Experiments and the Art of Being Global.* Oxford: Wiley Blackwell.

Rudnyckj, Daromir. 2010. *Spiritual Economies: Islam, Globalisation and the Afterlife of Development.* Ithaca, NY: Cornell University Press.

Rutherford, Danilyn. 2009. "Sympathy, State Building, and the Experience of Empire." *Cultural Anthropology* 24(1): 1–32.

Salamanca, Luis Jorge Garay. 2010. "The 1980s Crisis in Syndicated Bank Lending to Sovereigns and the Sequence of Mechanisms to Fix It." In Barry Herman, Jose Ocampo and Shari Spiegel, eds,, *Overcoming Developing Country Debt Crises,* 111–139. Oxford: Oxford University Press.

Samman, Amin. 2012. "The 1930s as Black Mirror." *Journal of Cultural Economy* 12(2): 213–229.

Sampson, Helen. 2013. *International Seafarers and Transnationalism in the Twenty-first Century.* Manchester: Manchester University Press.

Sampson, Helen, and B. Wu. 2003. "Compressed Time and Constraining Space: The Contradictory Effects of ICT and Containerization on International Shipping Labor." *IRSH* (48): 123–152.

Sanchez, Andrew. 2012a. "Deadwood and Paternalism: Rationalizing Casual Labour in an Indian Company Town." *Journal of the Royal Anthropological Institute* 18: 808–827.

———. 2012b. "Questioning Success: Dispossession and the Criminal Entrepreneur in Urban India." *Critique of Anthropology* 32(4): 435–457.

Sanyal, Kanyan, and R. Bhattacharyya. 2009. "Beyond the Factory: Globalization, Informalisation of Production and the New Locations of Labour." *Economic and Political Weekly* 44(22): 35–44.

Sarma, Jyotimoyee. 1969. "Puja Associations in West Bengal." *Journal of Asian Studies* 28(3): 579–594.

Schivelbusch, Wolfgang. 1987. *The Railway Journey: The Industrialization of Time and Space.* Berkeley: University of California Press.

Sennett, Richard. 2009. *The Craftsman.* London: Penguin.

Setser, Brad. 2010. "The Political Economy of the SDRM." In Barry Herman, Jose Ocampo and Shari Spiegel, eds., *Overcoming Developing Country Debt Crises,* 317–346. Oxford: Oxford University Press.

Sewell, William. 2012. "Economic Crises and the Shape of Modern History." *Public Culture* 24(2): 303–327.

Shah, Alpa 2006a. "Markets of Protection: The Maoist Communist Centre and the State in Jharkhand, India." *Critique of Anthropology* 26(3): 297–314.

———. 2006b. "The Labour of Love: Seasonal Migration from Jharkhand to the Brick Kilns of Other States in India." *Contributions to Indian Sociology* 40(1): 91–119.

———. 2007. "Keeping the State Away: Democracy, Politics and Imaginations of the State in India's Jharkhand." *Journal of Royal Anthropological Institute* 13(1): 129–145.

———. 2009. "Morality, Corruption and the State: Insights from Jharkhand, Eastern India." *Journal of Development Studies* 45(3): 295–313.

Shah, Alpa, and Stuart Corbridge. 2013. "The Underbelly of India's Boom." *Economy and Society* 42(3): 335–347.

Shever, Elana. 2012. *Resources for Reform: Oil and Neo-liberalism in Argentina.* Stanford: Stanford University Press.

Shore, Cris. 2011. "Espionage, Policy and the Art of Government: The British Secret Services and the War on Iraq." In C. Shore and S. Wright, eds., *Policy Worlds: Anthropology and the Analysis of Contemporary Power.* Oxford: Berghahn.

Shore, Cris, and Susan Wright. 1997. *The Anthropology of Policy: Perspectives on Governance and Power.* London: Routledge.

Shore, Cris, and Davide Pero. 2011. *Policy Worlds: Anthropology and the Analysis of Contemporary Power.* Oxford: Berghahn.

Sieber, R. Timothy. 1991. "Waterfront Revitalisation in Postindustrial Port Cities of North America." *City and Society* 5(2): 120–136.

Silver, Lauren. 2010. "Spaces of Encounter: Public Bureaucracy and the Making of Client Identities." *Ethos* 38: 275–296.

Simmel, Georg. 1908. "The Sociology of Secrecy and Secret Societies." *American Journal of Sociology* 11: 441–498.

Simondon, Gilbert. 1958. *Du Mode d'Existence d'Objets Techniques.* Paris: Aubier.

Simpson, Edward. 2006. "Apprenticeship in Western India." *Journal of the Royal Anthropological Institute* 12(1): 151–171.

Simpson, Edward, and K. Kresse, eds. 2007. *Struggling with History: Islam and Cosmopolitanism in the Western Indian Ocean.* London: Hurst and Columbia University Press.

Sivaramakrishnan, K., and Anne Rademacher. 2013. *Ecologies of Urbanism in India: Metropolitan Civility and Sustainability.* Hong Kong: Hong Kong University Press.

Sizek, Slavoj. 1999. *The Sublime Object of Ideology.* London: Verso.

Song, Jesook. 2009. *South Koreans in the Debt Crisis: The Creation of a Neo-Liberal Welfare Society.* Durham, NC: Duke University Press.

Spiegel, Shari. 2010. "Excess Returns on Emerging Market Bonds and the Framework for Sovereign Debt Restructuring." In Barry Herman, Jose Ocampo and Shari Spiegel, eds., *Overcoming Developing Country Debt Crises,* 140–160. Oxford: Oxford University Press.

Spreckley, Freer. 1981. *Social Audit: A Management Tool for Cooperative Working.* Leeds: Beechwood College.

Srinivas, Smirti. 2001. *Landscapes of Urban Memory: The Sacred and the Civic in India's High-Tech City*. Minneapolis: University of Minnesota Press.

Stafford, Charles, ed. 2013. *Ordinary Ethics in China*. LSE Monographs. London: Berg.

Steinmetz, George. 2010. "Colonial Melancholy and Fordist Nostalgia: The Ruinscapes of Namibia and Detroit." In Julia Hell and Andreas Schonle, eds., *Ruins of Modernity*, 294–320. Durham, NC: Duke University Press.

Stiglitz, J. E. 2002. "New Perspectives on Public Finance: Recent Achievements and Future Challenges." *Journal of Public Economics* 86: 341–360.

———. 2006. "Ethics, Market and Government Failure, and Globalization: Perspectives on Debt and Finance." In Chris Jochnick and Fraser A. Preston, eds., *Sovereign Debt at the Crossroads: Challenges and Proposals for Resolving the Third World Debt Crisis*. Oxford: Oxford University Press.

———. 2010a. *The Stiglitz Report*. New York: New Press.

———. 2010b. "Sovereign Debt: Notes on Theoretical Frameworks and Policy Analyses." In Barry Herman, Jose Ocampo and Shari Spiegel, eds., *Overcoming Developing Country Debt Crises*, 35–69. Oxford: Oxford University Press.

Stoler, Ann. 2002. *Carnal Knowledge and Imperial Power: Race and the Intimate in Colonial Rule*. Berkeley: University of California Press.

Strang, Veronica. 2005. "Common Senses: Water, Sensory Experiences and the Generation of Meaning." *The Journal of Material Culture*, 10(1): 92–120

———. 2004. *The Meaning of Water*. Oxford: Berg.

Strathern, Marilyn, ed. 2000. *Audit Cultures: Anthropological Studies in Accountability, Ethics and the Academy*. EASA Series. London: Routledge.

Struempell, Christian. 2008. "Conviviality and Modernity in a Company Settlement in South Orissa." *Contributions to Indian Sociology* 42(3): 351–381.

Struempell, Christian, and Jonathan Parry. 2008. "On the Desecration of Nehru's 'Temples': Bhilai and Rourkela Compared." *Economic and Political Weekly* 43(19): 47–57.

Subramaniam, Ajanta. 2009. *Shorelines: Space and Rights in South India*. Stanford: Stanford University Press.

Swyngedouw, Eric. 2004. *Social Power and the Urbanization of Water: Flows of Power*. Oxford: Oxford University Press.

———. 2005. "Governance Innovation and the Citizen: The Janus Face of Governance-beyond-the-State." *Urban Studies* 42(11): 1991–2006.

Sylla, Richard. 1988. "The Autonomy of Monetary Authorities: The Case of the US Federal Reserve System," In Gianni Toniolo, ed., *Central Banks' Independence in Historical Perspective*. Berlin: Walter de Gruyter.

Taussig, Michael. 1980. *The Devil and Commodity Fetishism in South America*. Chapel Hill: University of North Carolina Press.

———. 1997. *The Magic of the State*. New York: Routledge.

———. 1999. *Public Secrecy and the Labor of the Negative*. Stanford: Stanford University Press.

Tett, Gillian. 2010. *Fool's Gold: How Unrestrained Greed Corrupted a Dream, Shattered Global Markets and Unleashed a Catastrophe.* New York: Abacus.

Theret, Bruno. 1999. "The Socio-Political Dimensions of the Currency: Implications for the Transition to the Euro." *Journal of Consumer Policy* 22(1–2): 51–79.

Thompson, Eric P. 1967. "Time, Work-discipline and Industrial Capitalism." *Past and Present* 38: 56–97.

Thorat, Usha. 2002. "Developing Bond Markets to Diversity Long-Term Development Finance: Country Study of India." *Asia-Pacific Development Journal* 9(1): 45–63.

Thrift, N. 2001. "It's the Romance Not the Finance that Makes the Business Worth Pursuing: Disclosing the New Market Culture." *Economy and Society* 30(4): 412–432.

Thrift, Nigel, and John May. 2001. *Timespace: Geographies of Temporality.* London: Routledge.

Tomlinson, John. 2007. *The Culture of Speed: The Coming of Immediacy.* London: Sage Press.

Tomz, Michael. 2007. *Reputation and International Cooperation: Sovereign Debt across the Centuries.* Princeton: Princeton University Press.

Trebat, Thomas. 2007. "Argentina, the Church and the Debt." *Ethics and International Affairs* 21(1): 135–160.

Tsing, Anna. 2003. *Nature in the Global South: Environmental Projects in South and South-East Asia.* Durham, NC: Duke University Press.

———. 2005. *Friction: An Ethnography of Global Connection.* Princeton: Princeton University Press.

———. 2009. "Supply Chains and the Human Condition." *Rethinking Marxism: A Journal of Economics, Culture and Society* 21(2): 148–176.

———. 2015. *The Mushroom at the End of the World: On the Possibility of Life in Capitalist Ruins.* Princeton N.J.: Princeton University Press.

Upadhya, Carol, and A. R. Vasavi. 2008. *In an Outpost of the Global Economy: Work and Workers in India's Information Technology Industry.* New Delhi: Routledge.

Van Schendel, Willem. 2001. "Working through Partition: Making a Living on the Bengal Borderland." *International Review of Social History* 46: 393–421.

———. 2005. *The Bengal Borderland: Beyond State and Nation in South Asia.* London: Anthem Press.

———. 2006. "Stretching Labour Historiography: Pointers from South Asia." *International Review of Social History* 51: 29–261.

Veblen, Thorstein. 1924. *The Theory of the Leisure Class.* London: Allen and Unwin.

Veerkamp, Ton. 2007. "Judeo-Christian Tradition on Debt: Political, Not Just Ethical." *Ethics and International Affairs* 21(1): 167–188.

Venkatesan, Soumya. 2010. "Learning to Weave: Weaving to Learn . . . What?" *Journal of the Royal Anthropological Institute* 16(S1): 158–175.

Vijay, G. 2009. "Defragmenting 'Global Disintegration of Value Creation' and Labour Relations." *Economic and Political Weekly* 44(22): 85–94.

Vijayabaskar, M. 2011. "Global Crises, Welfare Provision and Coping Strategies of Labour in Tiruppur." *Economic and Political Weekly* 46(22): 38–45.

Vithal, B. P. R. 1996. "Debt Servicing and Budgetary Structure." *Economic and Political Weekly* 31(6): 349–354.

Wagner, Richard. 2013. *Deficits, Debt and Democracy: Wrestling with Tragedy on the Fiscal Commons*. London: Edward Elgar.

Wallman, Sandra. 1992. *Contemporary Futures: Perspectives from Social Anthropology*. London: Routledge.

Walsh, James P., Chanho Park and Jiangyan Yu. 2011. "Financing Infrastructure in India: Macro-economic Lessons and Emerging Market Case Studies." WP/11/181 IMF Working Papers.

Weber, Max. 1956 [1978]. *Economy and Society*. Berkeley: University of California Press.

———. 1994. "Parliament and Government in Germany under a New Political Order." In P. Lassman and R. Speirs, eds., *Political Writings*, 130–271. Cambridge: Cambridge University Press.

Wengle, Susanne. 2012. "Engineers versus Managers: Experts, Market-Making and State-Building in Putin's Russia." *Economy and Society* 41(3): 435–467.

Weszkalnys, Gisa. 2010. *Berlin, Alexandrplatz: Transforming Place in a Unified Germany*. Oxford: Berghahn.

White, Damian, and Chris Wilbert. 2006. "Technonatural Time-Spaces." *Science as Culture* 15(2): 95–104.

Wilson, Ara. 1999. "The Empire of Direct Sales and the Making of Thai Entrepreneurs." *Critique of Anthropology* 19(4): 401–422.

———. 2004. *The Intimate Economies of Bangkok: Tomboys, Tycoons and Avon Ladies in the Global City*. Berkeley: University of California Press.

Wilson, Ara, ed. 2012. "The Empire Debate: Hardt and Negri's Anthropological Encounter." *Focaal* 64 (Special Issue): 3–65.

Yanagisako, Sylvia. 2002. *Producing Culture and Capital: Family Firms in Italy*. Princeton: Princeton University Press.

———. 2012. "Immaterial and Industrial Labor: on false binaries in Hardt and Negri's Trilogy." *Focaal* 64: 16–23.

———. 2013. "Transnational Family Capitalism: Producing 'Made in Italy' in China." In Susan McKinnon and Fenella Cannell, eds., *Vital Relations: Modernity and the Persistent Life of Kinship*, 63–84. Santa Fe: SAR Press.

Yates, Michelle. 2011. "The Human-as-Waste, the Labor Theory of Value and Disposability in Contemporary Capitalism." *Antipode* 43(3): 1679–1695.

Zaloom, Caitlin. 2004. "The Productive Life of Risk." *Cultural Anthropology* 19(3): 365–391.

———. 2006. *Out of the Pits: Traders and Technology from Chicago to London*. Chicago: Chicago University Press.

———. 2009. "How to Read the Future: The Yield Curve, Affect and Financial Prediction." *Public Culture* 21(2): 243–266.

Zandi-Sayek, Sibel. 2000. "Struggles over the Shore: Building the Quay of Izmir, 1867–1875." *City and Society* 12(1): 55–78.

Index

and, 130; shipyard workers and, 124, 161;
  worship of, 44–45
Kolkata Port Trust, 20–21, 23–24; Austerity
  policy, 34–36, 105–8, 117, 120–21, 129,
  155–58, 198, 200, 207; Nehruvian policy,
  31–33
Krugman, Paul, 189

Laidlaw, James, 18
Lambek, Michael, 18
Latour, Bruno, 22
Law, John, and Ann-Marie Mol, 131
Liberalisation, India, 12–17
Li Puma, Edward, and Ben Lee, 18, 189
London Club, 196

Ma Ganga (Mother Ganges), 4, 22; worship
  of, 44–45; marine crew and, 71–73;
  marine officers and, 90–91
Ma Monosha (Mother Monosha), 184–86
Majhis (boatmen), 21, 99, 116–17; rights,
  documents and, 118–20
Marine Crew, 54–55, 84; East Bengali
  refugees and, 58–61; ethics of, 58, 62–66,
  66–69; Muslim, 58
Marine Officers, 53, 81–82; accidents and,
  145; as brokers, 82–83; cosmopolitanism,
  81; ethics of, 84–91; technology, affect
  and, 86–89
Marx, Karl, 177–78; on credit 8, 124; on
  fertility of labor, 18, 173; on time,
  149
Maurer, Bill, 18, 28
Mazzucato, Mariana, 206
McGoey, Linsey, 18
Miller, Danny, 18, 178
Mitchell, Timothy, 17, 178
Mohan, Rakesh, 17, 201
MOST (Ministry of Surface Transport),
  austerity policy and, 34–36, 41; planning
  and, 31–32, 105–8
Mukerjee, Pranab, 16
Mukherjee, Radhakamal, 21

Municipal bonds, 201–2
Murray Li, Tania, 17

Necropolitics, Achille Mbembe on, 54
Negri, Antonio, 172
Narain, Prakash, 39
National Union of Waterfront Workers, 21,
  39, 59–60
Nationalist melancholia, 57–58, 75–76
Nayachar Island, 44–45, 49

Paris Club, 196
Partition of India, 21, 39, 58, 67, 69, 85
Perrow, Charles, 130
Piketty, Thomas, 15, 209
Poovey, Martha, 18, 28
Port Sromik Union, 20, 23, 40, 54, 59–60
Postone, Moishe, 172
Predictive devices, 132–37
Private sector shipyards, 46–47, 154;
  bureaucrats and, 115–16, 155; Ma Ganga
  vessel and, 47, 57, 68, 89–90; short-term
  capitalism and, 156–61; virtual jetty and,
  47, 83
Public audits, 210
Public choice theory, 191
Public good, 80, 210
Public private partnerships, 24, 110–16, 121;
  family firms and, 79–80, 115–16

Quantitative easing, 198–99

Rakesh Mohan Infrastructure Committee
  1996, 201
Rangarajan, Chakravarti, 14
Rao, Narasimhan, 13
Ray, Bidhan Chandra, 54, 67, 72
Reinhart, Carmen M., and Kenneth S.
  Rogoff, 189
Res Publica, 5, 17, 155, 170, 209
Right to Information Act 2005, 109
Riles, Annalise, 17, 177
River Pilots, accidents and, 123, 129, 136,

Anthropology of Policy